Liberalization, Crisis, and Change in Colombian Agriculture

Liberalization, Crisis, and Change in Colombian Agriculture

Carlos Felipe Jaramillo

Routledge
Taylor & Francis Group

LONDON AND NEW YORK

First published 1998 by Westview Press

Published 2018 by Routledge
52 Vanderbilt Avenue, New York, NY 10017
2 Park Square, Milton Park, Abingdon, Oxon OX14 4RN

Routledge is an imprint of the Taylor & Francis Group, an informa business

A CIP catalog record for this book is available from the Library of Congress.

ISBN 13: 978-0-367-01065-2 (hbk)

To Cynthia and Daniel

Contents

Tables and Figures

Figures

Preface

Transcendental changes in economic policies have taken place throughout Latin America since the mid-1980s. The traditional import substitution strategy for economic progress has been replaced in most countries by market-oriented policies. Reforms have been extended to all sectors of the economy, including agriculture. These changes were initially expected to favor farmers in the region, since previous policies had been associated with an anti-agriculture bias. However, little is known about the actual fate of rural populations after reforms due to the absence of studies about the response of Latin American agriculture to recent policy changes.

This book provides an in-depth look at the impact of recent economic reforms on Latin American agriculture. It focuses on the experience of Colombia, a country with a large and complex agricultural sector. The bold attempt at reform initiated in 1990 posed strong challenges to Colombian agriculture, at a time when it still accounted for 20 percent of domestic employment, a fifth of gross domestic production and over a third of foreign exchange earnings. Challenges were compounded by the dual nature of the farming structure, which has traditionally consisted of two distinct segments: commercial farmers (who use modern technologies and hired labor), and *campesino* producers (who rely on family labor and more traditional production practices). Most importantly, *campesinos* have traditionally tended to specialize in the production of non-tradable staple crops, while commercial farmers favor export crops and import-competing grains and oilseeds. *Campesinos* also account for an important share of producers engaged in cultivation of coffee and maize.

The book describes and analyzes events in Colombian agriculture between 1990 and 1997. It highlights the critical role that macroeconomic factors play in determining agricultural outcomes and, in particular, the effect of the real exchange rate. The analysis provides preliminary answers to important questions: What was the nature of economic reforms for agriculture? Were reforms responsible for the agricultural crisis of 1992? How did policy-makers react to plummeting farm incomes? What were the effects of policy adjustments in the aftermath of crisis? What was the nature of structural changes in Colombian agriculture between 1990 and 1997? What forces explain these changes? The Colombian experience should shed some light on similar experiences that have been recently observed in other Latin American countries. It may also yield valuable lessons for other countries still in the early stages of agricultural policy reform.

There are two important limitations of the book that readers should bear in mind. First, it does not provide a detailed analysis of policies related to coffee,

Colombia's traditional export crop which accounted for about a tenth of agricultural gross domestic product in the 1990s. This is partly because this crop has been historically subject to special policies and institutions that have been studied extensively in Colombia. Most significantly, coffee policies have changed little in the 1990s and are only weakly related to the central theme of the book (i.e., effects of economic reform on agriculture). Second, the book contains only a partial treatment of developments related to the cultivation of illicit crops, a growing business in Colombia during the 1980s and 1990s. This is largely due to the dearth of credible statistics and studies on the evolution of this business and the impact on the rest of the economy. However, a discussion of this phenomenon is presented in Chapter 6, as well as some speculative analysis about the relationship between the drug sector and the rest of agriculture.

The book is intended for analysts, practitioners and students of Latin American development. It should also be of interest to policy-makers and, in particular, those dealing with agricultural and rural issues. Although written by an economist, the book is aimed at the broader audience of readers concerned with the results of recent economic reforms in Latin America. Definitions of key concepts are included in the text and an attempt has been made to minimize the use of technical jargon and complex models.

I have incurred many debts in writing this book. The original insights were gained in my tenure as chief of agricultural policies at the Departamento Nacional de Planeación (DNP) between 1992 and 1993. I am especially grateful to my mentors within the Colombian government at that time, Armando Montenegro and Rudolf Hommes and to former President Cesar Gaviria, whose sharp economic mind left an indelible imprint on the account told here. I am very grateful for the support of the Ministers of Agriculture who participated in the Gaviria administration, including Maria del Rosario Sintes, Alfonso López Caballero and José Antonio Ocampo. The entire staff of the unit in charge of agricultural policies at DNP collaborated in the gestation of this book in some form or another. My biggest debts were incurred there with Clara González, Raquel de Henao, Ivan Sombredero, José Luis Gómez, José Ignacio Vargas, Pilar Ruiz, Judith Barbosa and Ximena Rueda. Parts of Chapters 3 and 4 were extracted from an earlier book which received support from DNP and FONADE, who have both graciously ceded their translation rights.

I have large intellectual debts with some of the best academic observers of Colombian agriculture. Roberto Junguito and Albert Berry motivated and encouraged my research on the problems of the rural economy. My knowledge of Colombian agriculture has been enriched by valuable discussions with Juan José Perfetti, José Leibovich, Juan Luis Londoño, Jorge Ramírez, Edgardo Moscardi, Alvaro Balcázar, Absalón Machado, Fernando Bernal, Jesus Antonio Bejarano, Alvaro Francisco Uribe, Nestor Gutierrez, Carlos Federico Espinal and Jorge García García. While preparing this book, I had enriching discussions with Rafael Echeverry, Cecilia López and the group of researchers working on the Colombian government's Misión Rural. I also benefited from guidance from

Hans Binswanger and Alberto Valdés, as well as discussions with John Heath, Nicholas Krafft, Klaus Deininger and John Baffes at the World Bank.

The first two chapters of this book were possible due to the support of the MacArthur Foundation and the Agricultural and Natural Resource Economics Department of the University of Maryland at College Park, where Darrel Hueth was a gracious host. At Maryland, I also benefited from discussions with Bruce Gardner and Ramón López. The remainder of the book was written while the author was a staff member at Banco de la República in Colombia. I am very grateful to Miguel Urrutia, Director General, for supporting my efforts on this book. I also received valuable comments on earlier versions of the book from Leonardo Villar, Salomón Kalmanovitz and Enrique Ospina.

I must especially acknowledge the dedicated assistance of Edgar Caicedo, who accompanied me in this project from the beginning. It is in great part to his competent collaboration that I have been able to include graphs and tables to strengthen the arguments. I would like to acknowledge his special assistance in the analysis of variations in commodity returns presented in Chapter 6. The sections on rural labor markets and integration of agricultural markets benefited from joint work with Oskar Andrés Nupia. The section on the political economy of agricultural protection draws from preliminary work with Xavier Durán. Maria Cristina Guasca provided assistance in the preparation of the bibliography and the tables of contents.

I would also like to express my gratitude to my wife and son, who have supported me all along in this endeavor.

Carlos Felipe Jaramillo
Bogotá

1

Agriculture and Development Strategies in Latin America

A radical shift in development strategy swept through Latin America, in the second half of the 1980s. By the early 1990s, a new approach based on the integration of national economies to world trade flows and a greater reliance on market forces and private initiative had been adopted throughout the region, with the notable exception of Cuba. This more outward-oriented stance replaced "Import Substitution Industrialization" (ISI), the strategy followed by most Latin American countries in the post-war period.

The change in development paradigm had important consequences for Latin American agriculture, a sector of the economy that continues to provide the bulk of employment and foreign exchange in many of the economies of Latin America. The purpose of this chapter is to describe the nature of the change in development strategy undertaken across the region, by comparing the old paradigm with the new approach. Special emphasis is given to the implications of old and new policies on agriculture. This account will shed light on the origins and nature of the Colombian policy reforms of 1990 and 1991, described in more detail in Chapter 3.

The Strategy of Import Substitution Industrialization

By 1950, the large economies of Latin America were hosts to a budding manufacturing sector.[1] Established in the major cities, industries flourished as a consequence of the major disruptions in trade flows that resulted during the Great Depression and the Second World War. However, with international commerce gradually reestablished, governments throughout the region faced an important choice. One option was to resume free trade with the rest of the world, risking the rapid obliteration of nascent industries. The alternative, however, was to protect the new sector, implementing an explicit pro-industrialization strategy. Most countries in the region opted for a development strategy based on protection of urban-based industry.[2]

The reasons that led to the adoption of ISI policies at the start of the 1950s have been analyzed in an extensive literature.[3] Within national economies, the fledgling bourgeoisie lobbied for the new industries. From Chile, the United Nations Economic Commission for Latin America (ECLA) provided intellectual support. Implicit in the discussion was a rising skepticism of the opportunities for development offered by international trade. Most economies had followed explicitly pro-trade strategies since independence until 1929, with mixed results. The severe disruptions in world trade that ensued after the Great Depression instilled fears that international commerce flows were too volatile and disruptive for national economies. Further, ECLA's work tried to demonstrate that the prices of traditional—mainly agricultural—export commodities had been declining steadily since the late nineteenth century. Raúl Prebisch, then Director of ECLA, claimed that this was an inevitable trend and that attempts to achieve economic development by relying on exports of primary products were doomed to failure.[4]

Supporting anti-trade sentiments, the literature on development economics of the 1950s expressed doubts about the growth potential of economies based on exports of agricultural or mineral commodities. Industry was seen as the most appropriate sector to generate backward and forward linkages that would stimulate diversification of production throughout the economy.[5] Some believed in the importance of a government-assisted Big Push that would allow industry to surpass a minimum sustainable level.[6] Government involvement was critical because private savings were low and insufficient to finance the investments required. Taxation of primary products was seen in a favorable light since their supply was considered relatively unresponsive to economic incentives. These arguments formed the basis for growing support of government intervention in the economy to take the lead in industrialization efforts.

The implementation of ISI meant protecting industry from international competition. This was accomplished by means of high import tariffs, as well as explicit import controls. These policies raised prices of industrial goods in relation to goods and services produced in other sectors of the economy. Higher prices for industrial goods, including imported intermediate materials and capital goods, increased costs of export activities. Other policies associated with ISI included direct government subsidies to local industry, efforts to establish government-owned industries, and rationing of scarce foreign exchange in favor of protected sectors. In many countries, the domestic production of fertilizers and other agricultural inputs was promoted by tariff protection, although this frequently meant higher costs for farmers. The anti-export bias was reflected in overvaluation of the exchange rate, a consequence of macro policies and high import barriers.

Overvaluation of the exchange rate occurs when government action makes the price of US dollars (or any other foreign currency) in local currency lower than it would be otherwise. Such a policy is detrimental to the interests of domestic sectors producing exports or competing with imports, because it reduces the prices of goods measured in local currency. Agriculture was normally a loser when policies of this type were implemented. Export crops received lower prices and import-competing crops had to adjust their prices to those of cheaper foreign imports. Only protected industries reaped substantial benefits, as they were sheltered from import competition.

Exchange rate overvaluation caused by industrial protection was usually intensified by other policies. In many cases, countries adopted exchange rate levels (i.e., the price of foreign exchange in local currency) that were artificially low. Excess demand for foreign currency was rationed to prospective importers, with preference given to the purchase of inputs for industry. In other cases, multiple exchange rate systems taxed non-industrial sectors. Foreign exchange revenue from agricultural and other commodity exports was offered a low exchange rate. Importers of industrial inputs were also offered inexpensive foreign exchange while other imports were subject to higher rates of exchange.

Exchange rate overvaluation was also intensified by the tendency to enlarge government expenditures. Government outlays tended to concentrated disproportionately on labor and other non-tradable resources. This exerted upward pressure on the prices of non-tradable items, resulting in a further appreciation of the exchange rate.

Agriculture and Import Substitution

Agriculture was a major beneficiary of the free trade policies that were in place in most Latin American economies until 1929. With a comparative advantage in agricultural production, most economies relied on the sector as an engine of economic growth, with the exception of Chile, Peru and Bolivia. These countries relied on mineral exports. On the other hand, ISI policies had the practical effect of squeezing agriculture to accelerate manufacturing growth. This reflected the belief held by promoters of ISI that agricultural growth was not essential to industrialization.

ISI advocates were influenced by the perception that the fate of agriculture was only of secondary importance to growth, since food and fiber production are only a small share of the economic value added in developed economies. In point of fact, historical experience demonstrates that the share of agriculture in a country's labor force and total output declines with development. What was not acknowledged by policy-makers was that rapid agricultural growth must accompany—or even precede—general growth.[7] This was the case in all major industrialized economies of Europe and North America, as well as in Japan, South Korea and Taiwan.[8] In all these countries, the revolution in agricultural production occurred in the early stages of takeoff, greatly facilitating the transfer of labor, food supplies and savings to industrial centers. The combination of rapid growth in agricultural output and migration from the countryside to urban areas resulted in a sharp/rise in labor productivity. These factors were reflected in rising wages and living standards in rural sectors, which narrowed the gap with urban levels.

The success of agricultural revolutions in present-day industrialized countries reveals the importance of maintaining reasonable producer incentives and substantial government support through investments in research and extension, irrigation, communications and transport facilities. In some cases (i.e., Japan, Taiwan and Korea), agricultural performance was spurred by land tenure reforms, which increased incentives for private investment.

ISI has been defined as a "jump" strategy designed to bypass the stages of development that require investment in agriculture.[9] Under this strategy, agriculture is seen as a "resource reservoir" whose role is to supply labor, cheap food, foreign exchange and investment funds for industrial needs. Some elements of this strategy were put in place in the development experience of Japan and, more radically, in the USSR. The strategy was successful in Japan because it was implemented at a time when agriculture was already growing rapidly. Success was less clear in the USSR, although the country benefited from a large initial surplus relative to the subsistence needs of the rural population. However, some calculations suggest that agricultural productivity per worker in Latin America was below that of most present-day developed countries at the time they were beginning their industrial revolution.[10] Not surprisingly, agricultural supply shortfalls and inflation surges led by food prices became one of the key bottlenecks of post-1950 ISI experiences.

A variety of policies were implemented to keep agriculture subordinate to the needs of industry. Traditional exports were taxed to provide funds for government activities in support of protected sectors. Also, urban food supplies were regulated to keep wages low and stable. The methods used by governments to guarantee supplies of low-cost food in cities varied by country. In most Central American countries, import tariffs on grains were kept low and policies actively supported dependence on food imports. In other countries, including Colombia, Brazil, Chile and Mexico, policy-makers protected the production of import-competing crops, in order to save foreign exchange and stabilize domestic food prices. In many instances, large and powerful agricultural procurement agencies were established to purchase crops directly from farmers. These agencies often enjoyed a monopoly over imports of food grains. In urban centers, price controls and distribution of food through networks of government-owned shops were commonplace.

Despite these policies, there was room for measures to aid farmers. Much of agricultural policy in the ISI period concentrated in spurring the development of the sector through adoption of mechanical and agrochemical inputs. Many of these efforts were aimed primarily at large commercial farmers.

The overall effect of ISI policies on agriculture was to tax agricultural tradables, i.e., traditional export commodities as well as import-competing crops.[11] Even in economies where domestic foodstuffs were supported, the indirect macroeconomic effects derived from protection of the industrial sector and fiscal imbalances more than offset direct protection. A comprehensive study of agricultural policies in five Latin American countries (Argentina, Brazil, Chile, Colombia and the Dominican Republic) concluded that taxes on export commodities and import-competing crops amounted to 27.8 percent of farm income over the 1960-84 period.[12] Most of this effect was a result of indirect taxation stemming from protection of industry and exchange rate overvaluation. These interventions retarded the growth of these crops and limited their contribution to employment, exports and national income.

A glaring omission of most studies on post-war agricultural development in Latin America is the role played by sectors producing root crops, vegetables and fruits for local markets. In the majority of countries, these crops are primarily grown by *campesinos*. Since most of these crops are non-tradable (i.e., not traded in international markets due to limitations imposed by their low value and high transportation costs), the bias against tradable goods inherent in ISI did not affect them directly. Higher prices of industrial goods and agricultural inputs, however, were clearly unfavorable to producers of these crops. Nevertheless, compared with producers of commodity exports and import-competing crops, these *campesino* producers enjoyed more favorable incentives. In some of the large economies, these crops were sources of cyclical inflationary outbursts, a feature explained by periodic shocks in weather conditions and food demand.

The Results of Import Substitution Industrialization

By 1980, assessments of ISI results revealed a mixed picture. Economic growth had proceeded at a seemingly healthy, average annual rate of 5.5 percent for Latin America as a whole. Between 1950 and 1980, per capita incomes increased at about the same rate as the population (2.7 percent), from US$420 to US$960.[13] Much of this growth was concentrated in the larger economies (i.e., Brazil and Mexico) which enjoyed the advantage of large domestic markets. Output gains were also larger in the 1950s and 1960s, during the phase known as "easy" import substitution when industries were established to produce simple manufactures such as textiles, processed foods and building materials. As expected under ISI biases, economic expansion tended to be greater in industry and in urban centers. This process accelerated migration trends from rural areas to urban centers. By 1980, some 67 percent of the Latin American population resided in cities, up from less than 50 percent in 1950.

Social indicators reflected an improvement in living conditions, particularly in the early years of ISI. During the 1960s, the population living below the poverty line fell as a share of the total population from 51 percent to 40 percent.[14] However, this pace slackened sharply in the 1970s, when the proportion of the population living below the poverty line fell to only 38 percent by the end of the decade. As a consequence, the number of poor in the region increased from 113 million to 136 million between 1970 and 1980. Poverty was more prevalent among rural than urban residents. By 1980, the per capita incomes of 54 percent of the rural population were under the poverty line.

Another problem of ISI policies was that growth tended to come in spurts, as macroeconomic imbalances led to frequent economic disruptions. Policies that discouraged exports led to foreign exchange shortages that exploded periodically in balance of payments crises. Paradoxically, a strategy aimed at reducing dependence on outside markets increased vulnerability to price fluctuations in international commodity markets. Thus, many economies faced a recurrent "stop-and-go" cycle, punctuated by massive devaluations to restore balance in the external accounts.

Most significantly for long-term development, the pattern of growth promoted by ISI did not create a dynamic and productive industrial sector.[15] Most factories tended to be inefficient, and noncompetitive in foreign markets. Without competition from imports, there were few pressures to improve quality, design and productivity. Oligopolies and monopolies dominated the markets for specific goods, due to high barriers to entry of potential competitors. Industrial growth was based on expanding input use, and not enough on productivity increases. As a result, economic growth and improvements in living standards were limited, particularly in comparison with the East Asian miracle economies of Taiwan and South Korea. There is considerable debate about the extent of government involvement in the successful economies of East Asia and about the importance of productivity increases versus input growth.[16] However, the consensus view is that they benefited greatly by promoting exports at a time of rapid growth in international trade. With more inward-looking policies, Latin American countries missed out on the opportunities that were capitalized by East Asian economies.

In spite of the biases inherent in ISI, between 1950 and 1980, Latin American agriculture expanded at an average annual rate of 3 to 4 percent, a healthy pace by international standards. Growth was concentrated in the modern sector, represented by medium and large-scale farms. These segments of the rural population underwent a significant transformation, as traditional low productivity *haciendas* gave way to highly capitalized enterprises, adopting new technologies and farm machinery.[17] Most crop yields in this dynamic sector grew rapidly. However, the modernization process bypassed traditional smallholder agriculture, where few productivity gains were registered.

A key feature of the agricultural growth pattern of the post-war period was that it provided few new employment opportunities. This was largely a reflection of technological progress in mechanization and the adoption of new labor-saving production techniques. Between 1964 and 1979, the number of tractors in the region grew at an annual rate of 5.4 percent. In the same period, annual use of fertilizers increased from 10.4 kilograms to 39.1 kilograms per hectare, growing at an impressive annual rate of 9.2 percent.[18] Rapid diffusion of modern inputs was the result of two trends. One was the demonstration effect of North American farming, where labor-saving techniques had been highly profitable to farmers facing continuous labor shortages. The other was the result of favorable domestic policies, put in place by policy-makers who believed in mechanical and chemical-intensive farming as the wave of the future. Policies to favor rapid modernization of farming included low tariffs and subsidized credit for the purchase of imported farm machinery, government outlays to reduce the price of chemical inputs, as well as government programs to popularize the advantages of the new techniques among owners of medium and large-size farms. Unfortunately, the premature adoption of many labor-saving techniques resulted in low employment growth in rural areas, and contributed to persistent rural poverty, low wages and an accelerated outflow of inhabitants from the countryside.[19]

Agricultural growth after 1950 also exerted a negative effect on the environment. Area expansion for agriculture was often achieved at the expense of natural forests. Credit subsidies and public support for some crops led to conversion of forested lands with low agricultural potential. Fertilizer subsidies and lack of experience among farmers about the potential pitfalls associated with chemical products resulted in excessive application of Green Revolution inputs. Rivers and streams suffered the consequences. The absence of employment opportunities for the poor often led to deforestation of hillsides, erosion and overexploitation of low-quality soils.[20] All of these effects were compounded by the lack of attention paid by policy-makers to issues of natural resource depletion and environmental damage.

Towards a New Development Paradigm

Increasing foreign indebtedness and domestic fiscal imbalances exploded in a massive crisis throughout the Latin American continent, starting in 1982. The crisis was brought to a head by the sudden increase in international interest rates, a recession in developed countries, and depressed commodity prices. Led by Mexico, the major economies of Latin America announced their inability to service international debt obligations, spreading panic among lenders and halting all new capital inflows into the region. As a result, governments were forced to adopt massive adjustment programs designed to generate a trade surplus and the necessary foreign exchange to service debt payments. Imports were reduced drastically and exports were promoted. Governments cut expenditures, increased tax revenues and devalued the exchange rate, measures that contributed to profound economic downturns.

Farmers were hit hard by the ensuing economic crises. The growth rate of agricultural production dropped from the 3.5 percent annual rate of the 1970s to only 2.1 percent in the 1980s. Nevertheless, farmers did relatively well compared with their urban counterparts. In cities, retrenchment of government programs and the effects of devaluation produced unemployment and falling wage levels. As a result, agriculture grew faster than other sectors during the 1980s in most economies of the region. The more favorable performance was largely due to the high growth rates displayed by tradable crops, which responded vigorously to incentives provided by exchange rate devaluations. The volume of exports of agricultural commodities grew 3.6 percent annually between 1980 and 1991 while imports only increased by 0.3 percent in this lapse. Large profitability gains due to devaluation were obtained despite negative effects from cuts in subsidies and other compensatory measures, a result of fiscal austerity programs.

As governments muddled through painful economic adjustments, a favorable atmosphere emerged for the shift to a new development strategy. The era of import substitution was reexamined in a new light. New analyses charged that much of the manufacturing sector in the region, created under protective policies, was inefficient and had shown little capacity to penetrate export markets. This was in marked contrast to the success of East Asian economies. Also, the pattern of development had not been favorable to a rapid pace of employment generation due to subsidies on capital inputs and governmental regulations in labor markets that artificially increased the cost of employing workers.[21] In addition, ISI was associated in most countries with a rapid expansion of government, often resulting in bloated bureaucracies and layers of unnecessary regulation.

A new development paradigm gradually emerged, influenced largely by general disenchantment with ISI results, the massive economic crises of the early 1980s, and by free market ideas promoted, among others, by the International Monetary Fund and the World Bank. The new strategy was based on renewed optimism about the potential benefits of international trade, particularly in terms of providing opportunities for growth based on non-traditional products, a push for less governmental regulation and intervention in the economy, and the need to increase reliance on private sectors.

The new outward-oriented development strategy required liberalization of trade flows, as well as the removal of all previous subsidies and programs favoring industry. The effective operation of markets and private sector decisions required complementary measures to guarantee macroeconomic stability and lower inflation, a process that usually involved a balancing of fiscal accounts and control of monetary aggregates. In some countries where inflation had become an ingrown feature of the economy (as in Argentina and Nicaragua), stabilization was aided by the adoption of a fixed exchange rate regime, a process that often led to bouts of overvaluation while domestic prices fully stabilized.[22] In addition, the economies' favorable response to realignment of the relative prices of industry and other sectors required action to improve the functioning of factor markets. Thus, efforts were undertaken in most countries to deregulate labor and capital markets, to implement tax reforms and to privatize government-owned enterprises.[23]

A Preliminary Assessment

During the early stages of implementation of the new development strategy, agriculture was a clear winner. Adoption of a neutral stance at the macroeconomic level meant that subordination of farming to the needs of industry was effectively ended. Farming sectors could prosper, provided they had the comparative advantage required to succeed under the new rules. The new strategy was associated with the adoption of measures clearly favorable to agricultural interests, such as the elimination of all export taxes and quantitative restrictions, the removal of price controls, the reduction of tariffs on machinery and fertilizers, and the abolition of discriminatory exchange rate treatment.

Most significantly, devaluation of national currencies, usually undertaken as a first step in the adjustment programs of the second half of the 1980s, boosted the profitability of tradable goods. Devaluation was most favorable to tradable crops, particularly exportables for which a higher exchange rate meant greater profitability. Although both revenues and costs increased in terms of domestic currency, revenues increased by the full amount of devaluation; the rate of cost increase depended on the importance of imported inputs in production expenses. Crops more heavily dependent on labor costs (e.g., coffee) enjoyed higher increases in profitability, compared with those more intensive in tradable inputs. Exportables also benefited from the phasing out of export taxes.

Although import-competing crops benefited from the effects of devaluation, they were also subject to certain negative effects. First, domestic demand was generally low due to recessions associated with adjustment programs. Second, if they had enjoyed substantial protection in the pre-reform period, removal of this protection reduced the gains from devaluation. Furthermore, both exportable and importable crops were negatively affected by cuts in compensatory programs, including credit and input subsidies and government-sponsored support prices, resulting from adjustment programs and fiscal austerity measures.

While the local profitability of export production increased, marketing of excess supplies in overseas markets faced difficult prospects. On the one hand, adjustment programs and devaluation across Third World economies increased world supplies of farm goods and depressed world markets, particularly for tropical goods. By the same token, restrictive import policies and ballooning subsidies in developed countries generated increasing surpluses of temperate crops. Falling world prices for most agricultural commodities explain why export volumes increased by 38 percent between 1980 and 1990, while dollar revenues increased only by 1.1 percent.[24]

After 1990, important changes in global capital markets sharply altered the fate of tradable sectors, including agriculture. After nearly a decade of being kept out of global capital flows, the 1990s brought a new flood of foreign exchange to the large economies of Latin America (see Figure 1.1). The return of foreign financial flows affected countries undertaking economic reforms as

FIGURE 1.1 Capital Inflows to Latin America, 1987-1996 (US$ Billions)

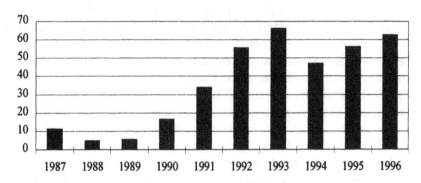

Source: Data from Inter-American Development Bank (1997).

well as those that had begun this process earlier. Several factors explain the return of foreign investors and lenders to Latin America. First, the reforms adopted during the 1980s and the resolution of debt issues generated optimism about future economic prospects. Second, poor investment prospects in developed countries in the early 1990s forced global investors to look for better alternatives elsewhere. Third, high interest rates in domestic Latin American markets promised better returns than in other parts of the world. In contrast to the 1970s, foreign banks were more willing to lend directly to the private sector in the 1990s. Finding more open economies, many overseas investors were willing to invest in new enterprises or shares of local businesses.

The massive increase in capital inflows into the major economies of the region caused real exchange rates to appreciate (see Figure 1.2). In some cases, appreciation was rapid and produced traumatic shifts in competitiveness across sectors of local economies. This induced policy-makers in several countries to restrict the flow of capital into their economies. In both Chile and Colombia, short and medium-term loans from foreign sources were subject to special taxes. These measures were only partially successful, as private companies smuggled in capital by over-invoicing exports or under-invoicing imports.[25]

There is a dearth of studies on what has happened to Latin American agriculture in the 1990s, after the currency appreciation process took effect.[26] Significant declines in the profitability of farming have been documented in seven Latin American countries during the 1990s.[27] The main factor underlying the decline in real domestic farm prices seems to be the appreciation of the exchange rate during the early 1990s, a phenomenon that was amplified by tariff reductions and, in some cases, by a fall in international prices. As was the case under ISI policies, falling exchange rates in the early 1990s dealt a blow to the

FIGURE 1.2 Real Exchange Rates, Selected Latin American Countries, 1987-1996 (Index 1990=100)

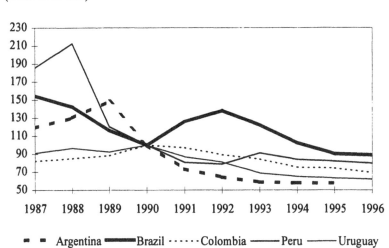

Source: Data from Inter-American Development Bank (1997).

profitability of tradable agricultural goods. This phenomenon is analyzed in greater depth for the case of Colombia in Chapter 6.

Pressure on the profitability of tradable farming activities has generated intense pressure to return to protectionist policies. These tensions have been more acute in countries experiencing rapid exchange rate appreciation and have led to counter-cyclical interventions, usually in favor of certain importable commodities. A striking finding is the concentration of compensatory measures on a few products in most countries. Favored crops include rice in the Dominican Republic, milk, wheat, sugar beet and beef in Chile and rice, coffee and beef in Colombia. The experience of Colombia with compensation measures and their impact on the liberalization of agricultural markets is the subject of Chapter 5.

In contrast to ISI times, exchange rate appreciation in the 1990s have also harmed the profitability of industrial goods. This is because falling exchange rates in the 1990s were greatly the result of exogenous changes in global capital markets. They have not resulted from government-imposed distortions. Winners include non-tradable sectors, especially service sectors, including construction and financial services. In some Latin American countries, short-term winners also included farmers who produce root crops, vegetables and fruits for domestic consumers. Moreover, some evidence suggests that rapid employment growth in service sectors increased wages in urban centers and attracted renewed migration from rural areas. This trend indirectly benefited rural labor interests by putting upward pressure on wages in the countryside (see Chapter 6). However, a complete assessment of the complex effect of appreciating exchange rates and global economic policies on Latin American agriculture in the 1990s remains to be done.

Conclusions and Plan of This Book

The new market-oriented paradigm that replaced ISI policies across Latin America since the mid-1980s has produced contradictory effects on agriculture. On the one hand, removal of implicit and explicit taxation measures has benefited farmers who had only a secondary role in the pro-industrialization era. Elimination of export taxes and price controls, and the lowering of input tariffs and other restrictions have spurred the profitability of many crops. On the other hand, fiscal austerity has led to the elimination of many compensatory programs that were used to bolster the profitability of important sub-sectors. Importable crops that enjoyed positive protection prior to reform have lost a great deal of their special treatment. All these changes have generated major shifts in relative incentives within agriculture, as will be illustrated in the following chapters for the case of Colombia.

Removal of the discrimination implicit in ISI measures did not lead to the general increase in farming incentives that some had predicted. The change in development strategy occurred along with negative trends that neutralized some of the expected gains and left certain deep-seated problems untouched. First and foremost was the unexpected appreciation of exchange rates, largely a result of exogenous trends in global capital markets after 1990. Appreciation, often associated with weak world prices in major commodity markets, led to substantial declines in producer prices of tradable crop during the first half of the 1990s. In Colombia, this phenomenon led to the agricultural crisis of 1992, discussed at length in Chapter 4. Exchange rate appreciation is greatly responsible for substantial change in the structure of Colombian farming after 1990, as will be illustrated in Chapter 6.

Second, attempts to emulate the experience of East Asia, where economies had been buoyed by rapid export growth, faced considerable difficulties in the realm of agricultural goods. During the 1980s, devaluation spurred exportable surpluses that faced excess supplies in world markets and barriers to entry in developed countries. As a result, prices in world markets fell continuously throughout the decade. In the 1990s, continued surpluses and the falling profitability of exportable commodities aggravated the situation. Hopes for the removal of subsidies and trade barriers for agricultural goods in the developed countries by including the sector in the General Agreement in Trade and Tariffs (GATT) during the Uruguay Round were not fulfilled. Instead, the global agreement imposed weak conditions for subsidy removal and lengthy periods for the partial elimination of subsidies.[28] This explains why Colombian *cam-*

pesino farmers fared better than their commercial counterparts after 1990, as will be discussed in Chapter 6.

Third, the new paradigm had little to say on the issue of how to address the profound heterogeneity of Latin American agriculture, including deep-seated rural poverty and a technologically backward segment of *campesino* farmers. Adjustment programs and fiscal concerns reduced funds for rural development programs and were generally unsupportive of policies that differentiated among groups of farmers. On the other hand, many smallholders have remained isolated from the effects of exchange rate appreciation, due to the lack of direct international competition in root-crops, fresh fruits and vegetables.

Finally, little progress was made towards reducing environmental damages associated with agriculture. Trade liberalization efforts and related crisis-management activities absorbed the bulk of government energies. Reduced profitability of tradable agricultural activities in the 1990s has made environmental concerns politically unpalatable. These have impeded progress towards enacting measures that would reduce the usage of harmful chemicals and penalize unsustainable use of natural resources.

The remaining six chapters of this book provide a detailed description of the Colombian experience with agricultural reforms. The second provides a review of trends in Colombian agriculture since 1950 and other background material. The third describes the agricultural reforms put in place in Colombia in 1990 and 1991. The fourth analyzes the agricultural crisis of 1992 and its principal causes. The fifth describes government policies in the aftermath of the 1992 crisis and evaluates the impact of policy adjustments on liberalization efforts. The sixth evaluates events in agriculture between 1990 and 1997, including the changing structure of Colombian agriculture and the post-1990 evolution of the welfare of the rural population. Chapter seven provides conclusions and lessons from the Colombian experience.

Notes

1. The discussion on ISI draws from Bulmer-Thomas (1994), Grindle (1986), Furtado (1976), and Sheahan (1987).

2. The smaller economies of Latin American with little industrial growth in the 1929-50 period did not explicitly adopt pro-industry policies until the 1960s (Bulmer-Thomas 1994).

3. See for example Hirschman (1968), Furtado (1976), Sheahan (1987), Bulmer-Thomas (1994) and Edwards (1995).

4. This appears in Prebisch (1950).

5. Hirschman (1958) was the principal proponent of the "linkages" approach.

6. The initial proponent of Big Push ideas was Nurkse (1953).

7. A comprehensive review of the need for an agricultural revolution prior to industrialization appears in Timmer (1988).

8. Comprehensive reviews of the early stages of agricultural development in the UK, the US, Japan, Taiwan and the USSR appear in Johnston and Kilby (1980).

9. See Timmer (1988).

10. Bairoch (1975) presents evidence suggesting that agricultural labor productivity in developed countries at the time of their takeoff was roughly similar to the levels achieved by Latin American countries in the 1960s.

11. Tradable crops are those with markets affected substantially by international trade and world prices. Within this category, it is important to distinguish between exportables and importables. Exportables are crops sold largely in world markets. Importables—also known as import-competing—are those in which local production is insufficient to meet domestic demand which is supplied in part by shipments from abroad. Finally, non-tradable crops are neither importable or exportable. Accordingly, they face no effective competition from outside markets.

12. The study is by Krueger et al. (1992).

13. Figures taken from Hirschman (1987).

14. Social indicators are taken from Gómez-Oliver (1994).

15. Some of the results of ISI policies are taken from Edwards (1994).

16. A comprehensive review of the East Asian growth experience appears in World Bank (1993).

17. A well-documented overview of the transformation from low to high productivity agriculture in Latin America appears in Grindle (1986).

18. Fertilizer and tractor information taken from Gómez-Oliver (1994).

19. The results of low employment growth in rural areas in Latin America are discussed in Urrutia (1991).

20. This process is well described in Heath and Binswanger (1996).

21. Regulations that increased the cost of labor included the high cost of dismissal, limitations on temporary contracts, and rigid minimum wage legislation.

22. Mexico followed a variant of the fixed exchange rate policy, announcing a predetermined rate of devaluation at a pace deliberately below ongoing inflation (Edwards 1994).

23. Inter-American Development Bank (1996) contains an excellent survey of reforms throughout Latin America.

24. Figures taken from Gómez-Oliver (1994).

25. An analysis of the relative success of taxes on foreign capital inflows in Colombia appears in Cárdenas (1995).

26. Among the few available partial evaluations are those of Valdés (1996) and de Janvry et al. (1997).

27. See Valdés (1996).

28. A review of the achievements of the final GATT agreement of the Uruguay Round appears in Ingco (1995).

2

The Uneven Development
of Colombian Agriculture

This chapter describes important features of Colombian agriculture and reviews developments in the period between 1950 and 1990. The first section provides background information, including a physical description, a review of the importance of agriculture to the overall economy, and an account of the principal crops and the dual farming structure. Trends in rural poverty and violence are also reviewed. In the second section, the major developments in Colombian agriculture between 1950 and 1990 are described. Five phases in trade and exchange rate policy are identified, including the agricultural boom of 1986-90. The distributional consequences of the postwar pattern of growth are discussed and a brief review of the conditions prior to the 1990 liberalization reforms is also provided.

Colombian Agriculture: Some Background

Physical Characteristics

Located in South America's northwestern corner, Colombia has a tropical climate.[1] Temperatures are relatively uniform throughout the year, with a daily average of about 20°C. However, daily variations can be substantial. Altitude is a key determinant of temperature and weather patterns. About 80 percent of the country's area is located between sea level and 1000 meters, where temperatures average 24°C. Another 10 percent is located above 1000 meters and below 2000 meters, with milder temperatures (17-24°C). The remaining 10 percent—above 2000 meters—is known as *clima frío*, with average temperatures between 12°C and 17°C. Although the intensity of rainfall varies widely, production of temperate crops in Colombia is affected by irregular rainfall patterns, high humidity and limited daylight in most areas.

Approximately 14 million hectares—12 percent of the country—have appropriate soil for farming. However, in the mid-1980s, only 4.1 million hectares were dedicated to crops. Low utilization of adequate areas seems to be a result of a poor road network coupled with negligible investments in irrigation, drainage and flood control. An additional 18.7 million hectares are appropriate for livestock operations. The remaining 79 million are suitable only for forest cover.

The main agricultural areas are located in the Andean and Atlantic coastal regions. However, agriculture in the area known as the Eastern Plains—*Llanos Orientales*—has been expanding rapidly since the 1960s, despite acid soils that limit the variety of agricultural activities. The Andean region is densely populated and farms tend to be small on hillsides and highland plateaus. According to one estimate, the average farm in the Andean region was 11 hectares in the 1970s, and 90 percent of plots in this zone had less than 5 hectares. Average farm size on the Atlantic coast was 50 hectares. As a result of poor soils, scant transportation facilities, and the predominance of extensive cattle-grazing, average farm size on the Eastern Plains was 160 hectares.

The Relative Importance of the Rural and Agricultural Economy

Traditionally, agriculture has been the single most important sector of the Colombian economy, accounting for a quarter to a third of economic output in the post-war period. However, its contribution has been falling steadily since 1950 (see Figure 2.1). By 1996, agriculture's share of gross domestic product (GDP) had declined to about 19 percent, due to the rapid growth experienced by other sectors of the economy.

Within Latin America, Colombian agricultural output usually ranks fourth, behind Brazil, Mexico and Argentina. Despite the gradual decline in its share of the local economy, the relative size of Colombian agriculture as a proportion of global output is still almost double the Latin American average (see Table 2.1). In 1990, agriculture accounted for 18.2 percent of GDP in Colombia, while the average contribution for Brazil, Mexico and Argentina was 10.3 percent.

Until the 1990s, agriculture was the country's main source of foreign exchange earnings, with coffee accounting for the bulk of exports. However, the success of non-traditional exports and the surge in mineral exports—coal in the 1980s and oil in the 1990s—contributed to reducing the importance of agriculture as a source of foreign exchange. While agriculture accounted for 67 percent of exports in 1970, its share in the 1990-95 period fell to between 30 and 40 percent.

In the early 1990s, agriculture was still the principal source of employment for over a third of the population living in rural settings. Nonetheless, the importance of agriculture as a provider of employment in the national economy has declined gradually during the postwar period. In the 1970s, it was estimated that about a third of the labor force worked in agricultural activities; this proportion has fallen to nearly 20 percent in the 1990s.

FIGURE 2.1 Agricultural Share of GDP, 1945-1995 (percent)

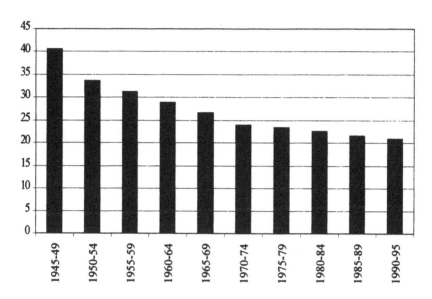

Source: Departamento Administrativo Nacional de Estadística (1997).

TABLE 2.1   Share of Agriculture in GDP (percent)

Country	1980	1990
Argentina	8.6	11.8
Bolivia	18.4	20.7
Brazil	10.5	11.5
Chile	7.2	8.2
Colombia	19.4	18.2
Ecuador	12.1	14.4
Mexico	8.2	7.5
Peru	10.2	13.9
Uruguay	14.5	14.6
Venezuela	4.2	5.0
Latin America[a]	10.1	10.9

[a]Includes Central American and Caribbean nations.

Source: Selected data from Comisión Económica para América Latina (1992).

Crops

The variety of weather conditions and adequate soils are reflected in Colombia's highly diversified agriculture. Historically, coffee has played an important role by providing foreign exchange earnings and employing a large share of the population on the Central Andean slopes. However, cattle-raising accounts for a larger share of value added than coffee. Other items that contribute significantly to agricultural value added include poultry, sugar cane, flowers, fruits, vegetables, rice and potatoes (see Table 2.2).

Exportable crops include coffee, bananas, flowers, sugar and cotton. Bananas have been a traditional export since the early part of the century. In the post-war period, cotton, sugar and flowers have prospered, aided by policies to promote non-traditional exports. Cotton has been an important export since the early 1970s, although production levels tend to swing widely due to changing international conditions and domestic policies[2]. On the average, legal exportable crops have accounted for 20 to 40 percent of domestic agricultural production since 1970.

Colombia is known internationally as a key source of illegal drugs.[3] This reputation began with growing exports of marihuana in the late 1970s and early 1980s. Cocaine processing and export became a booming industry in the 1980s and 1990s. Until the late-1980s, Colombian drug-traffickers relied on illegal imports of coca paste from Peru and Bolivia. Reliable data on trade flows of illegal crops are not available. However, in the late 1990s, it was estimated that Colombian drug exports yielded between US$2.0 and US$2.7 billion annually. Inflows for legal agricultural exports averaged around US$2.5 billion in the 1980s.[4] The impact on agriculture of developments in activities related to illicit crops in the 1990s is discussed in Chapter 6.

Importable crops include grains such as wheat, barley, maize, sorghum and rice and oilseeds (i.e., soybeans and oil palm).[5] Colombia also imported about 20 percent of its domestic consumption of dairy products in the 1980s. Since 1970, importable crops have accounted for 10 to 25 percent of the value of domestic agricultural production.

Non-tradable crops accounted for about half the value of domestic production in the 1980s.[6] This group of commodities features bulky, low-value crops, such as potatoes, cassava (*yucca*) and most fruits and vegetables. The perishable nature and high transportation costs normally associated with these crops limit prospects for international trade. Another important non-tradable is a sugar cane variety used to produce *panela*—a type of brown sugar. Beef production in Colombia is isolated from international trade because of the presence of hoof and mouth disease, which restricts entry to developed country markets. Although beef surpluses were exported in the late 1960s, exports in the 1980s and 1990s have accounted for only a marginal share of domestic slaughter. As a

TABLE 2.2 Share of Agricultural Output Value by Crop, Average 1980-1989

Crop	Value (1975 pesos)	Share (percent)
Annual Crops	29,669	24.5
Rice	5,983	4.9
Potato	5,651	4.7
Vegetables	5,012	4.1
Maize	4,001	3.3
Cotton	3,119	2.6
Sorghum	2,130	1.8
Bean	1,276	1.1
Soybean	1,225	1.0
Wheat	446	0.4
Barley	371	0.3
Others[a]	455	0.4
Permanent Crops	49,602	41.0
Coffee	15,432	12.7
Sugar Cane	7,490	6.2
Plantain	6,465	5.3
Panela Cane	5,831	4.8
Flowers	3,411	2.8
Cassava	2,483	2.1
Oil Palm	2,016	1.7
Banana	1,997	1.6
Other Fruits	1,638	1.4
Cocoa	1,306	1.1
Other[b]	1,533	1.3
Livestock	41,825	34.5
Cattle	28,027	23.1
Pork	2,678	2.2
Poultry	11,120	9.2
Total Farm Ouput	121,096	100.0

[a]Includes light tobacco, sesame, peanuts.

[b]Includes dark tobacco, yams, coconut and jute.

Source: Ministerio de Agricultura (1998).

result, beef has become a de facto non-tradable activity, with prices fluctuating independent of world trends.[7]

Dualistic Development

The development of Colombian agriculture has been affected greatly by the extremely unequal distribution of land. The pattern of land ownership, one of the most skewed in the world, is the legacy of Spanish colonization and the distribution of vast frontier lands to influential elites after independence.[8] As a result, a relatively small share of the population owns a large proportion of farm land and derives the lion's share of agricultural income. By contrast, in 1993, nearly 70 percent of Colombia's farmers worked plots of less than 5 hectares which represented less than 12 percent of the farmland and agricultural income.[9] Since 1960, the number of large farms has declined and the area covered by small farms (less than 5 hectares) has doubled. Despite these trends, the overall inequality of farm ownership has changed little since 1950.

Unequal land ownership is associated with two types of agriculture in Colombia. On the one hand, there is modern commercial agriculture, where farms tend to be large, flat and containing large tracts of good quality soil. Owners tend to be wealthy and educated. There are also the smallholders, known commonly in Colombia as *campesinos*. Farms in this sector tend to be located on hillsides; their soils tend to be poor and they are further away from adequate roads.

Commercial and *campesino* farms operate differently. Commercial agriculture uses modern technology, hires only wage labor and sells all its output on the market. In contrast, *campesinos* are low-income, use antiquated farming techniques and dedicate part of farm output to family consumption. However, they tend to apply more labor to production activities, partly due to the low opportunity cost of surplus family labor. In the 1970s, the ratio of labor to land was about eight times higher on farms under five hectares, compared with those above one hundred hectares.[10]

Campesino agriculture has accounted for about 50 percent of total agricultural production since 1960.[11] This sector has been the source of the bulk of the jobs generated by farming, as well as the food products for urban consumers. *Campesino* crops tend to be non-tradables, such as potatoes, cassava, plantains, fruits and vegetables, and cane for the production of *panela*. *Campesinos* are also involved in the production of some importables, such as wheat, barley, maize and beans. It is also estimated than some 30 percent of coffee output is provided by *campesino* farmers; nearly 80 percent of all coffee farmers in Colombia are classified as smallholders (see Table 2.3). In contrast, large farmers specialize in crops suited to the use of machinery (e.g., grains) or those requiring large-scale production to obtain economies of scale in processing, such as bananas, oil palm and sugar cane.

TABLE 2.3   *Campesino* Share of Area and Output, 1988 (percent)

Crop	Area	Output
Jute	100.0	100.0
Tobacco	96.1	95.8
Panela Cane	89.2	83.3
Cassava	86.1	86.8
Maize	80.1	68.6
Vegetables	75.5	78.7
Wheat	74.2	71.1
Cocoa	72.4	66.6
Fruits	69.3	74.1
Plantain	66.4	71.4
Potatoes	59.1	57.5
Barley	54.3	52.6
Rice	16.2	12.1
Cotton	9.3	9.0

Source: Departamento Nacional de Planeación (1990).

Rural Poverty and Social Indicators

The dualistic structure of Colombian farming is responsible for the tradition-ally high levels of poverty found in the Colombian countryside. In 1992, more than 4.2 million inhabitants of the rural sector, some 31.2 percent of the rural population, were found to be in extreme poverty. They accounted for nearly 70 percent of the population in this category in the entire country.[12] However, these figures represent some improvement over conditions in 1978, when 38.4 percent of the rural population was estimated to be in extreme poverty. Despite this apparent improvement, living conditions in the Colombian countryside continue to be substantially lower than in cities. In 1992, 24.1 percent of rural houses lacked sanitation services; the corresponding figure in urban centers was one percent. In the same year, about 20 percent of rural families were deemed to be living in extremely overcrowded conditions while in cities, this affected only 8.3 percent of households. Access to education in the countryside is limited. While 61 percent of the rural population had not finished primary education in 1992, the corresponding proportion in urban centers was 29 percent. In the same year, some 50 percent of rural households did not have access to drinking water. Life expectancy for rural Colombians in the early 1990s was three years less than in urban settings.

In comparison with other Latin American countries, the proportion of the entire population below the poverty line in Colombia is moderate. However, its distribution between rural and urban settings is atypical. In 1992, the proportion of the population in poverty was 3.6 times that in urban settings, which is substantially higher than in most other Latin American countries.[13]

Rural Violence

Violence has been endemic in the Colombian countryside since independence in the early nineteenth century. Periods of acute rural violence were registered several times in the 1800s. The unequal pattern of land distribution and high levels of rural poverty have often been blamed for social tensions in the countryside. These tensions, coupled with conflicts among the major political parties, explain the extended period of rural violence known as *La Violencia*, which left nearly one million Colombians dead between 1948 and 1964.[14] Guerrilla groups, paramilitary groups and private armies hired by drug-traffickers continued to account for high rates of violence in the 1970s, 1980s and 1990s. In the mid-1980s, it was estimated that about 8 percent of the total population and nearly 25 percent of the rural population were exposed to violent acts committed by left and right-wing groups alike.[15]

Post-war Economic Development

The Five Phases of Trade and Exchange Rate Policy

Colombia followed an import substitution industrialization (ISI) strategy during the post World War II period, as did most countries in Latin America. In addition to the classic recipe of protecting and promoting industry, the Colombian strategy included trade protection for importable crops and policies to foster the modernization of commercial crops. Most favored were crops linked to powerful agroindustrial interests (such as cotton, rice, and oilseeds) and food grains. The promotion of a few select crops under the ISI policy has been interpreted as a compromise between the interests of rural landowners and the rising industrial bourgeoisie.[16] The strategy created a niche for the production of importable foodstuffs and raw materials (e.g., cotton, oilseeds) and guaranteed urban centers stable supply of basic grains for urban workers. The policy also substituted food imports, in order to reduce the need to divert scarce foreign exchange resources away from industrial needs.

A complex array of policies was adopted to promote import substitution in agricultural crops, as well as food price stability for urban consumers. Tariffs were boosted in 1951. Law 26 of 1957 consolidated a system of subsidized credit aimed at producers of import-competing crops. The new law forced banks to direct 15 percent of their loans to farming activities at below market interest rates.[17] Government investment in agricultural research and extension was strengthened. Public investments in a handful of large irrigation projects were carried out between the early 1960s and the mid-1970s.

To stabilize prices and supplies, the government enacted a system of "contracts" between the public and private sectors for crops such as sugar, oilseeds and wheat. These contracts gave import permits to firms that agreed to purchase local crops (such as cotton, rice or oilseeds) at pre-arranged prices. Price levels were usually higher than those observed in world markets.

The National Food Supply Institute (INA, renamed IDEMA in 1968) was granted a monopoly on imports of most grains and a mandate to purchase crops directly in markets. While nominally acting to promote agricultural interests, INA also occasionally used its extensive powers to control—and even depress—prices, particularly in years of rising inflation. For example, in 1954, in the midst of booming coffee prices and escalating demand pressures, INA flooded local markets with imported food grains at prices reflecting unusually low tariffs.

Overall development policy varied substantially during the 1950-1990 period, reflecting key changes in trade policy. Five phases are clearly identifiable.[18] The first was the orthodox import substitution phase, lasting until 1967. During this phase, general economic growth was high but unstable and was punctuated by a series of stop-and-go cycles. These were related to the tendency towards overvaluation of the exchange rate and recurring balance of payments crises. On the other hand, thanks to an active agricultural policy that included protection from external trade, credit, research, extension and marketing activities carried out by the government, production and yields of targeted commodities increased substantially. These policies generally succeeded in fostering the expansion of commercial agriculture in relatively new crops (e.g., soybeans, oil palm and sorghum) as well as in some more traditional import-competing grains, such as rice, wheat, barley and maize (see Figure 2.2).

During the second phase (1967-75), the strategy was adjusted to include export promotion policies. The adjustment was the result of new attitudes on the part of policy-makers following a severe balance of payment crisis in 1966-67 that led to the design of explicit policies to promote non-traditional exports. These changes were incorporated in the landmark foreign trade regime outlined in Law 6 and Decree 444 of 1967. As a result of the new emphasis, a crawling peg regime for exchange rate management was adopted to prevent overvaluation. New measures to support exports were adopted, including the creation of the Tax Rebate Certificate (CAT), the establishment of subsidized credit channels for exports and expansion of the Vallejo Plan, a scheme to rebate tariff payments on inputs used in manufactures sold on world markets. Most of these measures counteracted, at least in part, the implicit taxation derived from industrial protection, and were a strong incentive to non-traditional export activities, including sugar, flowers and bananas. The anti-export effect of the import substitution strategy was much diminished in this period. As a consequence, the production of exportables and import-competing crops grew substantially (see Table 2.4).[19]

FIGURE 2.2 Areas Planted in Selected Commercial Crops, 1950-1970 (thousand hectares)

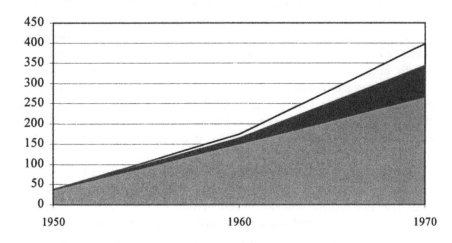

☐Cotton ■Sorghum ☐Soybeans

Source: Ministerio de Agricultura (1998).

TABLE 2.4 Growth Rates of the Value of Agricultural Production (annual average growth rates, percent)

| Crops | Phases of commercial policy | | | | |
	1951-66	1967-75	1976-82	1983-85	1986-90
Non-Tradable Crops[a]	2.3	2.6	1.6	1.7	2.5
Exportable Crops[b]	4.6	4.2	6.0	1.2	4.4
Excluding Coffee	8.3	7.0	3.2	3.6	4.1
Coffee	2.6	1.4	12.4	-1.7	5.6
Importable Crops[c]	3.0	3.8	3.5	0.9	10.9
Livestock	2.7	1.4	5.2	4.4	3.2
Total Farm Output	3.0	2.6	4.0	3.5	2.8

[a]Includes peanuts, potatoes, vegetables, *panela* cane, coconut, plaintain, yuca, yams, jute and fruits.

[b]Includes sesame, cotton, rice, sugar cane, cocoa, plantain for export, bananas, dark tobacco, flowers and coffee.

[c]Includes barley, beans, maize, sorghum, soybeans, light tobacco, wheat and oil palm.

Source: Author's own calculations and Ministerio de Agricultura (1998) data.

Agricultural growth was sharply reduced during the third phase of trade policy, between 1976 and 1982. In this period, the Colombian economy experienced a bout of Dutch disease, resulting from the massive increase in world commodity prices in the mid-1970s and, in particular, from the coffee booms of 1975-76 and 1978-79.[20] The rapid flow of foreign exchange into the country strengthened the Colombian currency, albeit temporarily, diminishing the profitability of tradable crops. To manage the potentially negative effects of a sudden abundance of foreign exchange, including runaway inflation, policy-makers reduced tariff and non-tariff barriers. This intensified competition and reduced prices for import-competing crops.

The negative effects of Dutch disease were aggravated after 1977 by expansive fiscal policies. Real public expenditure rose at an annual rate of 38.5 percent between 1977 and 1980. The bulk of this increase was for operating expenses. Due to growing government expenditures, the Colombian peso strengthened even further, rising in real value by 30 percent between 1975 and 1982.[21]

This strengthening of the peso up until 1982 (see Figure 2.3) coupled with lowered protection levels made tradable agricultural commodities more vulnerable to the sharp drop in world prices of 1982. When international markets weakened in that year, returns to tradable crops plummeted, producing the worst crisis experienced by Colombian agriculture in recent history. As shown in Table 2.5, the profitability of most tradable crops fell substantially, particularly during the 1980-82 period. A large share of the output gains of the 1967-76 period were erased as a result.

The fourth phase of trade policy was a period of crisis and adjustment, lasting from 1983 to 1985. Although Colombia did not face an overt debt and balance of payments crisis like the other large Latin American economies, shocks stemming from diminished international inflows, higher international

FIGURE 2.3 Real Exchange Rate, 1970-1990 (Index, 1986=100)

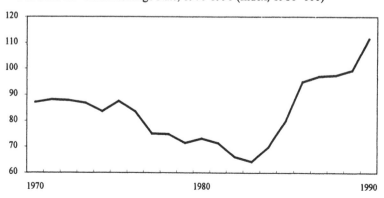

Source: Data from Banco de la República.

interest rates and recession in the developed countries forced important macro-economic changes. During this phase, government expenditure was reduced to accommodate a large adjustment in aggregate demand. Initially, foreign exchange imbalances were tackled by boosting tariff and non-tariff protection, which increased incentives for the production of commercial crops (see Figure 2.4). However, as of 1985, foreign exchange imbalances were attacked by accelerating devaluation of the exchange rate. Consequently, the real value of the Colombian peso fell by 35 percent between 1984 and 1986 (see Figure 2.3). These adjustments increased returns to importable and exportable crops by 10 percent and 6 percent, respectively, in the 1982-85 period.

The fifth and final phase of trade policy was the post-adjustment period of rapid recovery, which began in 1986 and ended in the first half of 1990. Due to its extraordinarily favorable effect on tradable agriculture, this phase is discussed in greater detail below.

The Agricultural Boom of 1986-90

The period between January 1986 and the first half of 1990 was very favorable for tradable crops. The profitability of many agricultural activities reached historically high levels in those years, as a consequence of decisions on macro-

TABLE 2.5 Return Indexes for Tradable Crops, 1980-90 (1990=100)

Commodity Group	1980	1986	1987	1988	1989	1990
Tradable Crops	90	110	106	108	95	100
Exportable Crops	91	116	109	114	94	100
Cotton	76	93	103	96	95	100
Rice	123	123	116	165	117	100
Coffee	80	132	110	111	80	100
Sugar Cane	94	101	103	99	97	100
Flowers	95	102	112	104	97	100
Importable Crops	88	94	96	90	99	100
Barley	68	87	91	86	86	100
Beans	53	87	79	81	88	100
Maize	107	102	112	93	99	100
Sorghum	74	82	85	89	100	100
Soybeans	98	102	91	97	112	100
Wheat	69	84	85	84	87	100

Source: Ministerio de Agricultura (1993).

FIGURE 2.4 Nominal Rate of Protection for Importable Crops, 1980-1990 (percent)

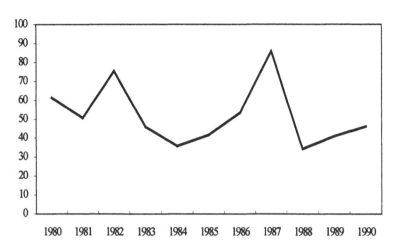

Source: Author's own calculations.

economic policy coupled with the favorable evolution of world commodity prices. The consequence was rapid growth in the output of tradable crops during this period (see Table 2.4).

The favorable juncture for tradable crops in the 1986-90 period was the result of three factors. The first was the evolution of the real exchange rate. After reaching historically high levels in 1986, it remained relatively stable until mid-1989 (see Figure 2.4). At that point, policy-makers decided to boost the rate again, devaluing the Colombian peso in preparation for trade liberalization, anticipated for 1990 (see Figure 2.3). It was felt that liberalization of the trade regime would generate a sharp increase in imports, which could be sustained only with a higher exchange rate. Devaluation also responded to fears about a potential balance of payments crisis, due to the sharp drop in coffee prices in mid-1989. As a result, between June 1989 and June 1990, the real exchange rate was devalued again, this time by 11.3 percent, establishing a new historical record and giving another boost to the profitability of tradable agricultural crops.

A second factor in the rise of tradable returns was favorable conditions in world commodity markets. International prices for most of Colombia's tradable crops increased above historical trends, particularly between 1988 and 1989 (see Figure 2.5). This upswing was due largely to the marked expansion in developed economies and, in some cases, to poor harvests in other countries.

FIGURE 2.5 International Price of Cereals and Oilseeds, 1980-1990 (US$ Dollars per ton, 1990=100)

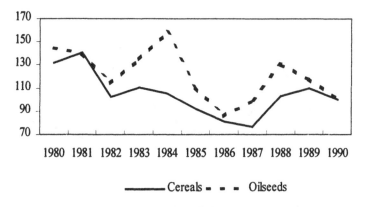

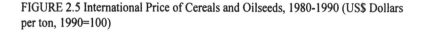

Source: Data obtained from World Bank (1994b).

The third factor that accounts for the positive performance of Colombian agriculture in the 1986-90 period was the minor reduction in protection for importable crops (see Figure 2.4). While protection for the main importable crops had stabilized at rates of 40 to 50 percent in 1985 and 1986, these levels dropped to between 30 and 40 percent in 1989 and 1990.[22] This reduction was due to the increase in world prices and the relative stability of domestic prices, thanks to policies that prevented the transmission of world prices to domestic producers.[23]

The increased profitability of tradable crops in the 1986-90 period was responsible for substantial increases in planted areas and production levels. As a result, agricultural GDP grew even faster than economy-wide GDP in 1987, 1989 and 1990 (see Figure 2.6). However, as later events would demonstrate, much of this growth was the result of planting on marginal land at relatively high cost. Production in these areas would prove to be short-lived.

The positive atmosphere surrounding the production of tradable crops in the 1986-90 period led many to believe that favorable conditions for this sector of Colombian farming would endure for some time. However, there were serious indications that these conditions were temporary. First, world market trends indicated that commodity prices would eventually resume their long-term secular decline. Second, as events would confirm, the pre-emptive devaluation of the exchange rate seemed excessive and sent an overly optimistic signal to producers of tradable crops.

FIGURE 2.6 GDP Growth, 1986-1990 (percent)

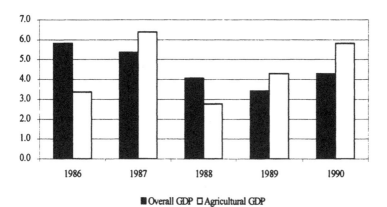

■ Overall GDP □ Agricultural GDP

Source: Departamento Administrativo Nacional de Estadística (1997).

The Distributional Consequences of Growth in Agriculture

Economic indicators reveal an impressive record of growth for Colombian agriculture in the 1950-90 period. Average annual growth in output was 3.5 percent per year, one of the highest rates in Latin America. However, this apparently acceptable record masks the uneven changing fortunes of commercial farmers, *campesino* producers and landless rural workers.

During most of the period, the bulk of agricultural growth was the result of output gains by commercial growers, a pattern that accentuated the dualism of Colombian agriculture. Starting from a modest technological base in 1950, large commercial farms underwent a substantial transformation, responding positively to supportive policies and the increasing availability of new production technologies. Green Revolution advances around the world provided improved seeds that were highly responsive to the application of fertilizers. In Colombia, these technologies were adopted in tandem with the mechanization of planting and harvesting tasks. Farmers were encouraged to modernize by government programs, which included subsidized credit, marketing support, import controls and research and extension services. The most significant transformations occurred in tradable crops and, importables, in particular. These were targeted to receive special protection as part of import substitution efforts. The crops that most benefited from this favorable treatment included oil palm, soybeans, rice, sorghum, cotton, sugar cane and bananas. This process was particularly intense in the 1960s and 1970s. After almost three decades of rapid expansion in output and productivity, yield gains by commercial crops slowed as of 1978.

TABLE 2.6 Sources of Growth of Agriculture, 1950-1987 (percent)

	1950-1987	1950-1980	1980-1987
Growth Rates			
Output	3.52	3.95	2.01
Area	1.41	1.50	1.23
Capital	2.80	3.22	1.37
Labor	0.57	0.49	0.70
Contribution to Growth			
Area	0.25	0.27	0.18
Capital	1.15	1.29	0.66
Labor	0.24	0.23	0.26
Total productivity	1.89	2.15	0.91

Source: Departamento Nacional de Planeación (1990).

The pattern of agricultural growth was particularly detrimental to the interests of rural workers. Despite high poverty levels and low wages in rural areas, agricultural growth between 1950 and 1987 involved growth in labor demand of only 0.6 percent annually, at a time when overall population growth rates were in excess of 2.5 percent (see Table 2.6). Accordingly, since the end of 1950s, agriculture's share of total employment diminished at a faster rate than would be expected, based on international patterns of development. In fact, international patterns indicated that agricultural employment in the Colombian economy should have been about 50 percent in 1987, at a time when it was only a third of total employment (see Figure 2.7).[24]

Low growth in labor absorption in the Colombian countryside since 1950 has been a direct consequence of policies to protect industrial and urban interests, and to promote large-scale mechanized farming. According to one estimate, commercial agriculture provided only 18 percent of the new jobs in rural areas between 1950 and 1980, due to heavy reliance on expansion of capital and land inputs.[25] In contrast, the crops that account for the bulk of employment are those associated with smallholders, such as coffee, plantains, cane for *panela*, fruits and vegetables In 1988, *campesino* crops accounted for nearly 70 percent of agricultural employment.[26]

Other factors that exacerbated these trends were the modest outcome of land reform efforts and the discouragement of all forms of land rental.[27] Between 1962 and 1990, redistribution of land by INCORA, the land reform agency, benefited 60,500 households out of an estimated total of 600,000 without access to sufficient land (see Table 2.7). Overall, these efforts have had little impact on the unequal pattern of land ownership.[28] However, land reform regulations have induced undesirable effects, such as the massive eviction of sharecroppers. This

FIGURE 2.7 Share of Agriculture in Total Employment, 1925-1985 (percent)

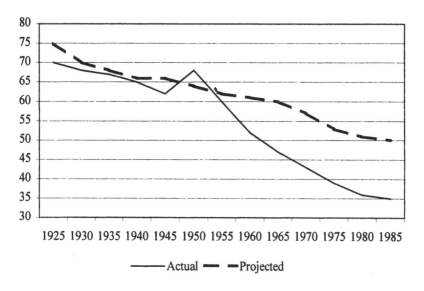

Source: Departamento Nacional de Planeación (1990).

TABLE 2.7 Land Distributed by INCORA, 1962-1990

Period	Families Benefited	Area (Thousand Hectares)
1962-1964	845	7.0
1965-1969	3,073	65.9
1970-1974	6,497	126.4
1975-1979	14,032	282.2
1980-1984	15,714	222.5
1985-1990	20,418	370.9
Total 1962-1990	60,579	1,075.0
Annual Average	2,089	37.1

Source: Jaramillo (1994).

seems to be a rational response to the fear of expropriation by large landowners, as well as to legal measures prohibiting land rental.[29]

The massive migration of rural inhabitants to urban centers and, to a lesser extent, to areas of new settlement, was largely a consequence of low employment growth in agriculture since 1950. The lack of opportunities for remunerative employment helped to increase social tensions that fed into violence in the Colombian countryside. Some studies suggest that areas of the country with the lowest rates of employment growth are where rural violence is most intense.[30] A vicious cycle operates in these areas. Narrowed access to land and employment increased the propensity for violence. In turn, violence diminished incentives for investment and employment. Rural insecurity reduced investment and biased investment patterns toward productive activities that are not labor intensive. Furthermore, the cost of hiring a large work force was potentially high in an atmosphere where workers might initiate violent reprisals against employers.

Rural workers did experience an improvement in their situation as of in the mid-1970s.[31] This seemed to be the result of declining population growth, increasing rural-urban migration and rapid dissemination of new coffee technologies that sharply increased the demand for labor. Demand for planting new tree stocks and for the ballooning harvest increased demand for rural employment and exerted a positive effect on rural wages.[32]

For *campesino* agriculture, the 1950-90 period was one of income stagnation.[33] The first phase, between 1950 and 1975, was one of stagnant or falling yields of traditional *campesino* crops, at a time when real prices remained stable. Commercial agriculture prospered, while *campesino* incomes deteriorated. After 1975, there were notable increases in the yields of some of the most important *campesino* crops. Initially, coffee growers were the first to benefit from the adoption of new technologies. Rural workers and smallholders with surplus family labor also benefited from the boost in labor demand throughout the coffee-growing region.

After 1975, non-coffee *campesino* growers started receiving some government attention, ending a long period of neglect. Owing to a resurgence in rural violence and an international wave of support for integrated rural development with emphasis on the welfare of poor farmers, the Colombian government launched efforts to assist selected *campesino* areas. These efforts included subsidized credit, technical assistance, marketing support, provision of social services and infrastructure, as well as the design of new technologies for *campesino* crops adapted to the ecological conditions of Andean slopes. Most of these efforts were channeled through a new agency, the Integrated Rural Development Fund (DRI), established in 1976 and supported by loans from the World Bank.[34]

Evaluations of DRI efforts demonstrate that farmers living in targeted areas displayed large gains in yields. The differences in yields between large-scale farmers and *campesinos* growing crops like maize, rice and coffee was reduced sharply between 1978 and 1988, due to productivity gains among *campesinos*.[35] Yield gains have been explained by the widespread adoption of new seeds and modern inputs such as fertilizers and pesticides. Other crops that benefited from yield gains include cane for *panela*, potatoes, beans, plantains, vegetables and fruits.

Despite yield gains among smallholders, prices for *campesino* crops dropped significantly between 1975 and 1990. This was the result of growing supplies in markets for non-tradable foodstuffs, which faced relatively inelastic demand. The reduction in prices offset most of the increase in productivity, leaving overall *campesino* income roughly stable. Thus, by the late 1980s, despite increasing state attention, income from the agricultural activities of *campesino* households had changed little since the early 1950s. This reflected the limits of policies aimed at promoting the production of traditional small-holder crops and highlighted the need to promote alternative crops among *campesinos*.

However, total income of a large proportion of *campesino* households showed some gains in the 1950-1990 period. These came from non-agricultural sources, including greater participation by female household members in non-agricultural activities. Between 1973 and 1985, the share of women in the economically active population of rural areas rose from 14 to 32 percent.[36] By 1993, commerce and service activities accounted for 11.2 and 14.7 percent of rural employment, respectively.[37] This diversification of rural incomes away from agriculture is responsible for some income gains, as well as a modest reduction in rural poverty levels.

The Pre-Liberalization Atmosphere

In mid-1990, when the administration of President Cesar Gaviria was pre-paring to initiate a massive trade liberalization program to spur growth of the Colombian economy, farming associations were still in an optimistic mood. Tradable crops experienced a boom, which was particularly strong in import-competing crops. The favorable situation was the result of high international prices, a devalued exchange rate and a government-sponsored Selective Supply Plan, which established attractive minimum support prices and guaranteed the marketing of crops.

What could be expected of a new market-oriented development strategy? Were there grounds to anticipate an important change in the returns to tradable agriculture as a result of reforms? A brief analysis of the situation of Colombian agriculture in 1990 provides some clues. ISI policies had taxed tradable crops via the overvaluation of the exchange rate. This is documented clearly in a comprehensive study of policies affecting four tradable crops—coffee, wheat, rice and cotton—between 1960 and 1983.[38] The study measured the effect of direct interventions on output and input prices as well as the indirect effects of industrial protection and macroeconomic policy on the exchange rate. The result was a tax of approximately 8 percent of sectoral value added. The authors of the study concluded that the proliferation of agricultural policies—tariff and non-tariff protection, credit and other input subsidies—were only sufficient to offset a portion of the anti-tradable bias of the development strategy. Similar findings in other Latin American countries showed that the Colombian pattern was not unique.[39]

The effects of ISI policies suggest that in the 1950-85 period, the anti-export bias of the trade regime worked in favor of protected urban-based industrial sectors and, to a lesser extent, non-tradable goods and services. The latter includes root crops, fresh vegetables and fruits, produced mostly by *campesino* agriculture. This may explain why *campesino* incomes did not deteriorate substantially during the period, despite government neglect until the mid-1970s.

In spite of the overall taxation of agriculture, the situation changed radically after 1985. Significant government policies to correct macroeconomic imbalances and devalue the Colombian peso redressed much of the previous biases. The exchange rate was successfully maintained at historically high levels, largely due to the virtual absence of new inflows of capital into the economy from external sources. These conditions stimulated the production of tradable crops in the 1986-90 period, apparently offsetting much of the implicit taxation traditionally associated with ISI. Whether government policies in this phase were sufficient to neutralize indirect taxation stemming from industrial protection is still an unresolved issue, given the lack of detailed studies on this period. However, it seems clear that whatever bias remained, it was drastically reduced during the late 1980s.

Thus, with the onset of trade liberalization, prospects for a continuation of the positive atmosphere enjoyed by tradable agriculture were not good. As to exportables, the collapse of the International Coffee Agreement in mid-1989 prompted a sharp slump in coffee prices, which fell to historical lows in subsequent years. Furthermore, as of 1990, the end of debt-crisis troubles and the reestablishment of macroeconomic stability in the large economies of Latin America led to a new phase of capital flows into the region. After a lengthy economic expansion, the economies of the developed countries stalled, depressing the demand for internationally traded commodities. The adoption of market-oriented reforms in Colombia would likely mean the removal of special policies favoring importable crops and a more neutral playing field for all farmers. Accordingly, in mid-1990, the likelihood of a reduction in the profitability of import-competing crops loomed large, although the magnitude of this reduction was unknown.

Notes

1. The discussion of Colombia's physical and meteorological characteristics draws from García and Montes (1988).

2. Cocoa and dark tobacco are minor exportable crops.

3. Studies on the economic impact of illegal crops in Colombia include Steiner (1996), Uribe (1997) and Rocha (1997).

4. For a detailed review of the possible extent of revenues and profits from the Colombian drug trade, see Steiner (1996).

5. Rice has been considered by some authors as an exportable, due to the production of occasional surpluses. However, the country has been traditionally nearly self-sufficient and government policies treated rice as an importable.

6. If beef is excluded, non-tradable crops account for about a third of agricultural GDP.

7. Valdés and Schaeffer (1995) obtain high levels of domestic protection in the 1990s for beef, assuming it is an importable commodity. However, the feasibility of large amounts of beef imports into Colombia is severely limited by the lack of refrigerated facilities. Also, domestic demand has traditionally favored fresh over frozen meat. The introduction of imported beef is also hindered by preference for local cuts, which differ from international standards.

8. The gradual distribution of lands to influential elites is carefully documented in Legrand (1986).

9. Admittedly, these figures exaggerate tenure inequality since farmland owned in small plots tend, on average, to be of higher quality than in large landholdings, due to the effect of unproductive areas in the latter.

10. Estimate based on Berry (1973).

11. See Berry (1991).

12. Estimates taken from World Bank (1994a).

13. The imbalance between rural and urban poverty is elaborated in World Bank (1994a).

14. Accounts of the causes and consequences of *La Violencia* appear in Oquist (1980).

15. Estimate taken from Bejarano (1988).

16. This view is formulated by García and Montes (1989). In the 1900-1950 period, policies shifted often between the contradictory goals of protecting agricultural production and supplying food to urban centers at low prices.

17. See García (1991).

18. These phases follow loosely those described by Ocampo and Villar (1992).

19. There is no agreement on the degree to which export promotion measures offset taxation on tradables derived from industrial protection. According to Berry (1992), the bias against tradable agriculture was effectively removed. The compensation was only partial for Garcia and Montes (1988) and Torres (1994).

20. The episode of Dutch disease in Colombia is described in Edwards (1984) and Kamas (1986). The effects on agriculture are discussed in García and Montes (1988).

21. Figure taken from Thomas (1985).

22. See Barbosa and Jaramillo (1994) for an analysis of protection policies and the stabilization of agricultural prices in Colombia.

23. Paradoxically, protection levels fell even while the Selective Supply Plan of the Ministry of Agriculture was being implemented (1988-90). This plan sought to stimulate production of importable crops by boosting support prices and restricting imports.

24. These calculations appear in Departamento Nacional de Planeación (1990).

25. The estimate comes from Berry (1992).

26. This figure appears in Departamento Nacional de Planeación (1990).

27. A provocative interpretation of the paralysis of land reform efforts in Colombia, arguably a result of the political power of commercial farmers who blocked attempts at redistribution, appears in de Janvry and Sadoulet (1993).

28. Once the initial political impetus of land reform was lost in the first half of the 1970s, INCORA's efforts focused on titling government lands in frontier areas, usually with detrimental environmental consequences.

29. Accounts of the undesirable effects of land legislation appear in Kalmanovitz (1978).

30. This conclusion is discussed in World Bank (1996).

31. The improvement in rural living standards of the 1970s is analyzed in Urrutia (1991).

32. The effect of technological change on coffee and its effect on wages appears in Errázuriz (1987).

33. Analysis of the stagnation of *campesino* incomes appears in Departamento Nacional de Planeación (1990) and Berry (1992).

34. A thorough review of DRI activities appears in Vargas (1994).

35. See Departamento Nacional de Planeación (1990).

36. Figures from Departamento Nacional de Planeación (1990).

37. Data from Reyes and Martínez (1994).

38. The study is by García y Montes (1988).

39. These findings are summarized in Krueger et al. (1992).

3

Apertura: The Reforms and Trade Liberalization of 1990-1991

In August of 1990, after taking office, President Cesar Gaviria announced the start of an ambitious period of economic reforms. The initial package of reforms was known as *Apertura*, indicating an "opening-up" of the economy to external markets. Gaviria argued that *Apertura* reforms were necessary to shake the economy out of its slow-growth pattern, by taking advantage of the opportunities offered by world trade. Strong political support facilitated the approval of many important legal reforms within the first year of his administration, including dramatic changes in trade, labor, and financial regulations.[1] Gaviria was also successful in promoting the election of a Constituent Assembly, which led to the approval of a new Constitution by the end of 1991.

This chapter provides a description of *Apertura* reforms, with respect to the agricultural sector. It outlines the key policies and the justification used in official documents, without attempting to assess their success. This task is left to the remaining chapters. First, a broad outline of *Apertura* reforms is presented. Second, agricultural policy changes are reviewed. Policies to benefit *campesinos* and to foster rural development are described in the third section. An assessment of the content of reforms is presented in the final section.

The Justification for *Apertura*

The key elements of Gaviria's *Apertura* reforms were published in the Economic and Social Development Plan (The Plan) for the 1990-94 period, which was entitled The Peaceful Revolution.[2] The Plan presented an analysis of Colombian development trends, the state of the economy at the start of 1990s, and described the major elements of *Apertura* along with the rationale for breaking with past economic policies.

The Peaceful Revolution argued that import substitution had kept domestic industry isolated from world markets and that substantial reforms were needed to avoid further stagnation in living standards. The Plan acknowledged that import substitution had paid important dividends in the past, resulting in a positive record of growth since the 1950s and in the development of a fledgling domestic industry. Nevertheless, economic performance had been losing steam since the mid-seventies, as reflected in falling per capita growth rates. The Plan attributed declining economic performance to a slowdown in the growth of factor productivity since 1974, the most important determinant of living standards in a modern economy.[3] The productivity slowdown seemed to be a result of the limits of a small domestic market and the technological shortcomings of enterprises sheltered from international competition. On the other hand, the development of exports, a potential source of growth, remained tied to the success of a few non-traditional products.

The Plan focused on three objectives designed to revitalize economic growth and raise living standards. The first called for more emphasis on market signals to allocate scarce resources. The second focused on increasing the role of the private sector in productive activities. The third redefined the role of the state in the economy and highlighted the need for a substantial reorganization of government agencies.

Several structural reforms were proposed to accomplish these objectives. The most important was trade liberalization, which was intended to eliminate the anti-export bias associated with import substitution by exposing domestic producers to international competition. This was to be accomplished by removing all non-tariff barriers and gradually lowering customs duties on all goods. The Plan also outlined structural reforms in regulations dealing with labor and financial markets.[4] More flexibility was introduced in labor markets, by reducing hiring costs and allowing for a greater diversity in employment contracts. In capital markets, reforms included removal of restrictions on entry into the banking sector, promotion of stock markets, elimination of foreign exchange controls, and adoption of a more favorable legal framework to promote foreign investment flows.

The Peaceful Revolution also underscored the need for less government intervention in economic affairs, including the elimination of discretionary and arbitrary decisions by public agencies. It was hoped this would broaden the scope of private activity and give market forces a greater role in resource allocation. The idea was to introduce transparent and stable rules to help manufacturers, merchants, industrialists and consumers make decisions with less risk. Enhanced private decision-making was expected to increase production in those areas where the Colombian economy displayed solid advantages.

Apertura and Agriculture

The Peaceful Revolution included two important areas of policy change for agriculture. First, it explicitly included agricultural goods within the trade liberalization program. This implied a dismantling of traditional government intervention in the form of import controls, support prices and direct crop purchases. A new, more liberal trade regime also meant that stable trading practices were to be established to avoid discretionary adjustments to protection levels and import flows, which had been the rule prior to 1990. Second, The Peaceful Revolution announced an ambitious ten-year plan for public invest- ment in irrigation and drainage facilities,[5] which was the Gaviria administra- tion's key priority to spur long-term agricultural development.

Other policy priorities for agriculture were fleshed out in the first two years of the Gaviria administration, but were not included explicitly in The Peaceful Revolution.[6] Policies to expand exports were reflected in the emphasis given to the negotiation of international trade agreements. Agricultural credit regulations were reformed to increase the participation of private banks in lending to farmers. *Apertura* policies also led to an important overhaul of government agencies, including those dealing with agricultural affairs. Programs to benefit *campesinos* were also fleshed out gradually. Key priorities included special subsidies for public investment in irrigation, a new approach to land reform, support for decentralized decision-making in the implementation of develop- ment projects, consistent with key provisions of the 1991 Constitution.

An account of agricultural reforms is presented below, starting with those explicitly included in The Peaceful Revolution: trade liberalization and the plan to boost investment in irrigation and drainage. This is followed by a review of policies concerning the promotion of exports, agricultural credit and institu- tional reorganization.

Trade Liberalization and Domestic Marketing Reform

The *Apertura* program for agriculture featured policies to liberalize trade flows and to deregulate domestic marketing. These included provisions to eliminate quotas, lower import tariffs and reduce government intervention in agricultural markets. However, The Peaceful Revolution gave agriculture special treatment, on account of its sensitivity to world price variations, the characteristics of production cycles, the existence of distortions in international agricultural markets stemming from pervasive subsidies in developed countries, and the oligopolistic nature of some trading channels. As a result, special stabilization instruments would benefit farm interests, including a special regime of compensatory measures to neutralize unfair trading practices.

The process to remove trade restrictions affected every sector of the Colom- bian economy, including agriculture. Trade liberalization occurred in two stages. The first took place in the period between late 1990 and the first two months of 1991, when all quantitative restrictions—such as quotas and import permits—were eliminated and a timetable was set for a gradual reduction of tariffs by 1994. In that year, import duties in every sector of the economy were to be set at the same level.

The plan gave special treatment to agriculture by calling for tariffs on farm products to be reduced at a slower pace than those on imports in other sectors.

However, by mid-1991, government licenses for all agricultural imports had been eliminated, as had IDEMA's monopoly over imports of food grains and oilseeds.[7]

The second stage began in February of 1992 when the tariff-reduction schedule was accelerated for all sectors, due to unexpected events. Instead of responding positively to tariff reductions, imports into Colombia declined in 1991. Apparently, investment decisions were postponed until further tariff reductions occurred. Additionally, increasing capital inflows created macroeconomic difficulties by putting upward pressures on inflation and on the value of the Colombian currency. Capital inflows were attracted by a number of factors, including improved economic prospects, high domestic interest rates, a recessionary environment in the developed countries, the end of the Latin American debt crisis, and a crackdown on illegal drug-related money in the United States.[8]

As a result of mounting macroeconomic troubles in 1991, the plan to gradually reduce import duties was abandoned, as was the special schedule for the agricultural sector. In February of 1992, the average tariff for the economy was reduced to 12 percent and five tariff levels were adopted: 0 and 5 percent for raw materials, intermediate and capital goods not produced in Colombia, 10 and 15 percent for other intermediate goods, and 15 and 20 percent for finished consumer goods.

As a result of these decisions, the average tariff for the agricultural sector fell from 31.8 percent to 14.0 percent between 1991 and 1992, which is slightly above the average for the economy as a whole (see Table 3.1). However, compared with other sectors, farm products enjoyed special treatment, particularly in terms of effective protection.[9] Between 1991 and 1992, the rate of effective protection for agriculture fell from 77.5 percent to 36.0 percent, while effective protection for the rest of the economy declined from 49.3 percent to 19.7 percent (see Table 3.1). This was a result of the greater difference between tariffs on inputs and consumer goods in the agricultural sector compared with other sectors of the economy.[10] In point of fact, the average tariff on raw materials and intermediate goods used in agriculture was 2.4 percent in 1993, when tariffs on these items in the rest of the economy averaged 10.2 percent. That same year, tariffs on capital goods for agriculture—mostly transport and hauling equipment—averaged 2.2 percent, while the average tariff on capital goods in all other sectors of the economy was 12.7 percent. Moreover, finished goods in agriculture benefited from greater protection levels than those produced by other sectors.

A price-band system was established in mid-1991 for eight sensitive agricultural products: wheat, barley, maize, sorghum, rice, soybeans, sugar and milk.[11] The system was designed to prevent the transmission of extreme highs and lows on world agricultural markets, while maintaining a reasonable degree of connection between local prices and external trends. Bands were expected to stabilize prices for the chosen commodities, as well as for a large number of

TABLE 3.1 Average Tariffs and Effective Protection Rates, 1991-1993 (percent)

	1991		1992		1993	
	Avg. Tariff	Effective Rate	Avg. Tariff	Effective Rate	Avg. Tariff	Effective Rate
Agricultural Goods[a]	31.8	77.5	14.0	36.0	12.7	30.8
Consumer goods	44.3	120.5	20.0	54.5	18.8	52.2
Food items	42.1	113.7	18.0	51.3	17.9	49.5
Pharmaceutical products	25.0	40.8	10.0	17.6	0.0	-15.1
Animal feed	31.9	100.2	14.0	47.2	13.7	44.4
Raw materials & interm. goods	14.6	15.7	5.6	6.8	2.4	-2.2
Other materials	12.1	12.0	6.1	8.7	6.2	4.9
Chemical products	17.2	19.4	5.2	5.1	0.0	-6.1
Capital goods for agriculture	15.5	14.5	10.5	15.6	15.4	15.4
Transport equipment	18.7	21.6	7.5	7.0	2.2	7.0
Non-Agricultural Goods	29.3	49.3	11.5	19.7	11.4	18.6
Consumer non-durable goods	40.5	66.8	16.8	28.2	16.4	26.7
Consumer durables	39.9	77.6	16.7	35.2	17.1	35.0
Fuels and lubricants	22.3	45.2	7.5	14.2	7.3	14.0
Raw materials & interm. goods	28.4	49.3	10.3	17.8	10.2	16.4
Construction materials	33.5	65.0	12.8	22.2	12.8	21.4
Capital goods for industry	21.1	26.8	9.5	12.6	9.4	11.9
Transport equipment	29.6	55.8	13.0	22.9	12.7	23.9

[a]Excludes variable tariffs from agricultural price bands.

Source: Departamento Nacional de Planeación, Trade Unit.

substitutes and by-products. Some 112 tariff items were chosen to benefit from the effects of price bands: eight for "indicative" primary products and 104 for substitutes and by-products such as flour, soybean meal and vegetable oils.

Frequent changes were made in the price band system after its establishment in 1991. The most important was its elevation in 1995 to an international regime for agricultural imports for the Andean Pact countries of Colombia, Venezuela and Ecuador. This change was accompanied by a widening of the system to incorporate price bands for pork, chicken parts, palm oil, soybean oil, white maize and raw sugar.

As a result of *Apertura* policies, the import substitution system, which had regulated domestic marketing for several decades, was dismantled between 1990 and 1991. Up until 1990, imports of grains and oilseeds had been restricted by prior licensing requirements and, at times, by IDEMA's monopoly over imports of the major food grains.[12] Furthermore, IDEMA intervened actively in the markets for these products, purchasing crops at support prices set to cover domestic production costs. Marketing restrictions were extended to several major export products, such as cotton and sugar. Exports required approval from the Ministry of Agriculture. Permits were granted only if agroindustrial firms, producers' associations and the government agreed on prices and supplies for domestic consumption.

Apertura policies included the elimination of IDEMA's monopoly on grain imports and a gradual withdrawal of direct intervention in markets, in order to allow greater participation by the private sector. Support prices were replaced by "floor" prices, set every six months.[13] In contrast to support prices, "floor" prices were based on international prices instead of production costs, and were meant only to offer a last-resort opportunity for crop sales to formerly supported commodities.[14] These prices were defined as the minimum import cost, determined by the "floor" price of the band for each semester, minus the cost of storage and transport.

The new policy also reoriented IDEMA's purchasing activities towards marginal areas, as an income-support policy for *campesinos*. However, the government allowed the agency to intervene occasionally in commercial farming areas as a buyer of last resort, in the event of disruptions in the market or serious problems with the sale of crops.

New restrictive guidelines for intervention by IDEMA transferred responsibility for the storage of food grains and oilseeds to the private sector. The agency's presence had kept private concerns from becoming significantly involved in this activity. As a result, private storage businesses in Colombia were severely underdeveloped.[15]

The shake-up in IDEMA's role had significant repercussions on its finances and the scale of its activities. Prior to *Apertura*, the agency covered losses on its marketing activities with profits obtained from its monopoly on key grain imports. With the elimination of this monopoly—and associated tariff exemptions—IDEMA's income was limited to revenue from the sale of products and to transfers from the national budget. Under the new system, crops purchased in marginal areas would be subsidized directly by the government. The reduction in IDEMA's revenues and responsibilities led to a sizable reduction in its staff from 3,378 employees at the end of 1989 to 1,516 at the end of 1993.

These reforms drastically reduced IDEMA's involvement in the purchase of crops and its share of grain and oilseed inventories. Total domestic purchases of grain declined 37 percent in volume between 1990 and 1993 (see Table 3.2). The number of purchasing centers in commercial farming areas declined as well. IDEMA also sold or leased the bulk of its storage silos and warehouses at ports to private storage firms, in order to make them more accessible to private agents. Its reduced role, coupled with mounting accusations of corruption and gross administrative inefficiencies, led to its liquidation in 1996.

Irrigation and Drainage Investments

The development plan of the Gaviria administration announced a significant boost in public investment in irrigation and drainage. This line of investment

TABLE 3.2 IDEMA Purchases, 1980-1993 (thousand tons)

Crop	Average 1980-89	1990	1991	1992	1993
Sesame	2.1	1.3	0.4	0.1	1.6
Rice	139.4	319.4	129.7	148.9	182.9
Barley	0.1	0.0	0.0	0.0	0.0
Beans	1.5	12.8	1.2	0.9	7.6
Maize	39.0	50.2	83.3	25.1	26.1
Sorghum	37.6	13.9	24.5	27.2	29.8
Soybeans	4.6	0.6	47.0	10.7	0.3
Wheat	26.4	25.0	32.5	7.2	0.0
Total	250.7	423.2	318.7	220.0	248.2
Purchases as share of domestic harvest (percent)					
Sesame	18.9	15.7	7.2	2.6	22.8
Rice	7.3	15.1	7.5	8.6	11.6
Barley	0.2	0.0	0.0	0.0	0.0
Beans	1.6	9.7	1.1	0.7	6.2
Maize	4.4	4.1	6.5	2.4	2.2
Sorghum	6.2	1.8	3.3	3.6	4.7
Soybeans	2.9	0.3	24.3	11.2	0.2
Wheat	38.7	23.8	34.6	9.5	0.0

Source: IDEMA.

had been virtually abandoned since the mid-1970s. The Plan justified this renewed emphasis by arguing that the shortage of farmland with a stable supply of water to cope with the cycles involved in farming was one of the primary constraints to the growth of Colombian agriculture.[16]

In 1991, the Social and Economic Policy Council (CONPES), a governmental body in charge of designing and approving all major policy changes, announced the Ten-Year Land Improvement Plan, at a total estimated cost of US$1.1 billion.[17] The Plan outlined ambitious goals for public and private investment in irrigation and drainage, and proposed a substantial increase in government funding. It also called for investments to benefit some 535,000 hectares of land during the 1990s, twice the amount covered by public investments in irrigation since 1950.

To accomplish these ambitious targets, the National Land Improvement Institute (INAT) was restructured and a regulatory framework was created to make investments in land improvement more effective. Laws 41 and 99 of 1993 include the relevant institutional and regulatory changes. Under the new policy regime, irrigation projects can only be constructed in areas where substantial local demand from farming communities exists. In contrast to past practices, beneficiaries were now expected to repay a pre-established portion of public outlays. Farmers were also required to participate in investment decisions, as well as in the management of irrigation districts. The recovery of a share of invested public funds was intended to facilitate greater coverage of the program. However, substantial subsidies would be allowed, including a smaller repayment requirement for low-income farmers. INAT was also authorized to contract the construction of irrigation works.

Aside from INAT-led investments, favorable lending terms and subsidies were also offered through public credit institutions, in order to stimulate private land-improvement efforts. Individual and collective borrowing facilities were created. In mid-1993, a Rural Capitalization Incentive was created to grant a 30 percent subsidy for investments in irrigation and drainage.[18]

Trade Agreements

A number of important changes were made in Colombia's export promotion policy as a result of *Apertura*. New emphasis was placed on the signing of international trade agreements that could expand markets for Colombian products. Trade liberalization also eliminated the need for policies to compensate for the effects of excessive protection. Consequently, export subsidies and other measures, which had been instrumental in compensating anti-export biases, until 1990 were phased out.

Trade integration with Andean neighbors received strong encouragement during the Gaviria administration. In 1992, a free trade zone was established between Colombia, Venezuela, Ecuador and Bolivia.[19] Quantitative restrictions and tariffs for most agricultural flows were eliminated that year.

A trade agreement known as the G-3 was signed in June of 1994 between Colombia, Mexico and Venezuela. It called for gradual trade liberalization, during a ten-year period, on approximately 60 percent of the agricultural products that were included in the treaty. Nearly 33 percent of all agricultural tariff items were excluded from the liberalization schedule. A 15-year tariff reduction program was established for a list of sensitive agricultural goods.[20]

A trade agreement with Chile was signed in December of 1993. It contemplated the elimination of all non-tariff barriers as of January of 1994, and established a tariff reduction program to be completed by 1999. Initial tariffs were readjusted to 75 percent of the levels prevailing in each country in 1993. The reduction was immediate for many products, and extended over a period of three years for products with considerable trade potential. The agreement also excluded sensitive agricultural products, particularly those covered by price bands. The list of exempted items accounts for approximately 8 percent of each country's non-mineral exports.

Aside from regional trade agreements, Colombia participated fully in trade discussions to include agriculture within the GATT multilateral agreement. Colombia was part of the Cairns group of countries, which pressured developed countries to commit to substantial reductions in their agricultural subsidies and to increase access to the their markets for commodities from developing nations. After eight years of negotiation, the Uruguay Round of GATT was signed in 1994, subjecting agricultural trade to multilateral rules.

The 1994 GATT agreement on agricultural goods included commitments related to trade liberalization in three areas: access to markets, domestic support and export promotion. As part the agreement, Colombia pledged high tariff ceilings for sensitive agricultural goods. The idea behind this apparently protectionist stance was to facilitate operation of the variable tariffs derived from the price-band system. The average bound tariff (i.e., the maximum import duty that countries agree not to exceed without penalty) on key Colombian importable crops covered by the price-band system was 148 percent; sugar was bound at the lowest level (111 percent) and maize at the highest (194 percent). Bound tariffs on substitutes or by-products in the price-band system fluctuated between 83 percent and 332 percent.

Tariff preference agreements with the European Union and the United States were also obtained under the Special Cooperation Program (SCP) and the Andean Tariff Preferences Act (ATPA), respectively. Both of these programs were offered to Andean Pact countries in order to encourage alternatives to the cultivation of *coca* in Bolivia, Colombia, Ecuador and Peru. The European Union program started in November of 1993, offering duty-free status for four years.[21] The ATPA program took effect in December of 1991 and is expected to remain in force until the end of 2001.[22]

Other Export Promotion Policies

Prior to 1990, the most important policy instrument used to subsidize non-traditional exports was the export subsidy granted through the Tax Refund Certificate (CERT).[23] The CERT was intended as partial compensation for an overvalued exchange rate and the anti-export bias associated with restrictions on imports. As a result of trade liberalization, the government planned to gradually eliminate the subsidy component of the CERT. The certificate would be redesigned as a genuine rebate on indirect taxes, allowing exporters to recover indirect taxes paid on imported raw materials.

In April of 1991, the six CERT subsidy levels (5, 6, 8, 9, 10 and 12 percent of the value of exports) were reduced to three (5, 8 and 10 percent). Furthermore, export products were reclassified into three categories, according to their nature and target market. The lowest subsidy rates were assigned to agricultural products and intermediate goods; the highest were reserved mostly for industrial goods.

As a result of CERT reforms, the value of export subsidies awarded to agricultural exports declined by half from US$50 million to US$25 million in the 1991-93 period. However, despite this overall reduction, the share of CERT subsidies granted to agricultural exports rose from 30 percent to 36 percent.

The Gaviria administration also supported a private-sector initiative to establish the Corporación Colombia Internacional (CCI) intended to support the development of new export products, particularly tropical fruits and vegetables. This non-governmental organization was established in November of 1992 with a government donation of US$3 million. It was created to identify products with export potential, to develop promotional activities and to certify the quality of export goods. However, the organization has not received the private support envisioned originally. As a result, the CCI has concentrated its activities in collecting and disseminating domestic and external price information. It is also involved in a joint-project with private investors to develop the export market for Colombian asparagus.

The Gaviria administration also streamlined export finance procedures and eliminated credit subsidies for exports. In 1992, the government converted PROEXPO, an export promotion fund, into the Foreign Trade Bank (BANCOLDEX). The new institution simplified its loan rediscount procedures and concentrated on providing new financial services for Colombian exporters, including pre-shipment collateral, international invoicing, loans to overseas buyers, export loan insurance and exchange risk coverage for exporters. As a result, by 1993, BANCOLDEX loans accounted for 35.5 percent of all credit for Colombian agriculture. The major beneficiaries of export credit reforms were producers and traders of bananas, flowers, sugar and cotton.

Credit Reform

Prior to 1990, agricultural credit at subsidized rates was available predominantly from public institutions. Three state-owned banks—Caja Agraria, Banco Cafetero and Banco Ganadero—were responsible for some 95 percent of all loans to farmers.[24] In addition, more than half of the funds channeled through these lending institutions were obtained from FINAGRO, a government-owned rediscounting fund for agriculture.[25] FINAGRO's resources came from forced investments imposed on commercial banks and other lending institutions, which were required to deposit a share of their lending portfolios in government bonds, earning below-market interest rates.

The Gaviria administration adopted measures aimed at luring private banks into providing credit to farmers. As a start, financial institutions were allowed to substitute forced investments for direct loans to farmers under the same terms offered by FINAGRO. Second, a plan to phase-out interest rate subsidies was announced in 1991 (see Table 3.3). Greater potential returns from higher interest rates were expected to attract new credit sources for farming. FINAGRO was asked to specialize in credit to *campesinos* and in medium and long-term loans for agricultural projects.

Attempts to reform Caja Agraria, a large loss-ridden agricultural bank, met with repeated failure throughout the Gaviria administration. Despite its virtual bankruptcy, strong resistance from political sectors and Caja Agraria's strong labor union blocked all attempts at reform. This failure led to the breakdown of negotiations between the government and The World Bank for a US$250 million development loan aimed at bolstering FINAGRO's funds for long-term lending.

Institutional Changes

Agricultural policy reforms related to *Apertura* prompted the reorganization of most agencies in charge of services for rural inhabitants, including the Ministry of Agriculture. New operational guidelines were issued, consistent with trade liberalization, with investment priorities stated in The Peaceful Revolution, and with the decentralization mandate outlined in the 1991 Constitution. Two of these changes—in agricultural research and environmental regulations— deserve special consideration.

Up until 1990, the bulk of government funding for research was channeled through a single national research agency: the Instituto Colombiano Agropecuario (ICA). This agency was also in charge of monitoring and preventing health and sanitation risks. The scheme was often criticized for its excessive centralization in a country with highly diverse agricultural conditions, and for poor results and administrative inefficiencies.

A new strategy to fund and organize agricultural research evolved in 1991 and 1992. The National Agricultural Science and Technology Council was assigned the task of defining national research strategies. It was also asked to provide guidelines for public spending on research programs to be carried out

TABLE 3.3 Maximum Interest Rates to Farmers, 1990-1995 (percent)

Farmer Category	1990-91	1992	1993	1994[a]	1995[a]
Small[b]	DTF-4[c]	DTF-2	DTF+2	DTF+4	DTF+6
Medium and large	DTF+4	DTF+6	DTF+6	DTF+6	DTF+6

[a]Maximum rates for 1994 and 1995 were superseded by provisions in Law 101 of 1993 which froze ceilings at their 1993 level.

[b]Small farmers are those with assets of up to US$17,500.

[c]DTF is the weighted average of short-term deposit rates of a sample of lending institutions.

Source: Monetary Board Resolution 77 of 1990.

by public and private agencies, including regional corporations, universities and other centers. The council was expected to allocate public research funds on the basis of technical criteria, by involving scientists and farmers in defining priorities. Most significantly, under the new guidelines, the government was allowed to commission agencies other than ICA to undertake research and the development of new agricultural technologies.

This policy fostered the establishment of semi-public and private research entities and competition for public research funds. As a result, the government and several producers' associations created the Colombian Agricultural Research Corporation (CORPOICA) in January of 1993, a semi-public agency to generate and transfer technology. The government leased the bulk of ICA's research facilities to CORPOICA, and transferred all research personnel to the new organization. ICA's institutional mandate was redefined, with an emphasis on its health and sanitation functions. However, resistance by ICA to the changes and legal battles about the transfer of assets and employees to CORPOICA resulted in a drawn out transition process.

The second institutional change was creation of the Ministry of the Environment in 1993. Up until that year, environmental policies dealing with the rural sector had been effectively under the control of the Ministry of Agriculture, and implemented by one of its agencies, the Institute of Natural Resources (INDERENA). In practice, this meant that agricultural concerns had always superseded environmental priorities. New legal provisions separated the functions of the environmental "sector" from those of agriculture, allowing the Ministry of Agriculture to retain authority over policies related to the productive aspects of forestry and fishing resources.

The law featured a substantial redefinition and decentralization of environmental management responsibilities. According to the new legal framework, national policies were to be set by the National Environment Council, presided over by the Ministry of the Environment. The Council includes most other agencies with substantial environmental responsibilities, such as the National Environment Fund, the Amazon Environmental Fund, the system of national parks, and a network of five scientific institutions and 34 regional environmental corporations. These entities, in conjunction with cities and towns having a population of more than one million people, are responsible for implementing national environmental guidelines within their jurisdiction.

Under the new regulatory framework, the government proposed creating the Forest Incentive Certificate, provided for in Law 139 of 1994. This initiative was meant to bolster reforestation activities and to reduce pressure on natural forests by developing a supply of plantation timber. The subsidy, available to plantations that conform with technical guidelines, covers 75 percent of the cost involved in the start-up operation of a plantation of native species for five years, or 50 percent in the case of non-native species.

Policies for Rural Development in the *Campesino* Sector

Up until 1990, successive governments had generally acknowledged that low-income farmers needed specific policies, because of special constraints facing *campesinos*. In the past, this view had justified greater credit subsidies for small farmers, targeted research and technical assistance, as well as investment in infrastructure targeted to rural areas.

During its first year in office, the Gaviria administration affirmed its commitment to many traditional *campesino* policies and adopted several new measures, such as special treatment for low-income farmers in obtaining access to public investment for irrigation and drainage, and technical assistance through a modernization and diversification program. The administration also continued with past *campesino* programs, including supply of credit from public sources, subsidized interest rates and land reform efforts. An ambitious investment package for the rural sector through the National Rehabilitation Plan, was also announced in 1991. Most of these policies appeared in various policy documents approved by CONPES. They loosely defined *campesino* policy in the first two years of the Gaviria administration.

Efforts to integrate these programs into a coherent strategy led to the approval of a CONPES paper on *campesino* and rural development policy in June of 1993.[26] The document highlighted the need for a new approach to rural development, emphasizing decentralization of decision-making and project implementation. It also had the dual objective of making *campesino* farmers more competitive and increasing the effectiveness of expenditures to reduce rural poverty through improved targeting efforts.

Strategies and Institutional Reforms

The CONPES document on *campesino* and rural development policy outlined two general strategies to accomplish the objectives of rural development. The first was the targeting of resources and programs to ensure that investments for rural development were intensified in areas where poverty indicators, unsatisfied basic needs and the extent of community participation in project funding and execution were highest. The second strategy was a heavy emphasis on decentralization, consistent with key provisions of the 1991 Constitution. As a result, a gradual transfer of duties and funding from the nation to Colombia's provinces and municipalities was announced, according to development plans proposed on a local and regional scale.

Several important changes at the local, regional and national level were proposed to adapt government institutions to the new policy guidelines and strategies. At the central level, the Vice-Ministry of *Campesino* Affairs and Rural Development was created within the Ministry of Agriculture to chair the newly established National Council on *Campesino* Affairs, Rural Development and

Agrarian Reform. The Council was given the responsibility of formulating policy and coordinating action for rural development.

A National Cofinancing System was created to assist towns and provinces in performing their new constitutionally-expanded functions, with an emphasis on social and infrastructure investments for the benefit of rural areas.[27] The system included public funds established to finance rural investment (DRI), urban investment (FINDETER), social investment (FIS) and the Social Solidarity and Emergency Fund (FSES).[28] These funds were instructed to finance public investments in towns and provinces, under the provision that local governments were required to share in project costs. New methodologies were designed to classify rural households according to unmet needs, in order to improve the targeting and efficiency of public expenditure. The Rural Investment Cofinancing Fund (DRI), originally established in the mid-1970s to fund rural development projects, was strengthened by adding to its list of potential projects, the funding of flood control works, housing subsidies and rural electrification programs.

The National Rehabilitation Plan (PNR), a social program established in the mid-1980s under the responsibility of the president's office to channel quick-disbursing funds for social expenditure was redefined to promote rural development, primarily in *campesino* areas. Its new strategy focused on funding poverty-relief projects in low-income areas, in conjunction with other state agencies. The PNR was also charged with promoting participatory democracy and assisting decentralization efforts. It was assigned the task of overseeing local government efforts to provide social and political participation by local communities. To this end, PNR representatives created Municipal Rural Development Committees as a forum where local elected authorities and citizens' groups could discuss priority investments for their communities.

The CONPES document on *campesino* and rural development also described government actions to promote smallholder organization, participation and training, particularly through the PNR. The Ministry of Agriculture was charged with managing resources to fund *campesino* organizations, via specific projects to be developed at the municipal level.

Special polices were ushered in to improve the situation of rural women. Measures were announced to encourage equal opportunity for participation in government programs, in the institutions where policies that affect community life are decided, as well as in greater access and control over productive resources.[29] Organizations representing rural women received government support and their participation in decision-making bodies was enhanced.

Modernization and Diversification

The Modernization and Diversification Program for Agriculture, approved by CONPES in October of 1991, was aimed at promoting technological changes needed to make farmers more competitive and at providing special governmental assistance during a transition period. The program concentrated on measures to improve conditions for production and marketing, with special emphasis on areas where wheat, barley, dark tobacco and jute were grown. These crops were typically grown by *campesinos* and were either largely uncompetitive or faced declining demand during the late 1980s.

The program's objective was to increase earnings for the 65,000 families who were producing the four targeted crops on 93,000 hectares.[30] It was designed to improve production efficiency in the targeted crops or assist farmers in switching to more profitable activities. Actions were announced to intensify research, technology transfer and investment in small-scale irrigation and regional marketing projects. The program also proposed temporary support policies, such as floor prices and purchase agreements with processors, while productivity improvements and diversification efforts were taking place.

The government encouraged agreements between farmers and agroindustrial buyers to guarantee the purchase of domestic wheat and barley harvests. These included coordinated public and private actions to support diversification efforts. Prices were agreed upon for the duration of these agreements. The barley agreement was signed in June of 1991 and remained in effect until September of 1993. The wheat agreement was signed in June of 1992 for a three-year period.

These measures were complemented by new guidelines for IDEMA crop purchases, which were refocused to benefit primarily low-income producers in outlying areas. IDEMA was authorized to subsidize the cost of transporting crops for *campesino* producers of products such as maize, beans and rice. In addition, the smoothing out of price fluctuations provided by price bands benefited a significant number of small farmers, particularly for crops like wheat, barley, maize and rice.

Land Reform

In 1992, CONPES approved a new land reform policy to facilitate access to farm land for low-income *campesinos*.[31] Thus, despite the apparent emphasis on pro-market policies, the Gaviria administration gave strong support to land redistribution on behalf of the rural poor. The policy paper argued that a change in strategy was needed due to the limited success of land reform efforts since 1961. During the 30 years of operation, the Instituto Colombiano de Reforma Agraria (INCORA) failed to reduce the concentration of land ownership significantly. Moreover, its financial and management capacities were unable to cope with the ambitious redistribution targets that had been set by successive administrations.

The CONPES document on land reform indicated that actions taken by INCORA between 1962 and 1990 had been seriously flawed. First, the high cost of land and program management led to excessive costs per beneficiary. Second, INCORA's selection of land for redistribution and its price-negotiation mechanisms resulted in a highly paternalistic process, allowed little participation to landless *campesinos* and bred corruption. Third, technical assistance efforts and investments in infrastructure were insufficient to improve the productivity of redistributed lands.

The CONPES document on land reform proposed a new revolutionary policy. The idea was to allow potential beneficiaries to negotiate freely with landowners and to select the land they wanted. Low-income beneficiaries could then apply for a direct subsidy from the government to cover as much as 70 percent of the value of the property. They were also given access to long-term credit from the government for the remaining 30 percent. The new policy was eventually reflected in Law 160 of 1994, which also approved a thorough reorganization of the land reform agency (INCORA). However, long congressional negotiations led to passage of Law 160 in the final days of the Gaviria administration. Hence, the application of the new policy was left to subsequent administrations.

According to Law 160, farm land that was left idle for a minimum of three years, employed to grow illegal crops or developed in violation of environmental regulations would be expropriated and redistributed to low-income *campesinos*. The new regulations also preserved INCORA's special powers to buy or expropriate land on behalf of indigenous communities. Furthermore, INCORA was assigned the special task of providing communal land rights for communities of African ancestry in the rainforests of the Pacific coast, as approved in the 1991 Constitution.

Investment in Irrigation and Drainage

Campesinos received special treatment through policies associated with the renewed emphasis on investment in irrigation and drainage. Under the new guidelines, low-income producers benefiting from public projects were entitled to a direct subsidy of 50 percent of investment costs. The subsidy could be supplemented with contributions from other public or private agencies. Furthermore, *campesino* beneficiaries of land improvement projects were entitled to special long-term financing arrangements to repay the unsubsidized share of costs.

Credit

Interest rates on loans to *campesinos* were not subject to the rapid adjustment to market levels approved for other farmers. Instead, they benefited from a special four-year plan to gradually remove caps on interest rates (See Table 3.3). An Agricultural Loan Guarantee Fund was also created to provide collateral for small rural loans, giving small farmers more access to credit. Loans extended to *campesinos* by private or public lending institutions were fully guaranteed by the Fund, provided farmers obtained backing from public or non-governmental agencies. The government also agreed to subsidize money-losing branch offices of *Caja Agraria,* in areas where they provided important banking services to small farmers.

Research and Technology Transfer

As part of the general overhaul of the agricultural research system, the National Council on Agricultural Science and Technology was instructed to emphasize research and development of new technologies for *campesino* crops. Given the high costs of organization facing *campesinos* and their low income, the government announced that research for smallholder crops would continue to be primarily funded from public sources.

The Gaviria administration thoroughly reformed public extension efforts. Prior to 1990, technical assistance for low-income farmers was available from a centralized group of extension workers who were employees of the Ministry of Agriculture, Caja Agraria and ICA. The system had been increasingly criticized for its administrative inefficiency and limited coverage. In an effort to support decentralization policies, the administration put into practice a new extension system centered around municipalities. Mayors of rural towns were instructed to set up Municipal Agricultural Technical Assistance Units (UMATAs), which were to provide farmers with free technical assistance, as well as advice on natural resource use and sustainable management practices. DRI was charged with promotion and cofinancing the creation of these new bodies.

A new institutional framework (The National Technology Transfer System, SINTAP) was developed to support provincial and municipal efforts in applied research and technology transfer. In order to strengthen this system, The National Agricultural Technology Transfer Program (PRONATTA) was launched, with a development loan obtained in 1994 from The World Bank. The program funds investment projects, technology transfer, testing of new varieties, training for UMATA extension workers and the development of databases and information systems on available technologies. PRONATTA also finances sustainable management projects, especially those involving soil, water, forests and fishing resources.

Income Diversification

The CONPES policy document on rural development highlighted the growing share of rural income derived from non-farming sources, a development that gives low-income families more opportunities for income diversification. To strengthen this trend, the government proposed measures to accelerate the development of opportunities in non-agricultural rural activities. An urban-based plan to promote the development of small businesses was expanded to cover rural areas, with funding from the International Fund for Agricultural Development (IFAD). In addition, DRI was charged with promoting small-scale agroindustrial projects. Along these lines, public credit agencies were instructed to promote agribusiness projects in *campesino* areas.

Conclusion

The reforms to agricultural policies and institutions proposed during the Gaviria administration was undoubtedly the most ambitious agenda for change that had been presented to Colombian farmers in several decades. The massive amount of changes and new measures reflected the reformist mood that swept the country in 1990 and 1991, in the wake of *Apertura* and approval of the 1991 Constitution. Few pre-1990 policies and institutions went unchallenged, as government officials proposed changes for virtually all areas of public endeavor. An important feature of the process was that the bulk of reform proposals came from the government's team of economists and planners. Few proposals were initiated by farming groups, many of which were on the defensive against what they saw as dangerous changes to a long-established order. This played against the durability and success of some of the proposed changes, since farmers did not feel a strong sense of "ownership" of the reforms.

The list of reforms contained many novel policies with extremely ambitious goals. Clearly, the government took substantial risks in proposing sharp breaks with the past on key issues. The most important breaks with the pre-1990 regime include the establishment of a trading system with transparent protection and marketing rules, the signing of trade agreements to expand horizons for Colombian exports, the renewed emphasis on irrigation and drainage expenditure, and the separation of environmental institutions from the agricultural realm. Equally ambitious were the new systems to provide for competition in the allocation of agricultural research funds, the cofinancing system to support decentralization efforts, and the transitional programs to assist crops that were likely to suffer from lowered protection. The new land reform scheme, providing direct subsidies to beneficiaries for land acquisition, was an imaginative proposal which attracted a great deal of attention from abroad.

Was the government over-enthusiastic in proposing reforms? Did it lack the capacity to put into practice such a long list of changes? These important questions have not yet been explored enough in studies about recent public policy changes in Colombia. On the one hand, there were some rapid successes: trade agreements with other Latin American nations, greater transparency of protection policies and the elimination of opportunities for corruption within government agencies.[32] However, as will be discussed in later chapters, some proposals became entangled in lengthy legal and operational disputes, which slowed their implementation. Others succumbed to insurmountable political and practical obstacles. The latter is the case of the plan to increase public expenditure on land improvement, which was slowed by political opposition to the implementation of new guidelines, the lengthy procedures required to secure development loans, and the contracting of extensive feasibility studies for new irrigation projects. As a result, the ambitious goals that had been established were not met during the Gaviria administration. Another important failure occurred when political pressure led to the introduction of politically-motivated projects through the National Cofinancing System. This move undermined the technical criteria that were supposed to guide the allocation of public funds. These policy failures will be discussed in more detail in Chapter 5.

There was also a general impression of failure with respect to implementation of the Modernization and Diversification Program. The agricultural crisis of 1992 (discussed at length in Chapter 4) created a sense of urgency, which did not conform to the more gradual timetable of the program. Another area where measures met with little success was in the promotion of new sources of agricultural credit. Although reforms improved conditions for agricultural lending, few private banks were persuaded to lend to farmers. Reforms to implement the new agricultural research system were also and costly. There were legal disputes about whether ICA research staff could be transferred to a non-governmental research organization. Also, ICA staff resisted the loss of research responsibilities and budgetary resources. In addition, discussions with INCORA and Congress about the precise content of new legal provisions for land reform led to the passage of a new law in the last weeks of the administration, leaving its application to the incoming government.

Within Colombia, substantial controversy arose over the "neo-liberal" (i.e., free-market) nature of *Apertura*, including its agricultural policies. The general thrust of economic reform was certainly guided by a greater trust in markets than had been the case before 1990. However, Colombian reform efforts emphasized the importance of state action, in particular, on behalf of the rural poor. Most significantly, agricultural policy reforms were moderate in comparison with those in other Latin American countries such as Chile after 1975 and Argentina in the 1990s. Trade liberalization was mollified by allowing sensitive agricultural products to enjoy higher tariffs than those applying to the rest of the economy and by the introduction of a variable tariff system (i.e., price bands) for more vulnerable crops. Agencies for government intervention in commodity and credit markets, such as IDEMA and Caja Agraria, were allowed to continue operating, even at substantial financial loss to the government. *Apertura* reforms also maintained the long tradition of special policies for *campesinos*. Low-income farmers enjoyed the benefits of a slow phase-out of interest rate subsidies, special subsidies for irrigation projects, IDEMA's continued purchase of their crops, continued land reform efforts, and sustained rural development expenditure.

Notes

1. Cepeda (1994) provides a lucid analysis of the political economy of the Gaviria administration's success in obtaining approval for a large number of structural reforms in 1990 and 1991.

2. The Plan was published in mid-1991 by Presidencia de la República and Departamento Nacional de Planeación (1991).

3. Some empirical evidence on the productivity slowdown appears in the Introduction of Hommes et al. (1994).

4. A thorough review of labor and financial market reforms appears in Hommes et al. (1994).

5. The plan called for investments in irrigation, drainage and flood control infrastructure.

6. Some of these policies were to be included in a second volume of The Peaceful Revolution which was never published.

7. The license required to import wheat remained mandatory up until mid-1992, when an absorption agreement was signed between the milling industry and the wheat-farming associations.

8. An analysis of the causes of capital inflows appears in Calvo et al. (1992).

9. Effective protection includes protection through lower taxes on imported inputs, and constrasts with nominal protection, where only output prices are compared.

10. Before 1992, tariffs on agricultural inputs were lower than those in other sectors.

11. Palm oil also enjoyed the benefits of the price-band system, since it was included as a soybean substitute in the processing of vegetable oils.

12. Domestic marketing policies are described in Silva (1994).

13. "Floor" prices are defined in Consejo de Política Económica y Social (1991a).

14. See Silva (1994) on the difference between support prices and "floor" prices.

15. The manner in which IDEMA handled storage, and its unfavorable impact on private-sector involvement in storage, is described in Hernández (1991). See Shonkwiler (1994) on the importance of storage in agricultural marketing with reference to Colombian agriculture.

16. The justification appears in Chapter III of Presidencia de la República and Departamento Nacional de Planeación (1991).

17. See Consejo de Política Económica y Social (1991b).

18. This incentive was provided for in the *Ley Agraria*, which is described in Chapter 4.

19. Peru declined to join at the time, arguing that it did not want to alter its flat tariff structure.

20. The list of agricultural exceptions includes the products covered by price bands in Colombia and Venezuela, and those targeted for domestic subsidies by Mexico. In addition, each country has three separate lists with products that require special import permits.

21. Bananas, sugar, strawberries and lemons are excluded from the SCP.

22. The ATPA does not apply to sugar, which continued to be subject to tariff-quota treatment.

23. In 1984, the CERT replaced the Certificado de Abono Tributario, an instrument which fulfilled a similar purpose.

24. Banco Ganadero, which had been partly owned by private agents, was fully privatized by 1992. Banco Cafetero was owned by the National Coffee Fund, and managed jointly by a private growers' association and the government.

25. Prior to FINAGRO's formal creation in 1989, the rediscount fund—Fondo Financiero Agropecuario—was located at the Central Bank.

26. See Consejo de Política Económica y Social (1993a).

27. The 1991 Constitution provided for a growing transfer of central resources to local governments, primarily for investment in education and health.

28. FINDETER and DRI were operating prior to the Gaviria administration. FIS and FSES were created during Gaviria presidency.

29. Policies for rural women appear in Consejo de Política Económica y Social (1994).

30. The Modernization and Diversification Program is described, in detail, in Consejo de Política Económica y Social (1991a).

31. The new land reform policy is outlined in Consejo de Política Económica y Social (1992a).

32. The elimination of import and export licenses, as well as varying tariff levels, rid the system of many opportunities to elicit under-the-table payoffs.

4

1992: The Agricultural Crisis

Colombian farmers remember 1992 as the year of the "crisis." In that year, farm production stagnated, with aggregate farming output remaining essentially unchanged with respect to 1991. This zero-growth scenario was the poorest performance of the sector since 1982. Annual crops[1] were particularly hard hit, as the real value of harvests fell by more than 12 percent, an unprecedented drop. This sharp contraction was interpreted by many as a clear symptom of the failure of *Apertura* measures for agriculture and, specifically, trade liberalization reforms. Among farmers, the situation created a hostile environment for the Gaviria administration, prompting a sharp wave of rural opposition to *Apertura* policies.

This chapter assesses agricultural events in 1992. First, it provides a detailed look at crop-level evidence on farm output, in order to uncover the nature of the crisis, its causes and effects. Second, it identifies factors that were directly responsible for the crisis, including the decline in international agricultural prices, acute drought conditions, the appreciation of the exchange rate, and the reduction in trade protection levels. The chapter also discusses other influences that may have contributed to aggravating the situation, including, the interruption of the flow of agricultural credit, the difference between local and international interest rates and the growth of rural violence. A summary of findings is presented at the end.

The Evidence

Interpreting the Data

Twice a year, Ministry of Agriculture officials are sent to all major farming regions to report on areas planted, harvest volumes and average yields for all crops. These statistics are compiled and aggregated to obtain national measures of agricultural output. Survey methods are still relatively rudimentary and thus, the figures are potentially subject to biases. However, since these official figures are the only evidence collected consistently for a substantial period of time, analysis of events in agriculture must begin with a close examination of these figures.

Statistics from the Ministry of Agriculture for 1992 reveal a slight 0.03 percent decline in farm output.[2] This aggregate figure is the result of a moderate decline in agricultural production (-0.7 percent) and an equally moderate increase in livestock output (1.2 percent) (see Table 4.1).

There are three different stories hidden in the virtual standstill in aggregate farm production. Two concern crops; the other reflects developments in the livestock sector.

The first story involves the dramatic drop in annual crop production in 1992. The value of output of these crops (aggregated with constant prices) declined 12.6 percent, greatly as a result of poor harvests in soybeans, barley, cotton, wheat, maize, and vegetables (see Table 4.2). All of the crops listed suffered declines of at least 10 percent in output, relative to the levels of 1991. The second contrasting story is that of the sharp increase in the output of permanent crops, excluding coffee. Production of these items increased on average (7.4 percent) in 1992, led by bumper harvests in sugar cane, flowers and fruits.

The first two stories are mirrored by variations in harvested areas. These fell by 285,300 hectares for annual crops (12.1 percent), while those in permanent crops (excluding coffee) increased by 54,900 (4.4 percent). Hence, reductions in crop output seem to respond to a great extent to farmers' decisions to reduce cropped areas. In the aggregate, harvested areas for annual and permanent products combined reflected a large drop of 230,400 hectares or 6.4 percent with respect to 1991 (see Table 4.3).

Although the reduction in planted areas seems to explain the bulk of output reductions in annual crops, it is also useful to look at crop yields in order to detect evidence of weather or pest-related problems. Table 4.4 displays diverse yield performance for annual and permanent crops. Yields of most cold-weather crops declined, including wheat (11.9 percent), barley (18.9 percent), jute (28.0 percent) and potatoes (0.6 percent). Poor performance in these crops reflects low rainfall levels in the Central Andean highlands. Cotton also exhibited a significant decline in yields (12.5 percent) as a result of both weather problems and pest-inflicted damages. Other crops that exhibited lower yields in 1992 as a consequence of *El Niño* effects, include oil palm, bananas, cassava, maize and cocoa.

Putting together the first two stories yields a negative picture of aggregate crop activity. In 1992, agricultural output (excluding coffee) declined by 0.7 percent. Coffee output, which traditionally has displayed high year-to-year variability, also declined by 0.5 percent, a development which contributed to further depressing output and agricultural employment in 1992. In summary, the figures suggest that the sector was buffeted by strong shocks that led to the reallocation of land and other inputs away from annual crops and towards permanent crops. The proportional reduction in areas is substantially greater than that for output, due to lower unit values among annual crops, relative to permanent ones.

TABLE 4.1 Agricultural Growth Rates, 1980-1992 (percent)

	1985-89	*1990*	*1991*	*1992*
Agriculture	3.4	8.2	4.0	-0.7
Annual Crops	4.1	2.5	-3.2	-12.6
Permanent Crops	4.6	6.8	5.4	7.4
Coffee	-0.9	24.1	13.9	-0.5
Livestock	3.5	3.5	3.0	1.2
Total Farm Output	3.5	6.6	3.7	0.0

Source: Ministerio de Agricultura (1998).

TABLE 4.2 Agricultural Production, 1991 and 1992 (thousand tons)

Crop	*1991*	*1992*	*Growth (percent)*
Annual Crops			
Rice	1,738.6	1,735.0	-0.2
Potatoes	2,371.9	2,281.4	-3.8
Maize	1,273.6	1,055.7	-17.1
Vegetables	1,272.1	1,142.4	-10.2
Cotton	414.5	306.6	-26.0
Sorghum	738.3	751.8	1.8
Soybeans	193.6	96.0	-50.4
Beans	108.0	119.8	10.9
Wheat	93.9	75.2	-19.9
Barley	102.4	56.0	-45.3
Permanent Crops			
Coffee	970.7	965.6	-0.5
Sugar Cane	1,661.7	1,839.3	10.7
Plantains	2,456.1	2,572.9	4.8
Panela Cane	1,092.6	1,175.6	7.6
Flowers	112.2	138.5	23.4
Oil Palm	290.9	290.5	-0.1
Cassava	1,645.2	1,651.0	0.3
Fruits	1,499.0	1,891.8	26.2
Bananas	1,521.3	1,629.4	7.1
Cocoa	58.1	54.9	-5.6

Source: Ministerio de Agricultura (1998).

TABLE 4.3 Areas Planted in Crops, 1991 and 1992 (thousand hectares)

Crop	1991	1992	Growth (percent)
Annual Crops	2351.6	2066.3	-12.1
Rice	435.1	423.6	-2.6
Potatoes	151.4	146.6	-3.2
Maize	821.8	695.7	-15.3
Vegetables	86.8	78.2	-9.9
Cotton	247.9	209.6	-15.4
Sorghum	256.5	245.0	-4.5
Soybeans	100.6	49.4	-50.9
Beans	133.7	127.0	-5.0
Wheat	47.3	43.0	-9.1
Barley	49.5	33.4	-32.5
Other[a]	21.0	14.9	-28.7
Permanent Crops[b]	1,253.6	1,308.5	6.2
Sugar Cane	116.5	119.7	2.7
Plantains	347.0	356.7	2.8
Panela Cane	196.1	191.9	-2.1
Oil Palm	97.6	108.5	11.2
Cassava	174.0	181.3	4.2
Fruits	93.1	112.1	20.5
Bananas	34.9	41.1	17.9
Cocoa	125.0	119.7	-4.2
Other[c]	69.4	77.6	11.8

[a]Sesame seed, peanuts and light tobacco.

[b]Excludes coffee and flowers.

[c]Yams, jute, export plantains, coconut and dark tobacco.

Source: Ministerio de Agricultura (1998).

The third story underlying farm output in 1992 was the moderate increase in livestock production. This performance reflected a heifer inventory build-up phase in cattle raising coupled with a sharp drop in slaughter, as well as rapid growth in the poultry industry. The latter sector benefited greatly from the upswing in beef prices (a close substitute) and reductions in feed grain prices (see Table 4.5).

TABLE 4.4 Agricultural Yields, 1991 and 1992 (tons per hectare)

Crop	1991	1992	Growth (Percent)
Annual Crops			
Rice	3,996	4,096	2.5
Potatoes	15,665	15,565	-0.6
Maize	1,550	1,518	-2.1
Cotton	1,672	1,463	-12.5
Sorghum	2,878	3,068	6.6
Soybeans	1,924	1,945	1.1
Beans	808	943	16.8
Wheat	1,985	1,749	-11.9
Barley	2,069	1,677	-18.9
Permanent Crops			
Sugar Cane	120,615	125,106	3.7
Plantains	7,077	7,213	1.9
Panela Cane	5,572	6,126	9.9
Oil Palm	2,980	2,677	-10.2
Cassava	9,455	9,108	-3.7
Cocoa	1,668	1,335	-19.9

Source: Ministerio de Agricultura (1998).

TABLE 4.5 Growth of Livestock Activities, 1990-1992 (percent)

	1990	1991	1992
Cattle	4.3	2.1	-2.2
Hogs	-11.2	6.0	-0.8
Poultry	4.7	4.8	9.4
Total Livestock	3.5	3.0	1.2

Source: Ministerio de Agricultura (1998).

The Crisis from a Historical Perspective

Was the 1992 contraction in farm output very severe by historical standards? Figure 4.1 displays growth statistics of those years when farm output exhibited abnormally poor growth since 1950, the first year for which consistent data are available. According to the data, the contraction of 1992 was the seventh largest in four decades. Agricultural output declines of 1 percent or more were observed in 1970, 1982, 1963 and 1953, suggesting a striking pattern: one major decline seems to occur about once every decade in Colombian agriculture. Unfortunately, little is known in Colombia about the potential causes of such medium and long-term cycles in agricultural performance.

Historical comparison reveals important differences between sub-sectors. The reduction in production observed in 1992 for annual crops is the largest

FIGURE 4.1 Agricultural Output: Worst Years on Record, 1950-1992 (percent)

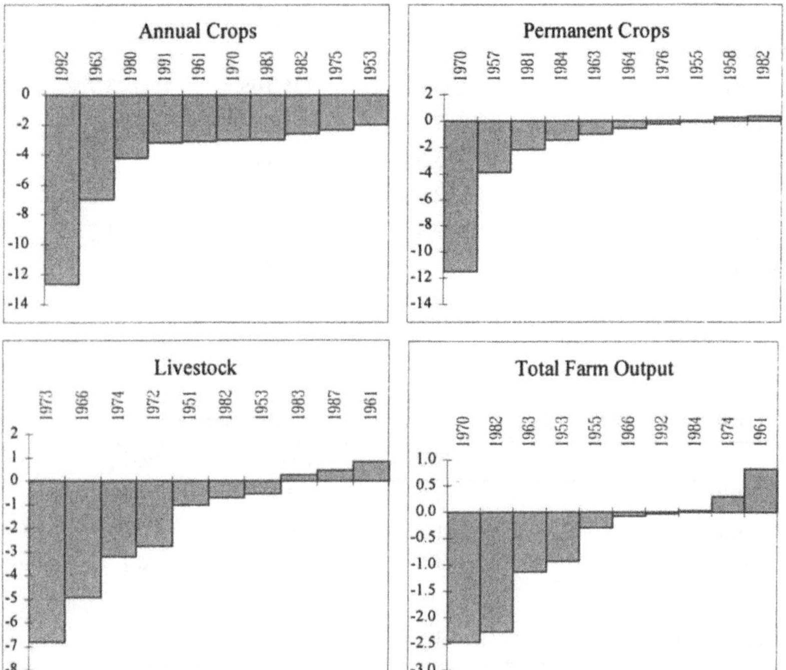

Source: Data from Ministerio de Agricultura (1998).

observed since 1950. For the case of livestock, the 1.2 percent growth rate is poor in historical comparison, significantly below the 1950-1990 average of 3.0 percent. However, it is not among the ten worst performance years. By contrast, 1992 was one of the best years on record for permanent crops, excluding coffee. For the latter crop, the decline observed in output (0.6 percent) is not extreme for a crop that has exhibited historically sizable annual fluctuations in production.

In summary, the downturn in agricultural production during 1992 was the result of historically low rates for annual crops and livestock, and unusually high rates for permanent crops. Historically low growth rates for annual and livestock sectors in 1992 have very different implications for farm income. In the case of annual crops, drops in production are usually reflected directly in reduced incomes for farmers. For the case of livestock, low output growth is characteristic of inventory build-up phases of the cattle cycle, when heifers are retained for breeding and slaughter levels fall below the norm. The impact on the income of cattle growers of these phases is often ambiguous due to the counteracting effects of rising prices and lower output levels.

Causes of Crisis

Many spokesmen of farming associations blamed trade liberalization policies for output drops in annual crops. They claimed that reduced protection facilitated entry of subsidized imports from world markets, which substituted for domestic crops.

Despite these claims, studies of the 1992 crisis have shown that farm income was affected by an unfortunate confluence of factors, which depressed profitability levels for some crops and increased yield risks for others.[3] The downturn in international prices, the drought, trade liberalization, and exchange rate appreciation are the causes most often cited.

International Prices

Between 1988 and 1989, world prices of certain important crops for Colombian farmers increased above long-term trends. However, they began to drop sharply starting in 1990 (see Figure 4.2). The main culprit was weak demand caused by the recessionary atmosphere in developed countries.

World prices of farm products reached critical levels in 1991 and 1992. In the latter year, real prices for widely traded agricultural products fell to record lows: 13.7 percent below the 1990 level, 32.6 percent below the average in the 1980s, and 58.0 percent less than the average level for the 1970s.[4] In particular, prices for cereals followed a steady downward trend. This was reflected in the fall of dollar prices for maize, sorghum, rice, wheat and barley by the end of 1992 (see Figure 4.3). International prices of some of Colombia's traditional

FIGURE 4.2 International Commodity Prices, 1988-1992 (US$, 1990=100)

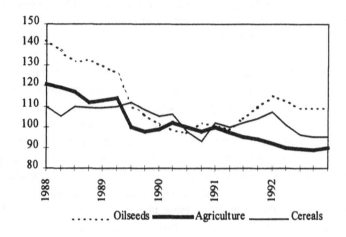

Source: Data from World Bank (1994b).

export crops also recorded drastic reductions, as was the case with coffee, cocoa, cotton and sugar.

Oilseeds were the only commodity group not to experience a major slump in international prices. The price of soybeans and palm oil on world markets rose slightly in 1992 (see Figure 4.3).

As in previous agricultural downturns, declining international prices exerted a negative effect on the profitability of importable and exportable goods. This influence may have been more acute after 1990, since trade liberalization should have made domestic markets more susceptible to fluctuations abroad. However, price bands cushioned this impact for most import-competing crops. As a result, the drop in international prices exerted a greater direct effect on prices of exportable crops.

Drought

In 1992, Colombia's main agricultural regions were affected by *El Niño*, the weather phenomenon associated with warming ocean currents in the South Pacific. For Colombia, *El Niño* is usually reflected in drought conditions in the central and northern areas of the country. Unfortunately for farmers in these areas, the drought of 1992 was one of the worst on record. The drought began in

FIGURE 4.3 International Prices, January 1990-December 1992 (US$ per ton)

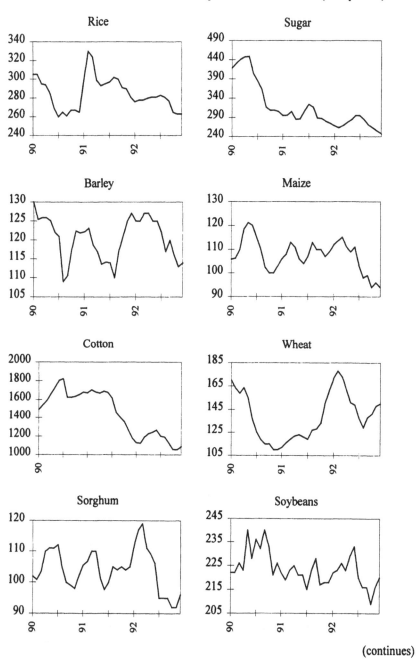

(continues)

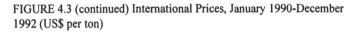

FIGURE 4.3 (continued) International Prices, January 1990-December 1992 (US$ per ton)

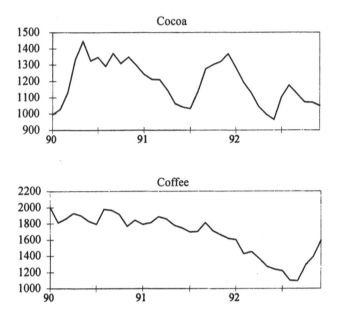

Source: International Monetary Fund (1998).

the final quarter of 1991 and lasted until the third quarter of 1992[5] (see Table 4.6 and Figure 4.4).

El Niño significantly reduced precipitation during the rainy season of the first half of the year. Rainfall was 40 percent below the average for April, when peak precipitation levels are registered in the Andean region. During the second rainy season of the year, the volume of precipitation barely reached 50 percent of historical averages.

Figures 4.5 and 4.6 display the extent of the drought in the first and second half of 1992, and the zones that were most affected. The drought was more severe in the Andean valleys of central (e.g., Antioquia and Norte de Santander) and southern (e.g., Huila) Colombia and throughout most of the Atlantic region, primarily on the coast and in the far north. Rainfall patterns were normal only in the Eastern Plains and in the Amazon region, which host little agricultural activities. Low precipitation levels were responsible for falling yields, as well as reduced plantings of rainfed *campesino* crops, such as wheat, barley, maize,

TABLE 4.6 Rainfall, Selected Agricultural Provinces, 1985-1993 (millimeters)

| | Provinces | | | | National |
Period	Atlántico	Antioquia	Norte de Santander	Huila	Average
1970-79[a]	801	1,678	931	1,331	1,185
1980-89[a]	830	1,688	865	1,348	1,183
1990	792	1,622	1,149	1,366	1,232
1991	508	1,595	433	1,087	906
1992	735	1,132	651	1,030	887
1993	1,243	1,581	558	1,514	1,224

[a]Annual averages.
Source: HIMAT (1993).

FIGURE 4.4 Average Precipitation Levels, 1970-1993 (millimeters)

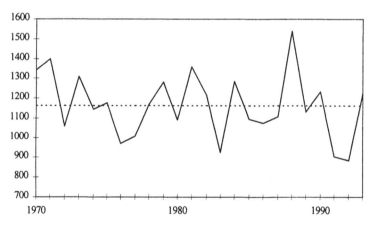

Source: Author's own calculations and HIMAT (1993).

FIGURE 4.5 Rainfall Levels, January-June 1992

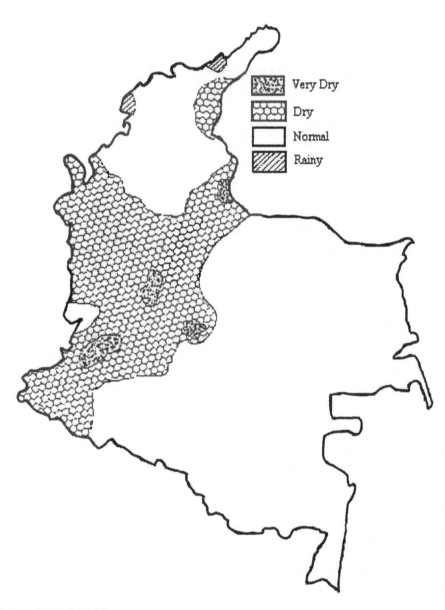

Source: HIMAT (1993).

FIGURE 4.6 Rainfall Levels, July-December 1992

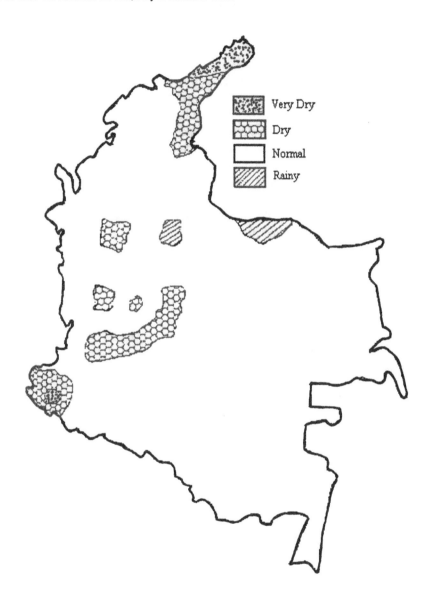

Source: HIMAT (1993).

beans and vegetables. Yields of cotton, traditionally an export crop, were greatly affected by the drought in the Atlantic coast area.

The Exchange Rate

Figure 4.7 displays the real exchange rate for the Colombian economy from 1990 to mid-1994.[6] After reaching a record high at the end of 1990, the real value of the peso appreciated 7.9 percent between 1990 and 1992. The unexpected strengthening of the domestic currency was a result of a growing surplus of foreign currency, due to large increases in overseas earnings in exports since the final quarter of 1990 and a marked slowdown in foreign exchange expenditures. Foreign exchange flows, spurred by an unusual upswing in export earnings and capital inflows, led to a sharp accumulation of international reserves, which increased from US$ 4.5 billion at the end of 1990 to US$ 7.7 billion by the end of 1992. The decline in imports was explained by the postponement of investment decisions, as agents awaited further tariff reductions.

The surge in inflows has also been explained by the improving prospects of the Colombian economy as a result of *Apertura* reforms. Part of a broader process observed in many Latin American economies, the upswing was sparked by renewed confidence in the region due to the favorable perception of economic policies. For the case of Colombia, inflows were greatly stimulated by the announcement of large oil finds in 1991 in the piedmont area of the Eastern Plains. The prospect of growing oil exports for the remainder of the decade gave

FIGURE 4.7 Real Exchange Rate, 1990-1992 (Jan. 1990=100)

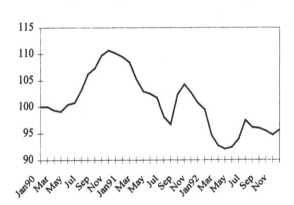

Source: Data from Banco de la República, Estudios Económicos.

foreign investors and creditors confidence in the economy's external accounts. The recession in developed countries, low interest rates overseas and a restrictive monetary policy in Colombia—which raised domestic interest rates dramatically—also helped to attract external flows.[7]

The appreciation of the Colombian currency affected negatively the domestic-currency price of exportable and importable goods, with a direct impact on profitability. In 1992, the aggregate index of output prices[8] increased by 17.8 percent, while the overall consumer price index increased 27 percent. The implicit drop in farm returns was partially offset by the decline in real prices in 1992 for most tradable inputs, including prices of fertilizers, insecticides and farm machinery (see Table 4.7). In aggregate, prices of agricultural inputs

TABLE 4.7 Prices of Agricultural Inputs, 1991-1992 (Index 1990=100)

	1991	*1992*	*Growth (percent)*
Agrochemicals	125.2	149.4	19.3
Manufactured in Colombia			
Fertilizers	125.4	140.9	12.4
Fungicides	122.9	156.0	26.9
Herbicides	123.7	152.1	22.9
Insecticides	118.0	142.4	20.7
Imported			
Urea	104.8	105.3	0.5
Insecticides	119.7	146.0	22.0
Fungicides	115.1	134.3	16.7
Herbicides	118.8	141.0	18.6
Fertilizers	115.7	123.1	6.4
Agricultural Machinery	114.0	126.0	10.5
Tractors	111.8	124.4	11.3
Other Machinery	116.4	127.0	9.1
Total Agricultural Inputs	120.8	140.3	16.1
Other Indexes			
Consumer Price Index	130.4	165.6	27.0
Producer Price Index	123.1	145.1	17.8
Producer Price Index for Agriculture	128.5	152.0	18.2
Rural Wages (*Clima Frío* Regions)	126.8	156.9	23.7
Rural Wages (*Clima Cálido* Regions)	127.5	158.4	24.2

Source: Data from Banco de la República, Estudios Económicos.

(except labor) increased by 16.1 percent, with those of imported fertilizers and machinery growing substantially below the average.

Diminished Protection

The returns to planting some importable crops were also affected by the reduction in import duties and the lifting of non-tariff trade restrictions. These factors exerted a proportionally greater effect on crops that had enjoyed considerable protection levels prior to 1990. Table 4.8 displays average tariffs between 1990 and 1993 for importable crops, including the tariff surcharge associated with price bands. A reduction in tariff protection is evident for most products between 1990 and 1992. For this period, the decline averaged 20.1 percentage points for the weighted average of the commodities included in the table. However, the reduction in official tariff levels may be a biased measure of real protection levels faced by farmers. On the one hand, Andean Pact agreements eliminated all tariffs for agricultural goods within the region starting in 1992, reducing protection for crops in which Ecuador and Venezuela could ship surpluses. On the other hand, tariff levels in 1990 did not capture the effect of quantitative trade restrictions in Colombia in effect at that time, as well as other domestic measures that altered the relationship between producer and world prices.

To deal with these measurement flaws, it is usually preferable to use nominal protection coefficients (NPCs), which yield better estimates of the aggregate effect of policies on trade protection. NPCs measure the actual gap between international prices and producer prices, measured in a common currency.[9] Table 4.9 lists NPCs for the major importable crops. Results show a sharp drop in protection at the border for oil palm and more moderate ones for rice, wheat, maize and soybeans between the 1986-90 average and 1992, proportionally greater than the reduction in tariff levels. In the same period, support levels

TABLE 4.8 Tariff Rates[a], 1990-1993 (percent)

Year	Rice	Barley	Maize	Sorghum	Soybeans	Wheat	Average[b]
1990	55.3	31.8	31.8	31.8	35.8	31.8	40.8
1991	42.8	23.1	29.0	29.0	34.6	37.7	33.9
1992	22.6	15.9	19.5	19.5	24.8	15.4	20.7
1993	36.6	23.9	43.2	32.5	16.6	16.0	35.7

[a]Includes basic tariff and variable tariff from price bands.

[b]Weighted by production value.

Source: Data from Ministerio de Agricultura, Dirección de Comercialización.

TABLE 4.9 Nominal Protection Coefficients for Importable Crops, 1986-1992 (percent)

Commodity	1986-90	1990	1991	1992
Rice	9	-9	-9	4
Maize	26	11	5	16
Oil Palm	47	48	2	-19
Sorghum	17	10	5	17
Soybeans	16	19	8	12
Wheat	21	37	27	11
Barley	33	43	36	36
Milk	41	25	31	42
Weighted Average	29	17	13	20

Source: Author's own calculations.

remain essentially unchanged for barley, milk and sorghum. Average protection for these eight commodities as a whole declined from 29 percent in 1986-90 to 20 percent in 1992.

The case of soybeans illustrates how protection may have been affected by Andean trade agreements. This crop, which had been grown with relative success in the Cauca Valley since the late 1950s, was affected dramatically in 1991 by the possibility of duty-free imports from Bolivia, under the provisions of the Andean Pact agreement. At the time, soybeans enjoyed great productive advantages in Bolivia, where virgin lowlands in the Santa Cruz region were being incorporated into the production frontier. Both land and labor costs in these areas were substantially less than in the Cauca Valley.

In spite of the tremendous logistical effort and the high costs of transportation required to bring soybeans into Colombia from Bolivia, import prices were initially lower than producer prices in the Cauca Valley.[10] With increasing imports, producer prices fell, prompting many farmers to turn to alternative crops (especially sugar cane) due to the high opportunity costs of farm land in the Cauca Valley.

Rice faced special problems as a consequence of lower trade barriers. Protection was reduced after 1991 beyond the government's intentions due to unfair import competition practices. In Venezuela, the price of urea—a key fertilizer in rice production—was controlled by the government below international levels. Also, rice exports enjoyed subsidies from a government program to promote exports.

As a result of this situation, some 65,000 tons of white rice crossed the border into Colombia in 1992. This, in addition to the 25,000 tons imported by IDEMA to prevent a shortage during the first half of the year, depressed domestic prices and lowered returns to rice farming. As a consequence, real producer prices of rice fell by about 10 percent in 1992.

Farm Returns

As expected, farm return indexes for most annual crops declined in 1991 and 1992, reflecting falling international prices, exchange rate appreciation, declining yields and, for some crops, reduced protection.[11] In the aggregate, returns for all annual crops dropped by 5 percent in 1992 with respect to 1990 (see Table 4.10). Sharp reductions in the profitability of maize, sorghum, soybeans, wheat, barley and cotton between 1990 and 1992 were primarily responsible. Rice and beans were the only crops to experience a slight increase in profitability in the same period.

For permanent crops, the aggregate returns index fell by 6 percent in 1992 with respect to 1990, greatly as a result of plummeting coffee prices. Excluding this crop, returns for these commodities increase by 5 percent for the same period, reflecting increased profitability in cassava, sugar cane and flowers. However, returns fell in oil palm, cocoa, bananas and plantains.

Table 4.10 also presents returns for crops classified as importable, exportable and non-tradable. The profitability of export crops as a whole registered a 10 percent drop between 1990 and 1992, while that of importable crops fell by 14 percent in the same period. By contrast, non-tradables crops saw their profitability ratio increase by 11.7 percent in the same period..

Assessing the Causes of Crisis

It is a difficult task to determine exactly how the 1992 crisis was influenced by each of the factors outlined above, particularly since each factor may have affected each crop or each region differently. Some aggregate evidence appears in a study that examined the key determinants of Colombian agricultural growth in the last few decades by using a simple econometric model (Jaramillo and Junguito, 1993). The study evaluated a large list of potential determinants of the annual growth rates of farm output, including variations in investment, precipitation, international prices, real exchange rates, trade protection and violence rates in the countryside. Results suggest that variations in investment, rainfall, exchange rates and trade protection levels were the key determinants of Colombian farm growth (see Table 4.11). Using the model to explain the 1992 drop in agricultural growth reveals that the key factors were drought and the decline in international prices. The decline in trade protection and the appreciation of the real exchange also contributed, although to a lesser degree.[12]

TABLE 4.10 Returns to Agricultural Activities, 1991-1992 (Index 1990=100)

Crop	1991	1992	Growth (percent)
Annual Crops	95	95	0.4
Rice	102	103	1.0
Potatoes	89	97	9.0
Maize	90	81	-10.0
Cotton	106	90	-15.1
Sorghum	81	86	6.2
Soybeans	89	86	-3.4
Beans	110	140	27.3
Wheat	88	82	-6.8
Barley	92	89	-3.3
Permanent Crops	96	94	-1.9
Coffee	96	69	-28.1
Sugar Cane	102	120	17.6
Plantains	88	91	3.4
Panela Cane	107	97	-9.3
Flowers	81	105	29.6
Oil Palm	77	63	-18.2
Cassava	116	183	57.8
Bananas	105	93	-11.4
Cocoa	89	87	-2.2
Beef	126	144	14.3
Importable Crops[a]	92	86	-6.3
Exportable Crops[b]	95	90	-6.1
Non-Tradable Crops[c]	98	110	11.7

[a]Rice, maize, cotton, sorghum, soybeans, barley, wheat and oil palm.

[b]Coffee, sugar cane, flowers, bananas and cocoa.

[c]Potatoes, beans, plantains, *panela* cane and cassava.

Source: Author's own calculations.

TABLE 4.11 Impact on 1992 Agricultural Growth (percentage points)

	Maximum Coeficient[a]	Minimum Coeficient[a]
Simulation 1[b]		
Weather	-5.2	-3.5
International Prices	-2.9	-0.5
Protection	-1.6	-0.5
Real Exchange Rate	+6.4	+2.0
Simulation 2[c]		
Real Exchange Rate	-1.4	-0.5

[a]Refers to alternative coefficients from equations estimated for agricultural growth.

[b]Changes with respect to expected growth, with independent variables at historical averages.

[c]Changes with respect to expected growth, with the real exchange rate set at its value of 1990.

Source: Jaramillo and Junguito (1993).

TABLE 4.12 Sources of Variation of the Domestic Price of Imports, 1992 (percentage change with respect to 1991)

		Explained by variations in:		
Commodity	Variation in DPI[a]	World Price[b]	Import Tariff[c]	Real Exch. Rate[d]
Wheat	2.9	26.6	-14.2	-5.1
Barley	-9.8	-4.1	-1.0	-5.1
Rice	-26.1	-12.4	-11.1	-5.1
Sorghum	-14.8	-6.8	-3.4	-5.1
Soybeans	-13.5	-4.9	-4.1	-5.1
Maize	-15.9	-8.0	-3.5	-5.1
Sugar	-16.7	-11.0	-1.4	-5.1
Milk	-0.9	12.5	-7.1	-5.1

[a]Variation in domestic price of imports in constant pesos: (1 + pct. change in world price) * (1 +pct. change in import tariff)* (1 + pct. change in real exchange rate)

[b]Percentage change in world price, deflated by world price index.

[c]Percentage change in import tariff, including price band effect.

[d]Percentage change in real exchange rate defined by Banco de la República.

Source: Author's own calculations.

An alternative methodology to rank the causes of the farm crisis of 1992 is to break down variations in the domestic price of imports, which reflects the cost of the imported commodity in the major consuming centers, once shipping costs, import tariffs and all other marketing costs have been added.[13] The results of an exercise along these lines is presented in Table 4.12, where the domestic price of imports is decomposed into three components: variations in international prices, tariffs and the real exchange rate. The exercise does not, however, capture the effects of other variables on production incentives, such as yields, input prices and other factors affecting the difference between producer prices and the domestic price of imports.

The variations observed between 1991 and 1992 in the domestic price of imports for the eight crops subject to price bands are presented in Table 4.12. Results show a decline in the domestic price for all products, except wheat. Declining prices for sugar, maize and sorghum can be attributed primarily to reductions in world prices and, to a lesser extent, to appreciation of the real exchange rate. International markets and the real exchange rate seem equally responsible for the drop in prices for barley and soybeans. The drop in rice prices seems to be explained by lower international prices and declining protection. In the case of milk, the decline was due primarily to a drop in protection and, secondly, to the appreciation of the exchange rate.

In short, although results vary by crop, the drop in international prices seems to be the dominant element in the explanation of variations in the domestic price of imports. The influence of exchange rate appreciation between 1991 and 1992 also turns out to be an important factor. On the other hand, the impact of reduced protection is significant only for the cases of wheat, milk and rice.

Aggravating Factors

Problems with the Supply of Credit

The effect of the supply of credit on agricultural output has been a controversial subject among economists. While some believe the supply of credit has an important impact on production decisions, for others it is not a key determinant of planting decisions. A comprehensive study commissioned by the government found that investment behavior has not displayed a significant association with credit supply in Colombia since 1970.[14] If this is the case, it is unclear what effect, if any, the slowdown in Caja Agraria lending activities in 1991 and 1992 exerted on the agricultural crisis. Yet, the fact that Caja Agraria was unable to respond to the credit needs of many farmers or to extend the payback period on their loans certainly aggravated the situation for some and delayed recovery for others.

Caja Agraria faced mounting financial losses throughout the 1986-1990 period. These were brought on by slow growth in financial earnings and the rising cost of its resources and administrative overhead.[15] Relative to those of commercial banks, personnel costs were high at most of Caja Agraria's 880 branches, transaction volume was low, and loan portfolios exhibited high default rates.[16] In 1991, these financial difficulties were aggravated when banking supervisors mandated an increase in pension fund provisions. This pushed Caja Agraria over the financial edge and led to a collapse in its lending operations. The situation was further complicated in 1991 by the rapid reduction in Caja Agraria's labor force, which led to serious administrative and operational problems. As a consequence, in that year, the value of new loans extended by the bank fell some 20 percent.

News about the financial difficulties of Caja Agraria and rumors that the government was considering its liquidation spread panic among farmers, many of whom opted to delay loan repayments until the situation was resolved. Overdue loans increased rapidly from 15.6 percent of the bank's loan portfolio in 1990 to 24.7 percent at the end of 1991, further aggravating the financial crisis and leaving Caja Agraria without funds to extend new loans.

The flow of credit to the farming sector was seriously affected by the crisis at Caja Agraria. Total credit for agriculture did not exhibit real growth in 1992. In the same year, Caja Agraria's new loan portfolio increased by only 10 percent, a rate well below inflation.

Some observers have pointed to the phasing out of interest rate subsidies as another aggravating factor of agricultural problems. However, maximum lending rates for agriculture were increased in 1991 and 1992 at a time when interest rates in the economy were falling. Table 4.13 displays changes in interest rates on farm loans between 1990 and 1992. Nominal rates for agricultural loans actually declined in 1992 as a result of generally lower interest rates

TABLE 4.13 Interest Rates for Agricultural Loans, 1990-1993
(annual percentage rates)

		Rates on Loans for:	
Year	*DTF[a]*	*Small Farmers[b]*	*Other Farmers[c]*
1990	36.6	30.8	39.6
1991	37.9	32.1	44.1
1992	27.7	25.0	36.2
1993	25.7	28.4	34.0

[a]Average deposit rate of commercial banks.

[b]Farmers with less than US$17,500 in assets.

[c]Farmers with more than US$17,500 in assets.

Source: Data from Banco de la República.

in the economy, despite the gradual elimination of interest rate ceilings. Hence, it does not seem likely that this factor had much of an effect on farming incentives.

In summary, it is likely that the 1992 crisis was aggravated by Caja Agraria's inability to help farmers deal with falling returns and liquidity problems. This credit squeeze affected disproportionately small farmers, since nearly all *campesino* producers with access to formal credit have been traditionally clients of Caja Agraria.

Interest Rate Differential

Another factor that may have further depressed returns in some crops was the result of financial incentives that favored storage of agricultural commodities abroad. Such incentives arise when, due to macroeconomic and financial policies, domestic interest rates rise substantially above international rates.[17] In these cases, if the domestic price of a product is similar to the import price, purchase of the local product implies financial and storage costs for the buyer that are less expensive abroad. Consequently, for domestic producers to compete with foreign crops, their output will need to be priced below world levels. By how much domestic prices will need to be reduced depends on how long the crop needs to be stored and on the magnitude of the gap between local and foreign interest rates.

Large interest rate differentials were recorded in Colombia during the latter half of 1991 and the early months of 1992, precisely at the time when annual crops were being harvested. The government's anti-inflationary policy in 1991 made domestic credit more expensive, pushing local interest rate levels to over 20 percent, in real terms. Simultaneously, foreign interest rates fell to record lows as a result of the recessionary environment prevailing in industrialized countries. Attempts at quantifying the effect of the interest rate differential for local farmers indicate that local prices may have fallen by as much 14.7 percent with respect to import prices in crops like sorghum, maize, rice and cotton.[18]

Rural Violence

Whether violence has been a significant drag on the Colombian economy is a controversial issue. Although the traditional belief is that violence generates an environment unfavorable to investment and economic growth, recent studies show that Colombia has been an atypical case in Latin America, combining the highest rates of violence of the region with positive and stable economic indicators.[19]

However, the violence originating from guerrilla activities, drug trafficking and other criminal activities has a more direct impact on agriculture than in most other sectors of the economy. This is clearly reflected in the findings of a study commissioned by the Colombian government, which attempted to quantify the combined influence of factors such as lowered investment levels, falling land prices and disruptions in input markets and communication and transport networks on agricultural activities. The study concluded that these factors impose a heavy burden on farmers and that they may have reduced agricultural GDP in the 1980s by 16 percent.[20]

The most common forms of rural violence clearly generate extra costs for Colombian farmers. Frequent kidnappings lead to absentee farming and diminished supervision of productive activities. Various forms of extortion by guerrillas imply additional costs for agricultural activities. Regional evidence for Colombia indicates that there is a close relationship between high levels of violence and low levels of investment in private irrigation projects during the 1980s.[21]

Despite the evidence cited, the effects of the drastic increase in violence rates on agricultural output between 1991 and 1992 is not easy to quantify (see Figure 4.8). Nevertheless, it seems likely that it constituted another factor aggravating the agricultural crisis.

Conclusion

This chapter has argued that a wide array of factors came together in 1992 to depress agricultural incentives and produce what was known as the "crisis."

FIGURE 4.8 Violence Rates, 1958-1993 (Homicides per 100,000 inhabitants)

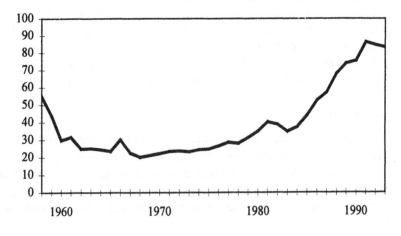

Source: Gaitán (1994).

However, output figures show that the crisis was in fact concentrated in annual, importable crops. For this sector of Colombian agriculture, production and prices suffered as a result of several mutually reinforcing factors: world prices fell below trend levels, the exchange rate rebounded after the excessive devaluation of 1989-90 (compounded by rapid capital inflows) and tariffs were reduced as a result of *Apertura* reforms. The sensation that the crisis went beyond importable crops (accounting for only 25 percent of agricultural production) was due to the intense drought which affected a wider array of crops (especially non-tradables) and declining returns for some exportable crops, especially, coffee, oil palm and bananas. The latter also were hit by falling world prices (except oil palm) and the appreciation of the peso.

Some of the factors which caused the 1992 crisis were of a short-term nature, such as the drought and the unusual depression of international commodity prices. However, other factors would prove to be persistent, including the appreciation of the exchange rate and efforts to remove restrictions to the free trade of agricultural goods. This explains why some of the changes in the production structure that were evident in 1992—the relative success of permanent and non-tradable crops over annuals and tradable commodities—would continue in later years. Also among the winners in this structural change would be those that managed to obtain disproportionately high protection levels, such as rice, sugar, beef and chicken.

Unfortunately, the 1992 crisis created a generally poor atmosphere for *Apertura* policies among most farming groups. This embittered the relationship between the private sector and the government and made excessively difficult advances in some of the joint efforts necessary to deepen long-term competitiveness of Colombian agriculture. This was the case with respect to fields such as agricultural research as well as investment in irrigation.

In addition, deteriorating incomes of traditionally important farming groups and political pressures from Congress pressured the government to propose emergency measures. These included some important modifications of the original *Apertura* plan. In the next chapter, these post-crisis adjustments are discussed as well as their impact on trade liberalization.

Notes

1. Discussion of agriculture in Colombia has usually distinguished between annual and permanent crops. The former display a plant-to-harvest cycle of six months or less. The latter have a productive life of more than one year. Also, annual crops are mostly importable crops, whereas permanent crops are a combination of export crops (e.g., coffee, and sugar cane) and non-tradables (e.g., cassava, plantains and *panela* cane).

2. Farm output includes production of crops and livestock.

3. See, for example, Jaramillo and Junguito (1993), Mora and Cortés (1993), Ocampo (1993) and Sanint (1993).

4. Figures refer to the commodity indexes published in World Bank (1994b).

5. See Himat (1993).

6. Figure 4.7 displays the real exchange rate indicator denominated as ITCR1 in Banco de la República (Colombia's Central Bank) data, calculated by using producer price indexes for Colombian and its major trading partners.

7. See Calvo et al. (1992) and Schadler et al. (1993) for more on capital inflows to Colombia and other countries of the region.

8. The aggregate index of farm output prices is obtained from the producer price index, calculated by Banco de la República.

9. The nominal protection coefficient (NPC) is defined as NPC = (P/P^*) - 1, where P is the producer price and P^* is the international price, both measured in a comparable location.

10. There were also reports that some of the soybeans imported from Bolivia originated in Brazil and Argentina.

11. Farm return indexes are defined as the ratio between the income generated by one hectare and the cost of inputs per hectare.

12. Jaramillo and Junguito (1993) argue that the appreciation hurt farming returns between 1990 and 1992 but that real exchange rate levels in both of these years were above long-term trends.

13. The domestic price of imports is the price of the imported product at a major consuming center, which includes FOB prices, insurance, international freight, docking and unloading fees, tariffs, other import fees and local transportation to processing centers.

14. See Departamento Nacional de Planeación (1990).

15. See Tobón (1994) for an analysis of Caja Agraria's troubles in the early 1990s.

16. See Hernández (1992) for a detailed analysis of financial problems of Caja Agraria.

17. A lucid analysis of the effect of interest rate differentials during agricultural trade liberalization in Mexico is found in Bivings (1992).

18. See Ruiz (1995).

19. See Consejeria para la Paz (1994).

20. See Departamento Nacional de Planeación (1990).

21. The study is by Dinar and Keck (1995).

5

The Aftermath of Crisis:
1993-1997

The 1992 crisis left a deep scar in many rural areas of Colombia. Influential groups of farmers affected by substantial losses and overdue loans asked the government insistently to modify *Apertura* policies. Under strong political pressure, the government adopted emergency measures throughout 1992, launched a formal recovery plan in the first half of 1993 and implemented a new Agrarian Law in 1994. New initiatives to boost depressed sectors were taken in 1994 and 1995 by a new presidential administration. The liberal policy regime proposed originally by the Gaviria administration was gradually modified by numerous crop-specific measures aimed at assisting farmers in recovering from the crisis.

This chapter looks at events in Colombian agriculture after the 1992 crisis and attempts to assess to what extent *Apertura* measures were affected by post-1992 policies. First, it describes government actions in the aftermath of the crisis. The review demonstrates the significant breadth of government efforts to cushion falling farm incomes, including the reversal of key liberalization measures for some crops. Second, the results of government efforts are assessed with a review of production trends after 1992. The analysis shows that despite intense government action, overall farm output continued to stagnate between 1992 and 1997 with continued declines in the production of annual crops. Third, protection levels are examined in order to assess the impact of post-1992 government actions on the trade liberalization efforts of 1990-91. Fourth, the degree of market integration after the 1990 reforms is tested, using a simple econometric model. And finally, a discussion of the political economy of agricultural protection in Colombia after the 1992 crisis is presented at the end.

Reforming the Reforms: Policies to Deal with Crisis

Responding to the First Signs of Crisis

Starting in early 1992, sharp drops in farm incomes in some areas generated strong pressure for compensatory action by the government. In spite of some delays in the flow of information from the agricultural regions to Bogotá, the government responded with emergency measures as soon as the first signs of crisis were detected. The first special measures were announced in early 1992, involving special refinancing terms for farmers affected by *El Niño*. Later in the year, grace periods and refinancing terms became more generous as the magnitude of the crisis in annual crops became apparent.[1]

In the first months of 1992, plans to withdraw IDEMA from crop purchases in important farming regions were postponed. Instead, the agency intensified its intervention in grain and oilseed markets during the second half of 1992. IDEMA was authorized to purchase rice, maize and sorghum at intervention prices, which were set substantially above official minimum guarantee prices. The reactivation of government intervention openly contradicted *Apertura* announcements of 1990 and 1991. Rice growers benefited from this measure, since IDEMA purchases prevented prices from declining further, after shipments of rice from Venezuela flooded domestic markets early in 1992.

In October of 1992, the government's Foreign Trade Council approved emergency measures to assist producers of annual crops.[2] The price band for maize was replaced by two new bands: one for white maize for human consumption and one for yellow maize, primarily for animal consumption. The new bands yielded greater protection levels. Also, US$29 million were budgeted for rescheduling of farm debts.

The collapse of cotton prices prompted the government to intervene in negotiations between the textile industry and producers' associations. Textile mills were pressured into offering higher prices to farmers during the first half of 1993. In addition, the government initiated negotiations with Venezuelan authorities to eliminate local subsidies and distortions in rice trade flows.

In October of 1992, the Ministry of Agriculture formally asked the Board of the Central Bank to authorize loans for crop storage in foreign currency. The purpose of this measure was to reduce the difference between domestic and foreign financing costs and, thus, avoid the negative effects on producer prices (as described in Chapter 4).[3]

In November of 1992, the government announced that export subsidy levels would be maintained throughout 1993, as a special concession to support exportable crops, which faced depressed low international prices and an appreciating exchange rate. Moreover, CONPES approved measures to extend guarantees needed for emergency loans to banana producers. These supports helped to buffer the impact of lower international prices and the effects of measures adopted by the European Community to restrict imports of bananas from Latin America.[4]

The Recovery Plan

The measures outlined above were taken in a haphazard way, as news of farming troubles reached Bogotá. By early 1993, the magnitude of the drop in income for producers of annual crops were well known. Moreover, powerful farming groups most affected by these events intensified their opposition to *Apertura* measures. In the first few months of 1992, the government prepared a Recovery Plan, spearheaded by José Antonio Ocampo, a highly respected economist and newly appointed Minister of Agriculture. The plan, officially announced in May of 1993, was designed to restore profitability and producer confidence in the short-term as well as to spur long-term competitiveness. The plan contained a long list of measures, including many of those already adopted since 1992. It also contained new provisions, some of them approved at the request of farming associations, which participated in a high-level commission established at the request of the Association of Colombian Farmers (SAC).[5]

The Recovery Plan was intended to boost producer confidence by giving positive price signals for crops affected by the crisis. Hence, a comprehensive revision of the method used to set minimum guarantee prices for IDEMA was announced, along with an increase in these prices for the second half of 1993. IDEMA was authorized to step up its intervention in the rice and bean markets, and expanded its range of action to include crops that had not been traditionally purchased by the government, such as cotton, jute, milk and silk cocoons. Renewed market intervention boosted the volume and value of agricultural products purchased by the agency by 20.5 and 98.7 percent, respectively, in 1993.

The Recovery Plan also featured important measures concerning trade policy. To discourage import flows and prevent import-tariff evasion (through under-invoicing of shipments), minimum import prices were adopted for 32 sensitive products. The methodology to calculate price band tariffs was altered to increase protection of processed food items. In addition, the tariffs on several pesticides and their chemical inputs were reduced.

Authorities also announced plans to create an import safeguard statute to deal with sudden surges in imports, stemming from distortions in international markets.[6] The idea was that high special tariffs would be imposed in the event of a serious threat to domestic production caused by a massive increase in imports. Special treatment would be reserved for agricultural goods, by allowing the mere perception of a threat to domestic farm production as justification for invoking the safeguard.

Imports of chicken parts and powdered milk were suspended temporarily in July 1993, while approval of the safeguard statute was still pending. In both cases, it was argued that large import shipments posed a serious threat to domestic production, and that local producers needed time to adjust to new market conditions.[7]

Colombian officials negotiated with Andean Pact neighbors to harmonize the methodology and coverage of the agricultural price band system and to consolidate a common external tariff for farm goods. Authorities also announced that export subsidies for agricultural goods under the CERT scheme would once again be maintained in 1994, with special benefits targeted to exports of bananas, flowers, shrimp, tuna and fruits.

Actions to boost the flow of agricultural credit in the Recovery Plan featured measures for capitalization and reorganization of Caja Agraria. In October 1993, an agreement was signed with the government's Fondo de Garantías Financieras (FOGAFIN) to provide US$183 million for capitalization of Caja Agraria between 1993 and 1994. According to the agreement, the government would assume Caja Agraria's future pension liabilities, which represented an additional annual contribution of nearly US$51 million. A plan to recover overdue loans was implemented, along with administrative reforms and a program for overall systematization of Caja Agraria operations.

Ad hoc efforts to provide debt-relief for farmers in 1992 were replaced by a comprehensive package to allow long-term rescheduling and ample grace periods, as ordained by Law 34 of 1993. These measures were to benefit all farmers affected by *El Niño*. Later in the year, the refinancing program established under the Law was broadened, and the number of crops that could take advantage of lengthened loan terms was increased to twelve. Nearly US$165 million in agricultural debts were refinanced through this plan; of these, US$95 million were channeled to coffee farmers. In addition, the government's Industrial Development Institute (IFI) extended US$76 million in loans to refinance banana producers.[8]

The Recovery Plan delayed removal of interest rate limits for *campesinos* until 1995. Also, interest rates on loans to other farmers were reduced by one percentage point, as a result of the removal of a tax traditionally used to provide funds for technical assistance.

The Agricultural Loan Guarantee Fund was authorized to provide collateral for farmers benefiting from refinancing deals. This facilitated access to working capital for farmers whose collateral had been exhausted. Law 69 of 1992 also created the legal framework for an agricultural insurance scheme for risks associated with weather disturbances and natural disasters. Studies were launched to create a Reinsurance Fund and to propose a scheme of government subsidies for the operation of crop insurance.

The Recovery Plan also included measures to cushion income declines among the poorest segment of the rural population: a rural employment plan was launched, focusing on regions where labor demand had been affected by declining agricultural production. The plan emphasized labor-intensive rural development projects in cotton-growing regions and areas affected by the coffee borer.[9]

Funding for the Modernization and Diversification Plan was increased to speed up the search for alternative crops for less competitive producers. The Plan was supplemented by a Technological Shock Program, designed to promote new cost-reducing technologies.

The Recovery Plan also included a wide array of measures for specific crops. The Price Stabilization Fund for cotton was launched and its operations, designed originally to stabilize export prices, were extended to smooth price levels in domestic markets. The government guaranteed a loan of US$12 million for the fund. Debts of cotton growers in the Atlantic coast were rescheduled. A subsidy was made available to farmers obtaining loans to drill deep wells in cotton growing areas of Cesar and La Guajira provinces. Moreover, the government encouraged a price-setting agreement between the textile industry and growers in 1993 and 1994. IDEMA intervened in the purchase of the 1993 domestic crop, granting producers a subsidy of US$127 per ton, 8.5 percent of market prices.

Rice farmers benefited from negotiations to remove production and export subsidies for competitors in Venezuela. A voluntary export restraint agreement was signed in order to reduce import flows from that country. IDEMA, the rice growers' federation (FEDEARROZ) and the millers' associations (INDUARROZ and MOLIARROZ) also agreed to establish prices jointly for the purchase of local harvests.

The Recovery Plan also gave a new boost to policies aimed at building long-term competitiveness and providing for sustained growth. Renewed emphasis was given to technological development and the need for funds from the World Bank to establish SINTAP, the program for technical assistance to small producers. Ambitious plans were announced to develop infrastructure and modernize marketing channels, extend the coverage of agricultural credit, and improve the flow of market information. Irrigation and drainage priorities were modified to provide small irrigation projects in areas with few such investments, such as the Eastern Plains and the Atlantic coast.

Public investments for agriculture increased substantially in 1993 and 1994, as a result of recovery measures. The real value of government spending in agriculture had declined by 7.5 percent between 1990 and 1992—excluding funds to rescue Caja Agraria. In 1993, the Ministry of Agriculture and its agencies were provided with a budget amounting to US$367.4 million for investment, reflecting a real increase of 8.9 percent with respect to 1992. The increase was due primarily to increased budgetary allocations for INAT projects for irrigation and drainage and for investment in rural housing and other development programs channeled through the DRI Fund.

Public funding for agriculture increased sharply again in 1994—by 24.4 percent in real terms, excluding investments earmarked for Caja Agraria. This substantial increase was mainly the result of additional resources for employment programs, assistance for development of new technologies, rural electrification and other rural development projects. The amounts earmarked for investments in irrigation and for crop purchases through IDEMA were also increased substantially. Greater funding was also allocated for subsidies to benefit *campesino* farmers, investment incentives and commodity stabilization funds.

Ley Agraria

The agricultural crisis of 1992 generated anti-government feelings among some influential farming groups, particularly those representing crops most affected by falling returns. During the first months of 1993, some of these groups met with members of the legislature to propose passage of legal provisions to dismantle *Apertura* measures in agriculture. They took advantage of the need for new legal provisions to develop Articles 64, 65 and 66 of the 1991 Constitution, which highlighted the strategic significance of agriculture to the Colombian economy. As a result, drafts circulated of a legal initiative that would reverse trade liberalization measures and provide generous short-term relief to farmers. These efforts culminated in December 1993, when Congress approved the General Agriculture and Fishing Development Act (Law 101 of 1993), which became known as *Ley Agraria*.

Despite its original motivation, the final version of the bill was a greatly altered one compared to the anti-*Apertura* drafts that had circulated early in the year. In legislative discussions, José Antonio Ocampo, then Minister of Agriculture, played an important role in modifying the original intentions of the proponents. More than half of the provisions of the approved text were included at the suggestion of the government, such as those concerning stabilization funds, rural development, technical assistance, subsidies for *campesino* families, refinancing regulations and crop insurance. Also, most of the provisions aimed at reversing trade liberalization were removed during legislative discussions.

Ley Agraria was the result of lengthy political negotiations between members of Congress, farming groups and the government. The result was a bill containing a variegated set of objectives, regulations, and instruments. In many areas, the law reiterated vague, lofty objectives, such as the need to extend credit to all farmers or ensuring that all international trade should obey "the principles of equity, reciprocity and national convenience," and that all agricultural policy be negotiated between the government and private groups.[10]

In addition to rhetorical sections, *Ley Agraria* also contained pragmatic provisions, which created key new instruments that widened the governments' arsenal to achieve development goals. These included the possibility of extending direct subsidies for crop purchases, on-farm capital investments and the creation of *campesino*-based agroindustrial enterprises.

Prior to *Ley Agraria*, the government had been legally barred from extending direct subsidies to farmers. Article 7 of the Law made this possible, allowing subsidies that would "protect farm incomes, natural resources and peace in the countryside." Explicit subsidies for purchase and storage of crops, on-farm investments, use of electrical energy in rural areas and crop insurance were authorized in the law. IDEMA was also allowed to extend direct subsidies to farmers without direct purchase of the crop. This new flexibility led directly to a reduction of crop purchases after 1994 and facilitated the elimination of the agency in 1997.

Ley Agraria also created the Incentive for Rural Capitalization (ICR), a direct subsidy for up to 40 percent of eligible on-farm investments. This subsidy was put in practice in early 1994 for irrigation investments, processing and storage structures and for projects that involved upgrading of production technologies. ICR funds are accessible to farmers who can obtain long-term investment loans from financial institutions. To avoid concentrating subsidies in a few large projects, regulations set the ceiling per beneficiary at roughly US$50,000.[11]

In order to alleviate the shortage of marketing and processing agents in many areas of the country, *Ley Agraria* created the EMPRENDER Fund, to provide capital contributions for new enterprises in marketing and processing of agricultural goods, which can be demonstrated to benfit farmers in marginal areas. EMPRENDER funding was made accessible to projects proposed by the private sector and territorial agencies. Enterprises benefiting from the Fund must share ownership with *campesino* groups. EMPRENDER funds can be extended for up to a maximum of 49 percent of total subscribed capital of the beneficiary enterprise.

Ley Agraria also included clauses to promote efficiency in agricultural markets. Provisions were included to foster the development of forward and futures markets. Also, extensive regulations were provided for the creation and operation of stabilization funds aimed at smoothing out price fluctuations in farm income and increasing export sales. The Law also provided modern rules for protection against unfair foreign competition, such as countervailing duties and minimum prices for the purposes of assessing import tariffs. Article 5 formalized the creation of a safeguard to be applied when there is proof of substantial damage (or threat of jeopardy) to domestic production.

Credit provisions of *Ley Agraria* included mechanisms for further refinancing of farm loans through the Agricultural Loan Guarantee Fund. Moreover, the Law ordained that interest rate ceilings in place in 1993 would be extended until 1995, effectively postponing the gradual phase-out announced by the Gaviria administration. The bill also stated that agricultural lending for *campesino* farmers should be subsidized and that farm loans should generally be extended at interest rates below those for commercial credit.

Ley Agraria also included provisions to strengthen decentralization efforts for rural development. The law mandated all municipalities to establish technical assistance offices (UMATAs) and Rural Development Councils for the purposes of setting local investment priorities.[12] A Vice-Ministry for *Campesino* Affairs and Rural Development was created within the Ministry of Agriculture to focus on the needs of the rural poor. The Law also allowed DRI funds to finance rural development programs in conjunction with *campesino* organizations or communities of organized producers.

Ley Agraria also set general guidelines for the creation of "parafiscal" funds, to be managed directly by agricultural associations, under contract with the national government. Financed by taxes on crop sales, these funds are aimed at promoting consumption and production of specific commodities. According to the Law, parafiscal funds may invest in research and development, technical assistance, production and marketing organization, export promotion, and consumption campaigns.

Agricultural Policies Under The Samper Administration

Farm issues were an important topic of debate in the presidential campaign of 1994. Candidates often spoke of the need to modify *Apertura* policies for agriculture. However, specific proposals for counter-reform did not surface. Candidates were aware of the potential costs of reneging on liberal trade policies, which would likely involve renegotiating trade agreements with Andean Pact nations, Mexico and Chile, as well as revising commitments under GATT.

Newly elected president Ernesto Samper, spoke in his campaign of the need to make trade liberalization measures "gradual and selective." After taking over in August of 1994, the new administration announced a new policy framework for agriculture, including measures to boost farmer confidence in the short-run and others for long-term development.[13] The latter were to a great extent a direct continuation of the programs pursued during the Gaviria administration. Plans were announced to continue with an emphasis on obtaining funds for large irrigation and drainage projects and for transferring investment and construction of projects to the private sector. Ambitious targets were announced for investments in water projects, including 42,000 hectares in small irrigation projects, 111,000 in medium and large irrigation schemes and 50,000 for rehabilitation of old projects. Research and development policies were to continue supporting the new institutional setup and the consolidation of CORPOICA. Technology transfer would be based on the SINTAP network and on strengthening municipal UMATAs. Trade and marketing policy would continue to be based on price bands, selective subsidies to crops facing difficulties, promotion of *campesino* enterprises through EMPRENDER and modernization of information systems for farmers and government. The administration also announced that it would continue studies to design an insurance scheme for farm-related risks.

Overall, Samper's plan for agriculture called for the continuation of *Apertura* policies as well as with the investment priorities proposed during the Gaviria administration. However, there were two areas where significant differences in emphasis arose. The first was in policies to benefit disadvantaged sectors, including *campesinos*, the rural poor and rural women. The second was the management of the short-run profitability crisis with trade policy tools.

With respect to social policy for the countryside, the centerpiece of Samper's rural development efforts was a strong push for market-oriented land reform—applying the subsidies for land purchase designed since 1992. The government announced a goal of financing subsidies for 1 million hectares to benefit 70,000 families between 1995 and 1998, as well as new efforts to decentralize the land reform agency. Furthermore, efforts were announced to establish *campesino* reserve zones, a new form of land ownership for communal management of land and natural resources, designed to prevent sales to land speculators in recently colonized areas.

Other measures designed to benefit disadvantaged rural groups included the expansion of the temporary rural employment program initiated in 1993. According to the Samper plan, the rural employment program was targeted to provide 23,000 jobs annually between 1995 and 1998. Financial cooperatives were given access to FINAGRO funds to extend agricultural loans. Ambitious targets were set for rural housing subsidies and a program to facilitate the access of rural women to government programs was implemented. In some areas of public investment, minimum targets were set for the number of female beneficiaries: 10,000 were to benefit from new loans from Caja Agraria, 1,000 from land reform subsidies, and 1,600 from land titling.

After 1995, Samper's original plan for agriculture suffered some modifications, particularly as a result of the political crisis arising from accusations of drug money contributions to his presidential campaign. In 1995, the government intensified efforts to fight drug trafficking, with emphasis on actions to promote the eradication of coca and poppy fields. In that year, the government launched a refurbished program to promote alternative activities (PLANTE), which included credit facilities and guaranteed prices for legal crops in remote areas as well as investments in infrastructure.[14] Efforts to control production of illicit crops generated strong anti-government feelings in frontier areas, particularly in the Guaviare and Caquetá provinces. As a consequence, in 1996 the government had to deal with 13 separate *campesino* protests ("marchas") involving some 400,000 demonstrators. These marches were often dissipated once government representatives agreed to concessions, usually involving unpaid debts and increased public investment.

Social policies for rural areas were also altered by subsequent events. In June of 1996, then Minister of Agriculture Cecilia López, convened a "rural social summit" which led to the signing of a "rural social contract" between the government and several major *campesino* organizations. The contract stipulated that government agencies would give priority to a large list of short-term measures and investments that were demanded by *campesinos*, in the areas of access to land, credit, health, education, social security, defense and natural resources.[15] Another unforeseen policy was the approval in June of 1996 of a law to create a "Solidarity Fund," designed to forgive debts of small farmers affected by weather disturbances, natural catastrophes or massive drops in producer prices.

According the Samper administration's plan for agriculture, the short-run crisis in annual crops would be tackled with the reinstatement of "absorption agreements" to be signed among producers, agroindustries and the government in order to force purchase of commodities at above-market prices. Similar agreements had been used in the 1950s and 1960s to support the development of import-substituting crops. In the new refurbished version, industries were induced to participate through an extension of tariff discounts on imports of their raw materials. Eventually, agreements were put in practice for wheat, sorghum, maize, barley and palm oil. The new government also announced the continuation of direct subsidies for cotton and soybean growers, designed to support farm incomes. Banana producers benefited in 1995 from an increase in CERT export subsidies from 2.5 percent to 5 percent of export revenues.

Absorption agreements were complemented with direct subsidies to farmers of sensitive crops and storage subsidies for the seasonal rice surpluses. These measures gradually substituted for direct IDEMA intervention, which had become increasingly inefficient and corrupt. As a result, the government announced in 1997 the liquidation of the agency, an announcement that was welcomed by farming groups.

To eliminate trade distortions with Andean neighbors, the Samper administration continued efforts to harmonize price band policies with Ecuador and Venezuela. An agreement was reached in early 1995, which led to the establishment of the Andean Price Band System. The agreement also resulted in the creation of new bands for chicken parts, pork, raw sugar, soybean oil and palm oil. The new system also included changes in methodology, which led to greater protection for some commodities.[16]

The Samper administration also fostered the signing of "competitiveness" agreements between the government and the main actors of commodity-based industries. Such agreements usually involved commitments on a number of joint actions to improve long-run competitiveness, including research, investments in infrastructure, quality improvements and greater coordination among producers and processors. Agreements were signed early on in Samper's term among producers and processors of textiles, cotton fibers, forestry and paper pulp. More difficult negotiation processes ensued in the feed grains, rice, oilseeds, milk products, forestry wood and furniture group.

The rice market received very special treatment during the Samper presidency. After extensive negotiations, the government and rice producers agreed in 1996 to a policy regime based on strict control of imports. A "policy" committee was created to decide import quota volumes, with the participation of the government, millers, producers and traders. Since then, the committee has banned permanently the importation of white rice, limiting the flow of imports to small quantities of paddy[17] in order to maintain a stable real price for farmers. Moreover, millers and a few select traders have been granted a monopoly on imports. Since 1996, rice has also benefited from a government storage subsidy designed to reduce seasonal price fluctuations.

Overall, by the end of Samper's term, the mood among farm groups was that the administration had not succeeded in improving conditions for farmers. As will be reviewed below, production of annual crops lost additional ground between 1995 and 1997. Profitability levels for most crops affected by the slump of 1992 continued to be depressed and farming groups complained about growing imports and the lack of access to credit. Furthermore, political scandals related to drug funds in the presidential campaign weakened the executive, while strengthening political criteria in the allocation of public funds and government posts. This affected the pace and effectiveness of implementation of many public programs. Farming groups complained of increasing levels of bureaucratic inefficiency and corruption.

Agencies related to agricultural development suffered disproportionately from the weakening of the executive. Most affected were those in charge of land reform (INCORA), rural development (DRI), irrigation (INAT), agricultural credit (Caja Agraria) and marketing (IDEMA). In 1996, the Samper administration considered seriously the possibility of closing down or merging several agencies, due to evidence of growing inefficiencies and corruption. Political resistance by powerful congressional groups led to the ousting of then Minister of Agriculture Cecilia López, before these plans could be carried out.

Institutional Failures 1993-1997

Some of the most important development initiatives for rural areas proposed during the Gaviria administration hinged critically on the successful implementation of ambitious investment plans and institutional transformations of government agencies. These were the cases of the market-based land reform initiative, the demand-drive push for investment in irrigation and drainage, the involvement of private farming groups in the management of agricultural research and the support of local governments through cofinancing funds. Although in-depth evaluations of the results of these reforms on a case-by-case basis are yet to be performed, by 1998, the general perception was that most of these initiatives had failed to meet expectations, contributing to the continued stagnation of Colombian agriculture after 1992.

The effort to grant direct subsidies to beneficiaries for the acquisition of land met with strong institutional and political resistance. Decades of managing land reform through local patron-client relations, dominated by regional politicians, made altering the status quo a difficult task.[18] Political forces interested in preserving traditional approaches supported INCORA staff in resisting changes. After the new land reform law was approved in 1994, the debate continued about implementation procedures, which had been left undefined in the law. Discussions within government and private sector representatives about the best way to implement the land purchase subsidy dragged on from mid-1994 to early 1997. Even after agreements were reached, the application of the subsidy faced practical difficulties: poor beneficiaries had to negotiate land purchases with powerful landowners. Also, in many areas of the country with high levels of rural poverty, potential beneficiaries had to struggle to find land in the market.

Despite the strong emphasis on land reform stated in the Samper plan, achievements were poor due to institutional resistance to new policies and implementation difficulties. By the end of 1997, only 224,000 hectares had been distributed, about 22 percent of the target announced in 1994. Further, most of the land was distributed using traditional policies involving direct purchases by INCORA. In 1996 and 1997, corruption scandals related to the land acquisition practices of the agency broke out in the national press.

Some of the practical difficulties of implementing a program of direct subsidies for land purchases may have been solved earlier if small pilot programs had been implemented to test the new scheme. With support from the World Bank, the government launched an experiment along these lines in four municipalities during 1996 and 1997. The program yielded important lessons. It illustrated how selection of the most promising beneficiaries could be best implemented by requiring the submission of "productive projects" by potential participants. Also, it demonstrated that successful implementation required greater decentralization of beneficiary and project selection, greater integration of land reform projects with local investment plans, and support for beneficiaries in the preparation of projects.[19]

The implementation of irrigation plans faced similar difficulties. During Gaviria's presidency, most efforts were directed to changing policies and obtaining formal approval through legal channels. The new policy thrust, based on financing projects proposed by groups of farmers, who had to commit to partial repayment of public outlays, faced resistance from inside and outside INAT. Many years of selection of projects and beneficiaries through regional patron-client relations were threatened, as well as the highly subsidized nature of traditional public irrigation districts. Institutional resistance within INAT was eventually defeated with the dismantling of labor unions and the reduction of the agency's labor force from 2,500 to less than 1,000. Substantial efforts were made to disseminate the new policies among farming groups and to secure foreign loans to finance large irrigation districts. Obtaining loans from multilateral institutions was more difficult than expected, in great part due to the poor implementation record of INAT in the 1980s with small irrigation projects funded by the World Bank.

The Samper plan called for implementation of the new policy in both small and large irrigation districts.[20] However, the weakening of the executive led to a greater influence of regional power bosses in the selection of projects and beneficiaries. High subsidy levels were established for both small and large beneficiaries and decentralization efforts were reversed with the reinvigoration of INAT's regional offices. Costly preparation studies absorbed the bulk of INAT's funds in 1995-97. As a result, by mid-1998, only 13,500 hectares had been constructed of the 110,000 hectares originally planned for large schemes; some 18,000 hectares of old districts had been rehabilitated, less than 40 percent of Samper administration targets. Only about half of the 40,000 hectares actually benefited from small irrigation projects. The bulk of the projects implemented since 1993 were those for which feasibility studies had been conducted prior to the approval of the new policies, including some with low rates of return. Most importantly, the costs per hectare of the irrigation projects undertaken since 1993 has averaged between US$4,500 and US$6,500, which are very high levels according to international standards. Costs are particularly high because the marginal benefits of irrigation investments are much lower than elsewhere. Due to favorable weather conditions, most irrigation projects in Colombia benefit areas where one six-month planting cycle occurs. In other tropical countries, such projects usually allow two planting cycles in previously unusable lands. In addition, costs of public irrigation are nearly double those incurred in private projects within Colombia, indicating poor selection of areas and heavy administrative overhead.

Another institution that suffered greatly from the weakness of the executive after drug-related scandals emerged was DRI, the cofinancing fund for rural development. However, DRI's problems began in the final years of the Gaviria administration. Prior to 1991, it was normal practice for the executive to negotiate with the legislative branch the inclusion in the annual budget of political projects that would benefit the constituencies of members of Congress who were supportive of the administration.[21] These projects were usually excluded from rigorous technical analysis in the National Planning Department and were known to feed regional patron-client relations. The 1991 Constitution, however, banned this practice, despite continuing pressures from politicians to have access to government funds for pet projects. Starting with the budget of 1994, political projects found their way into the budgets of cofinancing funds like DRI, which financed small infrastructure projects throughout most of the country.

The introduction of projects that were neither submitted by municipalities nor subject to technical review broke with a long tradition within DRI. In the past, DRI projects had to be submitted by local governments and underwent a lengthy process of evaluation, which included analysis of costs and benefits and coherence with regional development priorities. The introduction of political projects undermined the process and led to a confrontation with the World Bank and the Inter-American Development Bank, both of which had supplied a large share of DRI funds in the past. As a result, multilateral support for DRI ended in 1997, reducing resources for investment in rural development and increasing the share of politically motivated projects to over one third of the annual budget. A group of experts commissioned by the government to review government expenditures called for the dismantling of DRI and the other cofinancing funds in 1997. In 1998, with renewed multilateral support the government proposed changes to focus DRI activities on investing in broad development plans of local governments.

Implementation of new agricultural research policies proposed under Gaviria also moved exceedingly slowly. The creation of CORPOICA as a joint public-private agency to make research efforts more accountable to farmers' needs was mired from the start in legal controversy, involving the feasibility of transferring research staff from a governmental agency (ICA) to the new corporation. Institutional resistance to the change developed in ICA, where long-time staff members felt their importance had diminished with the transfer of research functions and funds to CORPOICA. Institutional conflicts weakened research and development interests and led to declining allocations from the national budget. The original scheme envisioned joint administration and financial support by government and private farming groups. By mid-1998, very little financial support had been received from private sources and the institution continued to be treated by the Ministry of Agriculture as a governmental agency. Moreover, CORPOICA continued to be highly centralized. Critics charged that it lacked focus, spending its scarce funds in many small projects with questionable overall impact.

The Performance of Agriculture After the 1992 Crisis

As demonstrated in the previous section, the 1992 agricultural crisis was followed by one of the most prolific periods in agricultural policy-making in Colombia's recent history. Did these intense efforts to aid farmers have a substantive effect on farm output after 1992? Official figures suggest that their effect was minimal. From 1993 to 1997, aggregate farm output edged upward at an annual rate of 1.4 percent, far below the post-war average of 3.5 percent (Table 5.1). This poor overall performance was the result of diverging trends in annual and permanent crops, not unlike those detected during 1992.

Annual crops did not recover after 1992. On the contrary, incomes and out-put for most of these crops continued to fall between 1992 and 1997. In this period, production of annual crops declined at an average annual rate of 1.3 percent. This dismal performance reflected the continued drop in production levels of cotton and most importable grains and oilseeds. Among the latter, the greatest output contractions were registered in barley, cotton, sorghum and wheat. The large cutback in cotton output increased import dependence for local textile mills.

Permanent crops—excluding coffee—performed better in the post-1992 pe-riod, growing at an average annual rate of 2.7 percent between 1992 and 1997. This positive rate reflected substantial output expansion of oil palm, fruits, sugar

Table 5.1 Value of Production 1992 and 1997 (Billion 1975 pesos)

	1992	1997	Growth (Percent)
Annual Crops	30.8	28.5	-1.3
Rice	5.2	6.0	1.1
Potatoes	7.3	7.0	3.5
Maize	5.2	4.5	-1.5
Vegetables	4.5	5.1	3.5
Cotton	1.9	1.2	-20.7
Sorghum	2.3	1.2	-16.5
Soybeans	1.8	2.0	2.6
Beans	1.1	0.9	-1.2
Wheat	0.6	0.3	-8.1
Barley	0.4	0.1	-21.6
Other annual[a]	0.5	0.3	0.5
Permanent Crops	43.0	55.9	2.7
Coffee	18.0	13.7	-8.2
Sugar Cane	9.2	12.2	3.0
Plantain	6.9	7.6	0.8
Panela Cane	5.9	6.9	1.6
Flowers	5.6	7.6	2.5
Oil Palm	3.9	7.1	9.0
Cassava	3.1	2.7	0.2
Fruits	2.9	5.8	4.6
Bananas	2.3	2.9	-1.3
Cocoa	1.6	1.5	-1.7
Other permanent[b]	1.4	1.6	1.2
Total Agriculture	96.6	98.1	-0.4
Total Livestock	50.4	65.7	4.4
Cattle	34.1	40.0	3.2
Pork	2.5	3.2	3.7
Poultry	13.8	21.7	6.3
Total Farm Output	147.0	163.7	1.4

[a]Sesame seed, peanuts and light tobacco.

[b]Yams, jute, export plantains, coconut and dark tobacco.

Source: Ministerio de Agricultura (1998).

cane and flowers. Rapid growth in production of oil palm led to the attainment of self-sufficiency for Colombia and the gradual increase of export shipments to neighboring countries as of 1993. The overall performance of permanent crops was diminished by the declines in production of exportable crops like cocoa and bananas.

Coffee production fell sharply after 1992. This was greatly a result of the reduction in new plantings that ensued after the international price collapse of 1989. Record crops achieved between 1990 and 1992 were followed by variable but declining harvests. As a result, coffee output declined at an average rate of 7.8 percent between 1992 and 1997.

The diverging performance of annual and permanent crops led to a net loss in output for aggregate agricultural production after 1992. However, this trend was partially compensated by the rapid expansion of livestock output. Livestock activities grew at a brisk 4.4 percent annually in the 1992-97 period, as a result of dynamic consumer demand for poultry and growing slaughter levels in cattle (without proportional decreases in herd size).

Overall, farm output grew at a mediocre rate of 1.4 percent annually between 1992 and 1997. The best year was 1994, when growth surpassed 3 percent mostly due to an upswing in the coffee harvest. On the other hand, aggregate performance in 1996 and 1997 was not too different from that registered in 1992. Clearly, government efforts to boost agricultural performance and, in particular, arrest the decline of harvests for annual crops were largely unsuccessful. Were the measures adopted ineffective? Were there stronger forces in action which prevented a recovery? Some clues on these matters are provided in Chapter 6, where a review of the causes of the mediocre performance of Colombian agriculture in the 1990s is presented.

Did Liberalization Survive the Crisis?

Pressures stemming from the 1992 crisis and its aftermath led to the modification of many liberalization measures originally announced in 1990 and 1991. This section evaluates the effects of these changes on liberalization achievements of 1990-91. The effects of modifications to *Apertura* on tariff and protection levels are examined first. Second, the degree of integration of local and international markets is evaluated.

Changing Protection Levels

Basic tariff levels (i.e., excluding price band effects) were not modified substantially after February of 1992, mostly as a result of Andean Pact commitments. Price band methodologies were, on the other hand, changed often, mostly with the intent of providing greater protection to crops. One way to determine if protection was changed significantly after 1992 is to examine actual tariff levels (including the effect of price bands). As shown in Table 5.2, crop-specific tariff levels have oscillated widely after 1992 in response to international price variations as well as methodological changes. Actual tariffs increased for all but one crop in 1993, probably as a result of measures to deal with the agricultural crisis. By 1997, most tariffs were above 1992 levels, with the exception of rice and soybeans. However, it is unlikely that 1997 tariff levels reflected an "equilibrium" situation. For instance, tariffs in 1996 were lower than those in 1992, due to the upswing in international prices of grains and oilseeds. It seems, therefore, more appropriate to evaluate whether protection was increased by comparing 1992 tariff levels with a multi-year average such as that for the years between 1994 and 1997.

Only minor changes in tariff levels are detected when tariffs in effect between 1994 and 1997 are compared with those applied in 1992. Only two exceptions can be noted: the tariff level for soybeans is 13 percentage points lower in the post-crisis period while that for milk is greater by 14 percentage points. Accordingly, tariff levels do not reflect a general move towards greater protection in the aftermath of the 1992 crisis.

As was explained in Chapter 4, the analysis of tariffs may not provide an accurate reflection of actual protection levels. On the one hand, there may be overt or hidden import restrictions that may result in higher effective protection. On the other hand, Andean Pact regulations allowed tariff-free trade for most agricultural goods across the borders with Venezuela and Ecuador. For these reasons, NPCs provide a superior measure of protection since they compare directly the price of the crop for Colombian producers with the relevant border measure of the international price. NPCs can also be used to examine changes in taxation (or support) levels for exportable crops.

Table 5.3 presents NPCs for nine commodities covered by the price band

Table 5.2 Tariffs on Price-Band Crops, 1992-1997 (percent)

Commodity	1992	1993	1994	1995	1996	1997	1994/97
Sugar	23	25	20	16	19	33	22
Rice	22	37	34	33	16	21	26
Maize	20	34	37	24	3	28	23
Sorghum	21	35	37	24	3	27	23
Soybeans	25	16	18	20	3	6	12
Wheat	16	16	15	9	2	19	11
Barley	16	24	21	13	3	17	13
Milk	24	49	75	33	16	28	38

Source: Ministerio de Agricultura (1998).

Table 5.3 Nominal Protection Coefficients for Price-Band Crops, 1986-1997 (percent)

Commodity	1986/90	1992	1994/97
Sugar	12	25	29
Rice	9	4	49
Maize	26	16	46
Oil Palm[a]	47	-19	-8
Sorghum	17	17	36
Soybeans	16	12	10
Wheat	21	11	10
Barley	33	36	32
Milk	41	42	16
Total[b]	25	21	23

[a]NPC calculated as exportable after 1993.

[b]Total weighted by crop production values.

Source: Author's own calculations.

scheme. The difference in protection levels between 1994-97 with those regis-tered in 1992 varies widely depending upon the crop. For the cases of rice, maize and sorghum, noticeable boosts in protection are detected. The NPC rate for rice jumps from 4 to 49 percent between 1992 and 1994-97. Over the same period, protection levels are 30 and 19 percentage points higher in 1994-97, for maize and sorghum, respectively. By contrast, a substantial drop in protection is registered for milk. Only minor changes are detected for wheat, sugar, palm, and barley. The aggregate production-weighted NPC for the nine crops increases slightly from 21 percent in 1992 to 23 percent in 1994-97. The evidence points then to a widely disparate behavior of protection levels in the aftermath of the 1992 crisis, with rice, maize and sorghum obtaining substantial gains in protec-tion.

NPC information also allows an assessment of whether "post-crisis" (i.e., 1994-97) protection levels were different from those prevailing in the period before *Apertura*. The comparison of average NPCs for the 1986-90 and 1994-97 periods yield noticeable increases in four of nine crops, and three substantial reductions. Increases are detected for the cases of rice (40 percentage points), maize (20 points), sorghum (19 points) and sugar (17 points). For the case of rice, this is clearly the result of the virtual reversal of liberalization policies that resulted from tight import controls particularly after 1996. For the cases of maize and sorghum, higher protection is largely a result of the operation of price bands and absorption agreements with local industry after 1994. For sugar, higher protection is a result of price bands and import restrictions to flows from Andean countries.

Reductions in protection of 25 percentage points or more occur for palm oil and milk. For the former, protection drops from 47 percent in 1986-90 to taxation of 8 percent in 1994-97. Much of this apparent drop can be explained by the loss of tariff protection implicit in the change in status from importable to exportable after 1993. For the remaining crops (soybeans, wheat and barley) protection levels in the post-crisis period have remained somewhat below pre-*Apertura* levels. Over the same period, the aggregate NPC fell from 25 to 23 percent, indicating only a moderate effect of liberalization measures on aggregate protection after the crisis.

Problems with the specification of appropriate international prices prevented the calculation of NPCs for poultry and beef. With respect to the former, trade restrictions and prohibitive tariffs have sheltered this activity from foreign competition. For the case of beef, large-scale imports have continued to be restricted by an underdeveloped cold-storage network and by the occasional use of sanitary restrictions. For both products, it is likely that NPC levels would reflect high protection levels in the post-*Apertura* period.

Did government policies affect protection levels of traditional exportable crops (excluding sugar)? Table 5.4 shows NPC levels for cotton, bananas, coffee and cocoa. All of these crops faced declining returns and production levels after 1990, leading to a shift to importable status for cotton since 1990. Protection levels exhibited additional reductions after 1992 for cotton, coffee and bananas, with that of cocoa remaining essentially unchanged. Moreover, cotton, coffee and cocoa displayed similar protection levels before and after *Apertura*. For cotton and cocoa, this meant no significant support nor taxation (NPCs near zero). For coffee it meant that the traditional export taxation burden continued at similar levels before and after *Apertura* (about 20 percent of export prices). A substantial reduction in the level of protection is detected only for bananas, largely as a result of cutbacks in the amount of export subsidies after 1990.

The above analysis demonstrates that despite the long list of government policies announced in the aftermath of the 1992 crisis, protection levels in the 1994-97 period were only increased significantly for three crops: rice, maize and sorghum. Moreover, the comparison of pre-*Apertura* and post-crisis NPCs reveals that on aggregate, liberalization measures resulted only in a slight decline in protection levels for importable crops (including sugar). However, the post-*Apertura* period exhibits disparate protection results across commodities. Crops like rice, maize, sorghum and sugar have been able to enjoy higher protection levels. Milk, palm oil, wheat, and bananas have seen their protection levels decline after 1990. Others like coffee, cocoa, cotton, soybeans and barley have seen their support levels remain unchanged.

Table 5.4 Nominal Protection Coefficients for Exportable Crops, 1986-1997 (percent)

Period	Cotton[a]	Bananas	Coffee	Cocoa
1986/90	2	9	-24	-9
1991	0	-13	-6	-22
1992	24	5	1	-8
1993	17	-4	-19	-11
1994	1	0	-32	-9
1995	2	8	-24	0
1996	12	-4	-12	-8
1997	-2	-20	-13	-9
1994/97	3	-4	-20	-7

[a]NPC calculated as importable after 1990.
Source: Author's own calculations.

As will be shown in Chapter 6, higher protection levels are greatly responsible for improved returns in rice and sugar since 1990. For the case of maize and sorghum, however, greater protection was not sufficient to compensate the depressing effect of other economic forces (world prices and exchange rate variations). Despite greater protection, domestic production of rice, maize and sorghum continued to fall after 1992 and growing imports were required to supply domestic needs. This apparent contradiction is explained in Chapter 6 by the downward trend of world prices and the unexpected appreciation of the Colombian currency throughout most of the 1990s.

In sum, after the 1992 crisis, protection levels were increased for only three crops. This result does not seem consistent with the large amount of policy measures taken after 1992. However, it is likely that efforts to increase protection levels in some crops were negated by restrictions derived from trade agreements, in particular, the Andean Pact agreement, which established common external tariff levels and mostly unfettered trade with Venezuela and Ecuador.

Changes in Market Integration

One of the objectives of trade liberalization efforts in Colombia and elsewhere has been to promote greater integration between domestic and world markets. In theory, *Apertura* measures should have increased transmission of world market signals to local producers for agricultural goods. However, price bands and the effect of measures taken in the aftermath of the 1992 crisis may have obstructed this process. This section evaluates formally the extent to which structural change occurred in the integration of agricultural markets as a result of *Apertura* reforms. Econometric tests are developed that take into account the special time series characteristics of agricultural prices. These tests are applied to 6 exportable (coffee, cotton, cocoa, beef, bananas and sugar) and 6 importable crops (rice, sorghum, maize, soybeans, palm oil and wheat).

Market integration, as defined in the economic literature, measures the extent to which international and local prices move in unison, reflecting the effect of unfettered trade flows. Available studies suggest that prior to the mid-1980s, transmission of world price variations was low, and often non-existent, in agricultural markets of developing countries.[22] The only available study on the subject for Colombia examines prices of six importable crops in the 1970-92 period and finds similar conclusions.[23] These findings have been interpreted as suggesting that governments across countries have a propensity to undertake interventions that stabilize and isolate domestic prices from external influences.

Increased integration should result in relatively constant NPCs that reflect stable non-prohibitive tariffs. However, the data does not reveal a general flattening out of protection levels after 1991 (see Tables 5.3 and 5.4), except for the case of cocoa where there seems to be strong covariation of world and domestic prices in the post-*Apertura* period. On the other hand, sugar and rice display upward trends in protection after 1991, corresponding to widening gaps between producer and world prices. By contrast, oil palm, wheat and soybeans exhibit downward trends in NPCs in the post-reform sample. For coffee, cotton, bananas, beef, sorghum and maize, NPC levels seem to have maintained a high degree of volatility after 1991, displaying no clear tendency for local and world prices to move in unison.

More formally, market integration can be tested by estimating an error correction model (ECM):

$$p_t^d - p_{t-1}^d = \mu + \alpha(p_{t-1}^w - p_{t-1}^d) + \tau(p_t^w - p_{t-1}^w) + v_t$$

where p^d and p^w are domestic and international prices respectively and v_t is an error term.[24] Prior to the estimation, all prices must be expressed in Colombian currency and deflated by the consumer price index.[25] The ECM allows for a useful economic interpretation of parameters: τ indicates how much of a given change in the world price of the commodity is transmitted to the domestic price in the current period (short-run effect). And α indicates how much of the past differential between domestic and world prices is eliminated in the following period (i.e., error correction coefficient). Values of τ and α near one reflect rapid adjustment of domestic prices to variation in world prices. The amount of adjustment of local prices to shocks in world prices that occurs after n periods is $1-(1-\tau)(1-\alpha)^n$. For values of τ and α close to one, a small number of periods are required for a total adjustment of the domestic price. If $\tau=1$, total adjustment is attained in the current period, while if $\alpha = 1$, complete adjustment is achieved by the second period.

The ECM formulation also allows testing for a structural break after *Apertura*. The test simply involves estimation of an unrestricted version of the ECM in which parameters are allowed to vary across pre and post-*Apertura* periods.[26]

Table 5.5 displays results of estimating the ECM for each crop for the restricted model (i.e., excluding the possibility of post-reform structural change).

TABLE 5.5 Restricted Model, 1970-1997[a]

Commodity	Constant	Adjustment Coeff.	Short-run Effect	R Squared	Durbin Watson	3-year Adjustment[b]
Rice	288.7	0.04	0.32	0.33	2.53	32
	(-0.08)	(-0.72)	(3.37)*			
Maize	843.1	0.22	0.08	0.17	2.78	53
	(-0.42)	(2.23)*	(-0.35)			
Sorghum	-717.0	0.08	0.09	0.07	2.61	0
	(-0.60)	(-1.28)	(-0.51)			
Wheat	-511.9	0.27	0.26	0.43	1.17	71
	(-0.37)	(3.49)*	(2.21)*			
Soybeans	-1744.2	0.10	0.24	0.22	1.93	24
	(-0.78)	(-1.57)	(2.24)*			
Oil Palm	-5090.8	0.06	0.17	0.11	2.04	17
	(-1.15)	(-0.69)	(1.74)*			
Cotton	34768.7	0.34	0.81	0.47	2.45	95
	(-1.13)	(2.27)*	(4.03)*			
Cocoa	-19977.3	0.22	0.34	0.79	2.52	69
	(-2.97)*	(5.31)*	(8.97)*			
Sugar	607.3	0.02	0.01	0.14	2.13	5
	(-0.77)	(1.95)	-0.64			
Coffee	-25850.0	0.11	0.35	0.62	2.47	35
	(-0.96)	(-1.34)	(6.07)*			
Beef	-19933.9	0.10	0.07	0.15	1.76	25
	(-1.41)	(2.00)*	(0.07)			
Bananas	93.5	0.15	0.39	0.34	2.46	39
	(-0.05)	(-1.09)	(3.51)*			

[a]T statistics in parenthesis. * denotes significance at the 5 percent level.

[b]Percent. Calculated using only significant parameters.

Source: Author's own calculations.

The only crops for which the short and long-run coefficients are both significant are cotton, cocoa and wheat. Particularly, for the case of cotton, it is found that a change of Col$100 in the world price in terms of local currency results in an adjustment of Col$34 in the current period and Col$14 in the following period. As a result, for this crop, 95 percent of world price variations are transmitted to domestic prices after three years. Short and long-term responses are somewhat lower than for cocoa and wheat. Changes in world prices lead to corresponding responses in current producer prices of 34 and 26 percent in cocoa and wheat, respectively. Three-year adjustment is 69 percent for cocoa and 71 percent for wheat.

By contrast, for the case of rice, soybeans, bananas, oil palm and coffee, only the short-term coefficient is significant. Short-term responses in local prices range from a low of 17 percent in oil palm to 39 percent in bananas. In these crops, the lack of significance of the adjustment coefficient implies that remaining differences are never adjusted and domestic and local price levels diverge in the long-run.

For maize and beef, the long-term coefficient is significant—22 and 10 per-cent—but no short-term integration is detected. The magnitude of the three-year adjustment is 53 and 25 percent, respectively. This suggests that local prices tend to respond with a lag to world price variations and that local prices are cointegrated with world prices. Finally, sugar and sorghum are two crops where statistically meaningful short or long-run relationships are not found. Local prices do not seem to respond to fluctuations in international markets.

To test whether *Apertura* reforms had any impact on the degree of integra-tion in agricultural markets, the unrestricted model was estimated for all prod-ucts, with 1991 as the year for the structural break (see Table 5.6). Tests for structural change do not detect any changes in short or long-run integration after 1991. A significant change in the three-year adjustment level is detected only for coffee, where it increases from 32 to 65 percent.

The empirical tests presented suggest several conclusions about the nature of the relationship between world and domestic markets for tradable commodities. Since 1970, minor exportable crops such as cotton and cocoa have exhibited relatively high integration with world markets. This is also the case of wheat, an importable crop for which foreign supplies have usually accounted for over three quarters of local consumption. For all these crops, no changes were de-tected in integration levels after reforms. This result is not surprising for cocoa, where government interventions have been virtually non-existent before and after reforms. The finding also indicates that attempts to protect cotton growers after the 1992 crisis have been overwhelmingly unsuccessful, as reflected in the sharp drop in output levels between 1990 and 1997. For the case of wheat, it suggests that despite import substitution policies, protection levels did not fluctuate substantially.

TABLE 5.6 Unrestricted Model, 1970-1997 (Reform Period 1991-1997)[a]

	Pre-Reform Period		Reform Period			
	Adjustment Coeff.	Short-run Effect	Adjustment Coeff.	Short-run Effect	3-year Adj.[b]	R Squared
Rice	0.06	0.32	-0.11	0.34	32	0.33
	(-1.8)	(3.17)*	(-0.49)	(-0.04)		
Maize	0.21	-0.03	0.24	0.53	51	0.21
	(2.08)*	(-0.13)	(-0.07)	(-1.01)		
Sorghum	0.05	0.01	0.23	0.28	0	0.1
	(-0.67)	(-0.03)	(-0.58)	(-0.67)		
Wheat	0.24	0.24	0.65	0.35	66	0.48
	(2.87)*	(2.01)*	(-1.33)	(-0.26)		
Soybeans	0.07	0.19	0.29	0.89	19	0.32
	(-1.11)	(1.77)	(-0.34)	(-1.42)		
Oil Palm	0.06	0.18	-0.08	-0.23	18	0.13
	(-0.65)	(1.74)	(-0.30)	(-0.62)		
Cotton	0.36	0.82	1.07	0.81	95	0.47
	(2.18)*	(3.58)*	(-0.64)	(-0.01)		
Cocoa	0.22	0.34	0.98	0.92	69	0.81
	(5.42)*	(9.04)*	(-1.63)	(-1.27)		
Sugar	0.02	0.01	0.03	0.07	5	0.15
	(1.78)*	-0.54	(-0.23)	(-0.54)		
Coffee	0.11	0.32	0.39	0.65	65	0.69
	(-1.42)	(5.51)*	(-1.08)	(2.07)*		
Beef	-0.04	0.38	0.19	0	27	0.25
	(-0.28)	(-1.42)	(-0.58)	(-0.66)		
Bananas	0.15	0.31	0.62	0.74	31	0.39
	(-1.06)	(2.32)*	(-0.54)	(-1.08)		

[a]T statistics in parenthesis. * denotes significance at the 5 percent level.

[b]Percent. Calculated using only significant parameters.

Source: Author's own calculations.

Crops that have traditionally been associated with strong political lobbies—including rice, oil palm, sugar, coffee, beef and bananas—have managed to avoid substantial changes in the degree of transmission of world price signals as well as in the relative volatility of producer prices. A powerful joint lobby of producers and processors may explain why sugar has managed to remain isolated from world market trends, by obtaining special protection and stabilization treatment from price bands. Similarly, rice, soybeans, oil palm, bananas, and coffee have displayed only partial short-term integration but substantial divergence between world and local prices in the long-term. For the case of rice, the absence of post-reform changes is clearly reflected in the large amount of compensatory measures extracted from the government after 1991, including price bands and import restrictions. For soybeans and oil palm, weak integration after reforms is the likely result of price bands. For coffee, results confirm that no substantive changes in taxation and stabilization policies have occurred after 1991.

Maize is a crop with a weaker lobbying group which has gained only short-term isolation. However, local prices tend to follow world trends in the long-run. This is the expected result of price bands, which seem to have closely substituted for prior policy instruments that provided only short-term isolation. For the case of beef, results reflect the importance of domestic factors in determining short-term price variations for a product in which Colombia is essentially self-sufficient. The presence of hoof and mouth disease has kept Colombian beef out of major markets, but the finding of long-term integration indicates that marginal amounts of exports and imports have kept domestic prices connected to world price trends in the long run.

In summary, empirical results indicate that after reforms none of the 12 commodities studied increased their level of integration with world markets. Three crops (cocoa, cotton and wheat) continued to exhibit strong integration while five (rice, soybeans, oil palm, coffee and bananas) have displayed some short-term sensitivity. Another two (maize and beef) follow world prices in the long-run and two more (sugar and sorghum) have remained effectively isolated from outside markets. This situation contrasts with results from Chile and Mexico, where in most cases three-year adjustment levels are significantly higher for comparable commodities (see Table 5.7).

Overall, the results suggest that the majority of tradable agricultural com-

TABLE 5.7 Price Adjustments after Three Years for Chile, Mexico and Colombia (percent)

Commodity	Chile	Mexico	Colombia
Rice	-	53	32
Maize	100	94	53
Sorghum	-	85	0
Wheat	91	57	71
Soybeans	-	91	24
Beef	59	-	25

Source: Baffes (1997) and Author's own calculations.

modities in Colombia have not exhibited a high degree of integration with world markets. Usually, lack of correlation between local and world prices indicates one or more of the following: pervasive government intervention, instability in protection levels, market power in the marketing chain, strong seasonal effects or measurement problems. Lack of integration seems consistent with stabilization and import substitution policies prevalent in the pre-1990 period. It does not seem consistent, however, with the spirit of trade liberalization reforms after 1990. The lack of correlation between domestic and international prices after *Apertura* is probably a result of government policies that have tended to stabilize domestic prices (including variable price bands, import controls, and absorption agreements). Market distortions and measurement problems may also play a role in some markets.

The Political Economy of Agricultural Protection

There is substantial academic debate about why trade policy differs from commodity to commodity.[27] Many economists have stressed the potential importance of economic and structural features of the markets for commodities to explain the degree of government support. However, some have pointed out that historical accident and other non-economic factors can also play an important role.

Whether producers should come together to lobby the government for protection depends largely on their perception of potential gains, relative to the costs of organizing. Economic factors that impinge on this decision include the costs of organizing, formulating a common position, preventing free-riding and mitigating opposition. Characteristics of commodities that have been usually considered to influence these factors are the number of producers, their geographical dispersion, and the importance of the commodity to each farmer's income. In a country like Colombia, the ease of access to power circles may be important and may be correlated with indicators such as producer income, educational level and the size of the average farm.

For some authors, public policy may be guided by certain objective principles that reflect the values of the particular society. For example, in certain contexts redistributional objectives may loom large, as well as the defense of the interests of the rural poor. Such aims may justify policies to support commodities produced by low-income farmers and those that generate substantial employment. Some governments may protect crops in which international markets are particularly distorted or in which there exists excessive world price volatility.

Regardless of the objective of policy-makers, the decision to support a specific commodity is usually a decision to redistribute rents to producers, at the expense of taxpayers' incomes and consumers' surplus. In such cases, it has been shown that redistribution is less costly when commodity supply or demand are inelastic.[28] Additionally, it is frequently argued that one of the least costly methods to protect a commodity is through import tariffs, which may also raise significant revenues for the government. Many studies have shown that importable crops are usually more likely to be protected than export crops.[29]

Policy inertia has also been advanced as an important determinant of protection levels. The idea is that regardless of the motivation for supporting (or taxing) a specific commodity, once the policy is in place, it is difficult to remove. Once producers gain from a specific measure, they may exert greater influence in opposing its dismantling.

Table 5.8 presents some empirical evidence on the potential determinants of protection for Colombian agriculture in the 1990s. NPC data indicates that the crops receiving the highest support after 1994 have been rice, maize, sorghum, barley and sugar. Crops receiving negative support (i.e., taxation) include coffee, bananas, cocoa, and oil palm.

The data suggests that crops most likely to receive high protection are importables (with the exception of sugar) as well as those which have received high protection in the past. In contrast, crops subject to explicit or implicit taxation during the 1994-97 period have been all exportable. Inertia in protection levels also seems to play a role in Colombia. Figure 5.1 shows that the sign

TABLE 5.8 Political Economy Indicators, Importable Commodities, 1994-1997

Commodity	NPC	No. of Producers	Geographic Concent.[a]	No. of Jobs[b]	Per Capita Income[c]	OECD PSE[d]	Price Volatility[e]
Rice	49	20,000	0.12	9.0	108.3	86.1	0.39
Maize	46	140,090	0.07	24.9	74.2	-	0.25
Sorghum	36	9,240	0.13	2.9	89	26.3	0.23
Barley	32	26,910	0.44	0.7	82.5	44.4	-
Sugar	29	1,000	0.61	8.3	106.3	55.5	0.64
Wheat	10	26,910	0.38	0.6	67.3	43.8	0.27
Soybeans	10	n.a.	0.47	2.1	108.9	26.3	0.23
Cotton	3	11,867	0.18	10.6	86.8	-	0.27
Oil Palm	-8	1,079	0.19	11.8	74.4	26.3	0.34

[a]Geographic Gini. Near zero indicates extreme concentration.

[b]Million man-days.

[c]Weighted per capita income in producing provinces, as percentage of national average.

[d]Producer subsidy equivalent average of OECD countries (percent).

[e]Coefficient of variation of monthly world price between 1986 and 1996.

Source: Author's own calculations with data from Departamento Nacional de Planeación, Ministerio de Agricultura (1998) and International Monetary Fund (1998).

FIGURE 5.1 Nominal Protection Coefficients for Major Commodities,
1986-1990 and 1994-1997 (percent)[a]

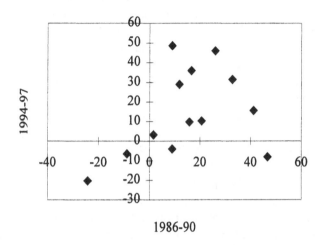

1986-90

[a]Crops: coffee, cocoa, cotton, sugar, rice, barley, wheat, maize, sorghum,
milk, bananas, oil palm and soybeans.
Source: Author's own calculations.

and level of support registered in the 1986-90 period seems to be an important
determinant of protection levels after 1994. However, this may simply reflect
the fact that importable crops were protected in both periods. Interestingly, oil
palm, a crop which was an importable in 1986-90 and exportable after 1994, is
an important exception to protection inertia. Its NPC drops from positive to
negative levels between the two periods.

Sugar seems to be the only exception to the importable-exportable dichotomy: it is an exportable that has been traditionally protected. However, the
protection afforded to this crop is largely a result of import-tariffs, which protect
the domestic market. Exports of surpluses (between 26 and 42 percent of local
production in the 1990s) usually fetch prices significantly below those prevailing in the Colombian market. Hence, while this crop is technically an exportable, public policies have clearly treated it as an importable.

It may also be significant that two of the crops that have most benefited from
post-*Apertura* protection are those in which world prices exhibit the highest
volatility levels: sugar and rice. It is well known that international markets for
both these crops are thin and unstable. Both crops also receive the highest
support among OECD countries, as measured by producer subsidy equivalent
measures.

The cases of rice and sugar also suggest that another important factor that may explain protection levels are certain features of the relationship between producers and processors of the commodity. In both these crops, millers are vitally interested in the health of domestic farming, since their fortunes depend on the availability of domestic supply. Not surprisingly, there is a certain amount of integration among both sugar and rice processors with production concerns. In both cases, a large share of the milled product is sold directly to disperse consumers, who have little bargaining power. This contrasts with commodities like cotton, soybeans and oil palm, all of which must compete with substitute raw materials in complex production processes. In the case of feed grains like sorghum and yellow maize, the local poultry industry has been allowed to substitute local supplies for imported ones. This has not been the case of white maize, used for human consumption, for which supplies in world markets are not widely available. In this case, local millers once again have a strong interest in maintaining production levels. In contrast, local agroindustry may use imported substitutes instead of the domestic supplies of wheat and barley.

The evidence does not suggest that the classic measures of costs of organization play an important role in determining protection levels in Colombia. Products receiving high protection levels include sugar, with only about 1000 producers in a reduced geographic area, as well as maize, with over 140,000 growers scattered over most of the country. For the latter crop, as well as for barley, it is possible that considerations related to the welfare of a population of predominantly poor farmers have played a role in high protection levels.

In summary, the evidence reviewed highlights certain factors that have impinged on protection levels of agricultural commodities in the 1990s. Crops obtaining high levels of protection are importable (or treated as such), face volatile (and distorted) world prices and tend to exhibit common interests with their processing counterparts.

Conclusions

The aftermath of the 1992 agricultural crisis was characterized by intense governmental efforts to facilitate recovery. Many new measures were adopted, including some that reversed *Apertura* principles. However, despite public efforts, production of annual crops affected by the crisis did not recover between 1992 and 1997. On the contrary, for most of the affected crops, output has continued to drop in later years. This apparent paradox is largely the result of powerful economic forces that will be explored in Chapter 6. In addition, the institutional collapse suffered by key government agencies in the mid-1990s rendered many of the government's efforts ineffective.

The analysis of NPC levels demonstrated that despite the announcements of the government, few changes in aggregate protection levels were recorded after

1992. There were noticeable increases in support for only three crops: rice, maize and sorghum. Along with sugar, these crops have been the only ones that have seen their protection levels increase after *Apertura*. For other crops, protection has either remained at pre-*Apertura* levels or lower. In a sense, widely diverging protection across commodities continues pre-1990 trends. Since the 1950s, some crops have enjoyed greater support levels than others, reflecting the relative power of producer groups as well as the priorities of policy makers. The choice of commodities that have continued to receive high protection levels after 1994 suggests that factors such as trading status (importable vs. exportable), world market distortions, lobbying power, the commonality of interests with processors and the income level of producers may have all played a role.

The analysis of integration between local and world markets demonstrated that most commodities in Colombia remain relatively isolated from world price changes. This indicates that stabilization of prices and support (or taxation) of agricultural products remain important policy priorities, even after *Apertura*. In the 1990s, the lack of integration between local and world prices is probably a result of price bands, import restrictions, market imperfections and other policies that prevent transmission of international price signals.

Notes

1. The refinancing measures are derived from Resolutions 04 and 012 of 1992 and resolutions 05, 08, 010, 011, 015 and 016 of 1993, issued by the Comisión Nacional de Crédito Agropecuario.

2. See Ministerio de Agricultura (1992) and Consejo Superior de Comercio Exterior (1992).

3. The Board of the Central Bank eventually turned down this petition.

4. See Consejo de Política Económica y Social (1992b).

5. Detailed description of measures associated with the Recovery Plan appears in Ministerio de Agricultura (1993) and Ocampo (1993, 1994a and 1994b).

6. A detailed analysis of the safeguard statute and its implications appears in Uribe and Leal del Castillo (1994).

7. The ban on milk imports was lifted in January 1994. The ban on imports of chicken parts was replaced in 1995 by a price band which yields prohibitive tariff levels.

8. See Consejo de Política Económica y Social (1993b).

9. These projects were financed primarily through DRI and PNR.

10. *Ley Agraria* created a National Agricultural Commission (Article 89) that would meet regularly to ensure that agricultural policy would be negotiated jointly between private and public interests. By 1997, this body had met formally once with little impact on government actions.

11. The maximum subsidy was set at 400 times the minimum monthly wage.

12. UMATA and CDR functions are described in Chapter 3.

13. The discussion of agricultural policies during the Samper administration is based on Hernández (1995) and López and Gómez (1997).

14. PLANTE is described in López and Gómez (1997).

15. See López and Gómez (1997).

16. See Torres and Osorio (1998) for an evaluation of the Andean Price Band System.

17. Paddy is an unprocessed form of rice. After milling, paddy is converted to white rice.

18. An assessment of land reform practices before and after the 1994 reforms appears in Hollinger (1998).

19. Lessons from the pilot programs are discussed at greater length in Deininger (1997) and Hollinger (1998).

20. A detailed evaluation of irrigation policy in the 1993-97 period appears in Ramirez (1998).

21. These projects were known as "auxilios parlamentarios."

22. See for example Hazell et al. (1990) and Quiroz and Soto (1993). Mundlak and Larson (1992) are an important exception to this consensus, although their findings have been questioned econometrically.

23. The study is by Rueda (1995).

24. The ECM can be obtained from the dynamic formulation of the relationship between local and world prices proposed by Hendry, Pagan and Sargan (1984):

$$p_t^d = \mu + \beta_1 p_t^w + \beta_2 p_{t-1}^d + \beta_3 p_{t-1}^w + v_t$$

where μ and β_i $(i=1,2,3)$ are parameters to be estimated, and v_t denotes the error term. Using this model, it is possible to deal with non-stationarity in the variables. Imposing a homogeneity restriction, the formulation can be expressed as an ECM:

$$p_t^d - p_{t-1}^d = \mu + \alpha(p_{t-1}^w - p_{t-1}^d) + \tau(p_t^w - p_{t-1}^w) + v_t$$

where $\alpha=1-\beta_2$ and $\tau=\beta_1$. In this relationship, inferences about the parameters will be valid if the differenced series are stationary. The dynamic model described can be used to estimate the amount of adjustment that has occurred after any given period of time (Baffes, 1997). In the current period, $n=0$, the amount of adjustment (k) takes the value of the short-run parameter τ, which can also be expressed as $k=1-(1-\tau)$. In period $n=1$, k takes the value of $\tau+(1-\tau)\alpha$, which can be decomposed into the effect of the previous period (τ), and the feedback effect, $(1-\tau)\alpha$ or $1-(1-\tau)(1-\alpha)$. Following the geometric sequence, the amount of adjustment after n periods is:

$$k = 1 - (1-\tau)(1-\alpha)^n$$

25. For ECM estimation, international and producer price series were available for the 1970-97 period for rice, maize, sorghum, wheat, barley, soybeans, palm oil, cotton, sugar, coffee, bananas and cocoa. World prices are taken from monthly series from the

IMF's International Financial Statistics. Producer prices were assembled from diverse sources, including producers' associations, the Ministry of Agriculture and Colombia's Producer Price Index. For the case of coffee, domestic and international prices were obtained directly from the Colombian Federation of Coffee Growers. Augmented Dickey-Fuller (ADF) and Phillips-Perron tests indicated that, with the exception of producer prices of rice, all price series are integrated of order one and the differenced series are stationary.

26. An F-test is used to test jointly whether parameters are equal across sub-periods.

27. The discussion in this section draws from Gardner (1987), Lavergne (1983) and Olson (1985).

28. See Gardner (1987).

29. See World Bank (1986).

6

Colombian Agriculture
During the 1990s

Government policies in the aftermath of the 1992 crisis were insufficient to reactivate production of most annual crops. Clearly, deep economic forces maintained a depressing influence on many agricultural activities. As suggested in Chapter 4, these forces included macroeconomic events which appreciated the Colombian peso. Despite the apparent failure of public action, some agricultural activities exhibited substantial output dynamism, leading to substantial changes in the structure of Colombian agriculture.

What is the nature of this change? Why did some agricultural activities grow while others contracted? What was the effect of this transformation on the welfare of the rural population? This chapter presents preliminary answers to these questions. The first section examines changes in the structure of production and the performance of agricultural exports and imports since 1990. The second section attempts to explain production performance by examining the evolution of profitability indicators. The most important factors that have affected economic incentives for agriculture are analyzed, including international prices, real exchange rates and trade policies. The third section reviews changes in the standard of living of rural inhabitants.

Structural Changes

Production and Areas

Colombian agriculture was buffeted by strong economic forces after 1990. Some of these forces played an important role in reshaping the structure of the sector. This section identifies the nature of these changes by assessing the evolution of production and cropped areas between 1990 and 1997. Generally, aggregate performance of Colombian agriculture in the 1990-97 period did not compare well with the pre-1990 record. The sector grew at an annual rate of 2.2 percent, substantially below the post-war average of 3.5 percent. The mediocre performance of Colombian agriculture after 1990 can be better understood by examining separately its three main subsectors: annual and permanent crops, and livestock activities. Of these, annual crops have performed worst in the

TABLE 6.1 Value of Production, 1990 and 1997 (Billion 1975 pesos)

	1990	*1997*	*Growth (percent)*
Annual Crops	35.6	28.5	-3.2
Rice	6.9	6.0	-2.1
Potatoes	6.3	7.0	1.4
Maize	5.6	4.5	-3.1
Vegetables	4.8	5.1	0.8
Cotton	3.4	1.2	-15.1
Sorghum	2.8	1.2	-12.3
Soybeans	2.3	0.9	-13.5
Beans	1.9	2.0	0.5
Wheat	0.7	0.3	-10.5
Barley	0.5	0.1	-23.8
Other annual[a]	0.4	0.3	-5.1
Permanent Crops	43.0	55.9	3.8
Coffee	18.0	13.7	-3.9
Sugar Cane	9.2	12.2	4.0
Plantain	6.9	7.6	1.4
Panela Cane	5.9	6.9	2.2
Flowers	5.6	7.6	4.3
Oil Palm	3.9	7.1	8.5
Cassava	3.1	2.7	-2.1
Fruits	2.9	5.8	10.1
Bananas	2.3	2.9	2.9
Cocoa	1.6	1.5	-1.6
Other permanent[b]	1.4	1.6	-5.4
Total Agriculture	96.6	98.1	0.2
Cattle	34.1	40.0	2.3
Pork	2.5	3.2	3.4
Poultry	13.8	21.7	6.5
Total Livestock	50.4	65.7	3.8
Total Farm Output	147.0	163.7	1.5
Exportable Crops[c]	47.6	46.8	-0.2
Importable Crops[d]	24.7	22.1	-1.6
Non-Tradable Crops[e]	74.7	94.8	3.4

[a]Sesame seed, peanuts and light tobacco.
[b]Yams, jute, export plantains, coconut and dark tobacco.
[c]Coffee, sugar cane, flowers, bananas and cocoa.
[d]Rice, maize, cotton, sorghum, soybeans, barley, wheat and oil palm.
[e]Potatoes, beans, plantains, *panela* cane and cassava.
Source: Author's own calculations and Ministerio de Agricultura (1998).

1990s. Output of these crops fell continuously from 1990 to 1997, at an average annual rate of 3.2 percent (see Table 6.1). Contractions were particularly strong for cotton (15.1 percent annually) and for importable grains and oilseeds. Among the latter, the greatest reductions were registered in barley (23.8 percent), sorghum (12.3 percent), soybeans (13.5 percent), wheat (10.5 percent), and maize (3.1 percent).

By contrast, permanent crops—excluding coffee—exhibited on the whole positive output growth through most of the 1990-97 period. Aggregate output increased at an average annual rate of 1.5 percent between 1990 and 1997, somewhat below the post-war average (3.5 percent). This performance reflected substantial output expansions for oil palm (8.5 percent annually), fruits (10.1 percent), sugar cane (4.0 percent), flowers (4.3 percent) and bananas (2.9 percent). There were also large output gains in minor crops, as in the cases of jute and yams. Most noteworthy, the rapid expansion of oil palm output led to the attainment of self-sufficiency and the initiation of export shipments to neighboring countries since 1993. Despite the positive overall performance of permanent crops, production of minor exportable crops like cocoa and dark tobacco declined in the 1990s.

Coffee fortunes fluctuated sharply between 1990 and 1997, yielding an overall negative trend. As was mentioned in Chapter 5, production fell sharply after 1990 as a result of the reduction in new plantings that ensued after the international price collapse of 1989. Record crops achieved between 1990 and 1992, at a time when world markets exhibited the lowest real prices on record, were followed by variable and declining harvests. However, farm incomes partially recovered in 1994 and 1997 due to short-lived price spikes. By the end of the period, production levels declined due to low investment. The 1997 harvest reached only 10.8 million bags, 17 percent less than in 1990.

The evolution of planted areas in the 1990s mirrors almost identically the structural changes in crop output outlined above. In 1997, some 3.1 million hectares were planted in annual and permanent crops, almost 700,000 less than were planted in 1990 (see Table 6.2). The bulk of the reduction can be attributed to annual crops. Areas planted in these products fell from 2.5 million hectares in 1990 to 1.6 in 1997. Cereals and soybeans were responsible for the bulk of this reduction. Cropped areas contracted between 1990 and 1997 for rice (4.1 percent annually), maize (5.4 percent), soybeans (14.0 percent), sorghum (14.0 percent), wheat (12.5 percent), and barley (24.8 percent). In addition, cotton areas dropped at an annual rate of 16.9 percent.

By contrast, the areas dedicated to production of most permanent crops—excluding coffee—increased, from 1.24 to 1.45 million hectares between 1990 and 1997. The most significant increases were recorded in areas dedicated to sugar cane (5.5 percent annually), fruits (8.5 percent), oil palm (6.9 percent), and bananas (3.7 percent).

Opposite tendencies in annual and permanent crops combined for a 1.5 per-

TABLE 6.2 Areas Planted in Crops, 1990 and 1997 (thousand hectares)

Crop	1990	1997	Growth (percent)
Annual Crops	2,495.5	1,620.8	-6.2
Rice	521.1	390.0	-4.1
Potatoes	161.4	166.8	0.5
Maize	836.9	573.4	-5.4
Vegetables	87.6	95.8	1.3
Cotton	200.5	61.3	-16.9
Sorghum	273.0	102.6	-14.0
Soybeans	116.2	43.5	-14.0
Beans	164.6	135.3	-2.8
Wheat	56.7	23.6	-12.5
Barley	54.3	9.6	-24.8
Other[a]	23.3	18.9	-3.5
Permanent Crops[b]	1,243.7	1,448.2	2.2
Sugar Cane	114.8	168.3	5.5
Plantains	344.8	379.1	1.4
Panela Cane	199.6	209.9	0.7
Oil Palm	89.7	145.1	6.9
Cassava	207.3	181.8	-1.9
Fruits	70.9	129.0	8.5
Bananas	32.4	42.0	3.7
Cocoa	120.7	109.6	-1.4
Other[c]	63.5	74.6	2.7

[a]Sesame seed, peanuts and light tobacco.

[b]Excludes coffee and flowers.

[c]Yams, jute, export plantains, coconut and dark tobacco.

Source: Ministerio de Agricultura (1998).

cent increase in total agricultural output between 1990 and 1997. This mediocre rate was, however, greatly compensated by the rapid expansion of livestock output, which grew by 30.3 percent between 1990 and 1997 (see Table 6.1). All livestock activities enjoyed rapidly expanding production, led by the poultry industry, which increased its output at a 6.5 percent annual rate between 1990 and 1997. Demand for poultry had shown substantial dynamism in the 1980s, but the sector blossomed fully after *Apertura*, boosted by lower broiler and egg real prices as well as changing consumer preferences. On the other hand, cattle slaughter levels increased sharply starting in 1993, initiating one of the largest liquidation phases of the Colombian cattle cycle on record. Continued increases in beef supply through 1997 were coupled with large investments in new herds, associated with the conversion of areas previously planted in annual crops to pastures. Much of the investment in new herds incorporated new breeds and production technologies, often concentrating on the simultaneous production of milk and beef.

Expansion of permanent crops—excluding coffee—and contraction of annuals since 1990 changed the structure of Colombian agricultural output. The former group increased its share of the value of agricultural output from 44.5 percent in 1990 to 57.0 in 1997; annuals dropped from 36.9 percent to 29.1 in the same period (see Table 6.3). Coffee, the most important traditional export crop, lost importance by dropping from 18.6 percent of agricultural output to only 13.9 by 1997. In addition, livestock activities increased their share in total farm output from 34.3 to 40.1 percent between 1990 and 1997.

Did structural changes between agricultural activities reflect realignments consistent with underlying comparative advantage? This is an issue of debate among Colombian observers. For some, overall changes reflect the effect of the removal of protection practices for importable crops, which had been in effect since at least the 1950s. The new structure displays a greater preponderance of permanent crops, in which Colombia seems to possess greater comparative advantage. However, changes were also highly influenced by the structure of protection levels in the post-*Apertura* period. For instance, it is unclear whether the success of sugar was greatly dictated by the effect of the price band. As will be seen below, structural changes also reflected Dutch disease-type effects, as a result of exchange rate appreciation in the 1990s, as well as the impact of changing relative prices in world markets.

Yields

Per hectare yields increased for most crops in the 1990s. Most impressive were gains in annual crops, which in most cases were at least 10 percent greater in 1996-97 with respect to those achieved in the 1987-90 period (see Table 6.4). Yield growth for annual crops was greatly a result of the concentration of production in the best agricultural lands. Marginal areas, where costs were high

TABLE 6.3 Shares of Value of Production, 1990 and 1997 (percent)

	Shares of:			
	Agricultural Ouput		Total Farm Output	
	1990	1997	1990	1997
Annual Crops	24.2	17.4	36.9	29.1
Rice	4.7	3.7	7.2	6.1
Potatoes	4.3	4.2	6.5	7.1
Maize	3.8	2.7	5.8	4.6
Vegetables	3.3	3.1	5.0	5.2
Cotton	2.3	0.7	3.5	1.2
Sorghum	1.9	0.7	2.9	1.2
Soybeans	1.5	0.5	2.4	0.9
Beans	1.3	1.2	2.0	2.0
Wheat	0.5	0.2	0.7	0.3
Barley	0.4	0.1	0.6	0.1
Other annual[a]	0.3	0.2	0.5	0.4
Permanent Crops	175.8	182.1	163.1	170.9
Coffee	12.2	8.4	18.6	13.9
Sugar Cane	6.3	7.5	9.6	12.5
Plantain	4.7	4.6	7.1	7.7
Panela Cane	4.0	4.2	6.1	7.0
Flowers	3.8	4.7	5.8	7.8
Oil Palm	2.7	4.4	4.1	7.3
Cassava	2.1	1.6	3.2	2.7
Fruits	1.9	3.5	3.0	5.9
Bananas	1.6	1.8	2.4	2.9
Cocoa	1.1	0.9	1.7	1.5
Other permanent[b]	1.0	1.0	1.5	1.7
Total Agriculture	65.7	59.9	100.0	100.0
Cattle	23.2	24.4		
Pork	1.7	1.9		
Poultry	9.4	13.3		
Total Livestock	34.3	40.1		
Total Farm Output	100.0	100.0		
Exportable Crops[c]	25.1	23.1	38.1	38.6
Importable Crops[d]	17.8	13.0	27.0	21.7
Non-Tradable Crops[e]	57.2	63.9	34.8	39.7

[a]Sesame seed, peanuts and light tobacco.

[b]Yams, jute, export plantains, coconut and dark tobacco.

[c]Coffee, sugar cane, flowers, bananas and cocoa.

[d]Rice, maize, cotton, sorghum, soybeans, barley, wheat and oil palm.

[e]Potatoes, beans, plantains, *panela* cane, cassava, and livestock.

Source: Author's own calculations and Ministerio de Agricultura (1998).

TABLE 6.4 Agricultural Yields, 1987-1990 and 1996-1997 (tons per hectare)

Crop	1987-90	1996-97	Growth (percent)
Annual Crops			
Rice	4,388	4,536	3.4
Potatoes	14,995	16,209	8.1
Maize	1,393	1,667	19.7
Cotton	1,656	1,771	7.0
Sorghum ⁄	2,781	3,256	17.1
Soybeans	1,945	2,109	8.4
Beans	759	992	30.7
Wheat	1,754	2,153	22.8
Barley	1,830	2,051	12.1
Permanent Crops			
Sugar Cane	123,429	171,104	38.6
Plantains	6,464	6,983	8.0
Panela Cane	5,285	6,030	14.1
Oil Palm	2,941	3,178	8.0
Cassava	8,684	9,684	11.5

Source: Ministerio de Agricultura (1998).

and yields were low, were withdrawn from production. For the case of rice, output per hectare only increased slightly, despite the reduction in areas.

Yields also increased sharply for many non-tradable commodities, including cassava, *panela* cane, yams, jute, and coconuts. Yield growth in these crops was largely a result of improved agricultural practices and technological innovations.

Despite yield improvements since 1990, low productivity continues to be a key constraint to increasing the competitiveness of annual crop production in Colombia.[1] This relative disadvantage is greatest for crops like rice, wheat, barley and maize. Although lower yields can be compensated partially with lower costs, growing rural wages have diminished the cost advantage that Colombian farmers enjoyed in the past. By the mid-1990s, Colombia was among the leading countries in productivity per hectare in crops like sugar cane, oil palm, coffee and bananas—all permanent crops. However, much lower relative yields are detected in crops like maize, barley, cotton and wheat, as revealed by a comparison of Colombian yields with those of the leading countries and world averages (see Table 6.5).[2] Colombian yields are somewhat above

TABLE 6.5 Agricultural Yields in International Comparison, 1990-1994

Commodity	Average yield (tons per hectare)			World Ranking[b]	Colombian yield relative to:	
	World	*Leader[a]*	*Colombia*		*World*	*Leader*
Rice	3.6	8.3	4.1	28	1.14	0.49
Barley	2.0	6.2	2.0	53	0.97	0.32
Maize	3.9	9.8	1.5	90	0.39	0.16
Sorghum	1.4	5.8	3.0	12	2.16	0.52
Wheat	2.3	8.1	1.9	61	0.83	0.23
Beans	0.7	5.0	0.9	50	1.36	0.18
Soybeans	2.0	3.4	2.0	19	1.02	0.59
Cotton	1.8	4.5	1.6	29	0.92	0.36
Potatoes	13.4	42.7	15.4	48	1.15	0.36
Cocoa	0.4	2.3	0.5	19	1.05	0.20
Sugar Cane	60.5	110.0	91.3	11	1.51	0.83
Cassava	9.7	22.7	9.7	25	1.01	0.43
Coffee	0.6	2.1	1.0	12	1.75	0.46

[a]Country exhibiting the largest yield in FAO data as reported by Balcázar (1998).
[b]Colombia's yield position among all countries producing the commodity.
Source: Balcázar (1998).

world averages in soybeans, rice, potatoes and cocoa, but remain far below those of the leading producers.

Agricultural Trade

Apertura reforms had a strong impact on overall international trade flows in the 1990s. Imports into the Colombian economy grew rapidly from 15.5 percent of GDP in 1990 to 46.9 percent of GDP in 1997. Exports also grew, albeit at more moderate rates, increasing from 20.7 percent to 32.6 percent of GDP between 1990 and 1997.

The overall pattern of trade growth was mirrored in agriculture. Official figures indicate that import flows of agricultural goods grew at a historically high annual rate of 26.8 percent between 1991 and 1997, in US dollars, while exports only increased at 7.4 percent (see Tables 6.6 and 6.7). However, it is likely that official trade figures overestimate food import growth: before *Apertura*, many markets in the Atlantic coastal region were supplied by contraband items, usually smuggled through the border with Venezuela. After *Apertura*, much of these flows became legal and surfaced in official statistics.

TABLE 6.6 Agricultural Imports, 1991-1997 (US$ Millions)

	1991	*1997*	*Growth (percent)*
Total	378.6	1,886.9	26.8
Primary Products	229.0	1,217.9	27.9
Yellow maize	1.6	263.8	84.6
Wheat	69.3	189.1	16.7
Soybeans	18.0	105.1	29.4
Fruits	17.8	95.3	27.9
Barley	21.1	56.1	16.3
Legumes and vegetables	27.8	95.6	20.6
Rice	0.1	71.7	105.1
Cotton	1.2	84.6	71.4
White maize	0.1	15.0	91.4
Milk and milk products	5.9	3.1	-11.0
Other primary	66.0	238.4	21.4
Processed Goods	149.6	669.1	25.0
Soybeans	25.7	148.5	29.2
Soybean oil	14.8	82.2	28.6
Processed cereals	1.0	50.4	66.1
Palm oil	26.4	36.1	5.2
Sardines	16.0	29.5	10.1
Processed legumes and vegetables	1.8	31.1	47.1
Other processed	64.0	291.3	25.3

Source: Ministerio de Comercio Exterior (1998).

Despite the flaws in import statistics, the increase in foreign inflows of food-stuffs was nonetheless substantial after 1990. This growth reflected large increases in imports of primary and processed products (see Table 6.6). Among raw materials, substantial increases were registered in cereals and oilseeds. The value of imports of cereals multiplied sixfold between 1991 and 1997. Imports of yellow maize jumped from US$1.6 million in 1991 to US$263.8 million in 1997, while those of rice went from US$0.1 million to US$71.7 million in the same period. Furthermore, the value of imports of wheat and barley was multi-

TABLE 6.7 Agricultural Exports, 1991-1997 (US$ Millions)

	1991	*1997*	*Growth (percent)*
Total	2,736.2	4,269.5	7.4
Primary products	2,441.7	3,553.4	6.3
Coffee	1,336.4	2,258.9	8.7
Bananas	395.8	467.7	2.8
Flowers	280.3	544.6	11.1
Shrimp	4.7	49.0	39.0
Fruits	49.8	44.8	-1.8
Farmed shrimp	25.5	37.3	6.3
Yellow-finned tuna	0.0	30.9	-
Other primary	349.1	120.3	-17.8
Processed products	294.5	716.1	14.8
Coffee products	62.2	163.2	16.1
Raw sugar	43.7	122.5	17.2
White sugar	29.4	116.1	22.9
Sugar products	9.9	71.1	32.9
Processed tuna	3.9	47.7	41.9
Palm oil	1.1	41.9	60.3
Processed cereals	10.8	36.3	20.2
Tobacco	39.2	24.6	-7.8
Other processed	94.4	92.6	-0.3

Source: Ministerio de Comercio Exterior (1998).

plied by more than two-and-a-half times. In addition, the value of soybean inflows increased five fold between 1991 and 1997. There were also substantial increments in the imports of fruits—mainly apples, pears, grapes and peaches from Chile and the US—and processed vegetables.

Among processed products, the largest increases were recorded in vegetable oils and processed cereals, legumes and vegetables. In particular, the value of imports of processed oilseeds increased from US$65 million in 1991 to almost US$260 million in 1997.

Rapid growth of agricultural imports since 1990 has generated heated controversy in Colombian farming circles. For advocates of local production, import growth is a clear reflection of diminished protection and policies which favor consumption of imported items over domestic goods. However, rapid growth of food imports has reflected fast-growing local demand and improved welfare levels of Colombian consumers.[3] Demand growth resulted from lower prices of tradable foods, a direct consequence of *Apertura*. Low income segments of the population, which spend a larger share of their income in food, have benefited greatly from this trend.

Agricultural exports managed to grow in the 1990s, despite unfavorable trends in the exchange rate and falling international coffee prices. The total value of agricultural exports grew at an annual rate of 7.4 percent between 1991 and 1997. Flowers and shrimp exhibited the highest rates of growth among primary goods. A positive development has been the relative success of agroindustries in penetrating foreign markets. However, export growth was substantially greater in processed goods (14.8 percent annually) than in primary products (6.3 percent) (see Table 6.7). The value of export flows increased at rates of over 15 percent per year for products like palm oil, processed tuna, sugar products, processed cereals, and coffee by-products.

Explaining Structural Changes

Supply Response

Structural changes in Colombian agriculture in the 1990s were the result of substantial output changes of many crops. What motivated farmers to increase or decrease production so dramatically in this period? While the literature points to a large number of potential determinants of agricultural production, much of economic analysis shows that the key factor that explains short and medium-run output swings is expected farm profitability. Many empirical studies have documented the positive response of farmers to expected returns—usually approximated by real producer prices.[4]

Colombian farmers seem to respond actively to economic incentives, much like their counterparts in other countries. Table 6.8 displays short and long-run elasticities of output for a sample of crops, estimated using annual data for 1970 to 1997.[5] Elasticities measure the response of annual output to changes in return indexes. All elasticities turn out positive and most are statistically significant. Short-run elasticities range from 0.14 for sugar to 0.94 for soybeans. In most cases, long-run elasticities are substantially higher, ranging from a low of 0.40 for cocoa to 2.38 for coffee. Short-run elasticities are lower for permanent crops (e.g., cocoa, bananas, coffee), due to lengthy plant-to-harvest cycles.

TABLE 6.8 Price Elasticities, Selected Crops (1970-1997)

Crop	Short Run	Long Run
Annual Crops		
Rice	0.50	1.27
Maize	0.15	1.14
Cotton	0.45	1.67
Sorghum	0.35	1.51
Soybeans	0.76	0.94
Wheat	0.20	0.89
Barley	0.42	1.61
Permanent Crops		
Coffee	0.32	2.33
Sugar Cane	0.14	1.22
Plantains	0.14	0.30
Panela Cane	0.23	1.11
Bananas	0.07	0.83
Cocoa	0.06	1.41

Source: Author's own calculations.

Farm Returns

The analysis of supply response indicates that expansions and contractions in agricultural activities in Colombia are greatly determined by swings in the returns that farmers expect. Hence, the analysis of return indicators should reveal a great deal about the underlying reasons for the structural change recorded during the 1990s.

Table 6.9 compares return indexes for the main crops between 1986-90 and 1994-97. Indexes are calculated as the ratio of per hectare income to per hectare costs, assuming constant yields. Figures suggest that returns fell sharply after 1990 for most annual crops. Between 1986-90 and 1994-97, returns dropped by more than 20 percent for barley, wheat, maize, and soybeans. By contrast, farm profitability increased for beans, potatoes and plantains. Returns remained essentially unchanged for rice, flowers and *panela* cane.

The situation is less dramatic for permanent crops. Returns dropped by more than 15 percent for oil palm, cocoa, bananas and coffee. On the other hand, returns increased sharply for cassava (39.5 percent) and sugar (28.5 percent). Profitability in cattle growing fell more moderately by 5.5 percent.

The results described are broadly confirmed by a similar analysis of return

TABLE 6.9 Returns to Agricultural Activities, 1986-1997 (index 1990=100)

Crop	1986-90	1991-93	1994-97
Annual Crops			
Rice	114	104	114
Potatoes	84	92	131
Maize	103	84	71
Cotton	96	98	90
Sorghum	103	97	82
Soybeans	105	90	76
Beans	119	127	153
Wheat	95	86	65
Barley	93	89	65
Permanent Crops			
Coffee	108	75	92
Sugar Cane	106	127	141
Plantains	86	87	91
Panela Cane	86	101	83
Flowers	98	100	99
Oil Palm	114	70	56
Cassava	108	147	160
Bananas	93	94	65
Cocoa	140	86	88
Beef	122	133	115
Importable Crops[a]	106	91	84
Exportable Crops[b]	107	94	104
Non-Tradable Crops[c]	91	103	113

[a]Rice, maize, cotton, sorghum, soybeans, barley, wheat and oil palm.

[b]Coffee, sugar cane, flowers, bananas and cocoa.

[c]Potatoes, beans, plantains, *panela* cane and cassava.

Source: Author's own calculations.

indexes adjusted for yield changes. With this method, returns are adjusted ex post with the aim of capturing income changes due to variations in production per hectare. However, in some cases the magnitude of the drop in returns is not as large for the measure corrected for yield changes. This is because of the apparent yield increases that occur as a consequence of the removal of marginal lands from production. Also, in cases when profitability increases after 1990, as in rice and potatoes, increasing yields make ex post returns higher. An important exception is coffee, where both yields and prices fell, making ex post returns lower.

In sum, most crops have seen their returns fall after 1990, with the exception of some non-tradable activities like cassava, potatoes and beef. Only two tradable crops, namely sugar and rice, managed to increase profitability levels after 1990.

What are the causes of declining economic incentives for most tradable activities after 1990? A way to answer this questions is to decompose return indexes into factors related to foreign trade and government policies, extending the accounting methodology proposed by Quiroz and Valdés (1994). Return indexes (RI) are defined as the ratio of producer prices (P) to a constant elasticity cost index (CI), reflecting the key components of cost for each crop:

$$CI = P_f^\alpha P_i^\beta P_p^\delta MS^\gamma W^\lambda$$

In this equation, P_f, P_i and P_p are the prices of fertilizers, insecticides and pesticides, respectively, MS is the cost of machinery services and W are agricultural wages. The parameters α, β, δ, γ, and λ are the cost shares associated with each one of the cost components. The particular functional form chosen assumes constant elasticity of substitution among all factors.

Since consistent information about the annual cost of machinery services (MS) is unavailable for most farm activities, it is approximated by the product of the nominal local interest rate and the price of new farm machinery:

$$MS = IP_m,$$

where I is the local interest rate (in nominal terms) and P_m is the price of farm machinery in Colombia.

In order to quantify the original sources of variation in the aggregate cost index, the prices of tradable inputs are decomposed into world prices, the real exchange rate and a residual which essentially captures trade policies:

$$P_f = P_f^{cif} RER(1 + \varepsilon^f),$$

$$P_i = P_i^{cif} RER(1 + \varepsilon^i),$$

$$P_p = P_p^{cif} RER(1 + \varepsilon^p),$$

$$P_m = P_m^{cif} RER(1 + \varepsilon^m),$$

where P_f^{cif}, P_i^{cif}, P_p^{cif}, and P_m^{cif} are the international prices (in constant US dollars) of fertilizers, insecticides, pesticides and machinery, respectively, RER is the real exchange rate and $(1 + \varepsilon^f), (1 + \varepsilon^i), (1 + \varepsilon^p), (1 + \varepsilon^m)$ are residual terms, measuring trade policies and other distortions that inhibit equality of local and foreign prices in each input market. In these formulations, all import prices are deflated by the consumer price index and expressed in constant Colombian pesos.

In a similar fashion, the following simple identity can be used to decompose real producer prices:

$$P = P^b RER(1 + \varepsilon),$$

where P is the local producer price in constant pesos, P^b is the border price of the commodity in real US dollars and $(1+\varepsilon)$ is a residual term, capturing the effect of trade policies and other market imperfections which inhibit equality of world and local prices. The border price is approximated by CIF prices for the case of importables and by FOB prices for exportables.

Putting these equations together, annual variations in return indexes can be decomposed into changes due to international commodity markets, the real exchange rate, world prices of tradable inputs, wages, domestic interest rates and a residual capturing government policies and other imperfections:[6]

$$\hat{P} = \hat{P}^b + b\hat{RER} + \sum_{j=1}^{4} c_j \hat{P}_j^{cif} + d\hat{W} + e\hat{I} + f\hat{RES},$$

where a circumflex denotes percentage rate of change (i.e., logarithmic differences). The four terms in the summation correspond to the changes in the international price of the four tradable input prices. RES is a residual term which captures the effect of all trade policies and market imperfections in input and output markets that prevent local prices from equaling world prices.

Table 6.10 shows the return decomposition for 11 important tradable commodities, comparing average returns for 1994-97 with those for 1990. Results suggest that world prices and the real exchange rate have both exerted a negative influence on the profitability of most crops over the period. The only

TABLE 6.10 Determinants of Changes in Returns, 1994-1997 vs 1990 (percent)

Commodity	Return	World CIF Price	Real Exch. Rate	Policies and others	Input CIF Prices	Wages
Cotton	-5	-16	-14	18	4	0
Bananas	-42	-29	-23	8	2	0
Coffee	-8	35	-25	-17	1	-1
Sugar	35	-26	-12	61	4	0
Cocoa	-12	-3	-24	13	2	0
Rice	14	-29	-9	41	5	1
Maize	-47	-32	-28	16	-1	-1
Oil Palm	-59	19	-17	-68	3	0
Sorghum	-20	-36	-11	19	4	0
Soybeans	-27	-26	-7	-6	5	0
Wheat	-43	-21	-10	-20	4	0

Source: Author's own calculations.

exceptions are coffee and oil palm, for which international prices were both substantially higher in 1994-97 than in 1990. The appreciation of the real exchange rate depressed returns for all crops, with an effect ranging from 7 percent in the case of soybeans to 28 percent for the case of maize.

Reductions in world prices of tradable inputs have exerted a largely positive, albeit small effect on crop returns. The greatest effect is a positive influence of 5 percent in the returns of rice and soybeans.

Variations in local interest rates between 1990 and 1994-97 have also exerted a small positive effect on returns. The most significant effects are detected in sugar and soybeans, crops in which machinery costs are significant.

Rural wages do not exert a substantial influence on commodity returns between 1990 and 1994-97. This simply indicates that real rural wages have not varied substantially between the two periods.

Finally, the residual, which captures the effect of trade policies and other market imperfections, shows great disparity across commodities. For sugar and rice, this factor has more than compensated for the depressing effect of world prices and real exchange rates. It also explains why these crops are the only ones that exhibit higher returns in 1994-97. For crops like cotton, bananas, cocoa, maize and sorghum, greater protection was not sufficient to compensate the depressing influences of world markets and exchange rate variations. By contrast, reduced protection (or greater taxation) aggravated the slump in producer incentives for the cases of wheat, soybeans, coffee and oil palm. For the latter crop, a large share of the apparent drop in protection is associated with its transition from the importable policy regime—which allows crops to benefit from import tariff protection—to the exportable status after 1994.

It may be argued that the comparison of returns with conditions prevailing in one year (i.e., 1990) could be misleading. Table 6.11 displays results of a decomposition of returns, in which the situation of 1994-97 is compared to that of 1986-90. The results indicate that all commodities were net losers from trends in the real exchange rate and world prices. However, there are significant differences in variations in returns and policies. For some crops, returns decrease precipitously, largely as a result of negative trends in world prices, the exchange rate and declining support levels. This group includes bananas, oil palm, soybeans and wheat. For others, returns fell despite compensatory policies, due to the overwhelming effect of international markets and exchange rate appreciation. This group includes coffee, cocoa, maize and sorghum. A final group includes those commodities for which returns did not decrease (sugar, cotton and rice) greatly as a result of increasing support from government policies (for sugar and rice) and higher domestic prices due to dwindling supplies for export (for cotton). Returns remained flat for cotton and rice but increased substantially for sugar.

The results highlight the disparate nature of protection policies after 1990. In a period in which world prices declined and the exchange rate appreciated, some crops were able to obtain large benefits from trade and marketing policies and others did not. This is, of course, the result of the wide array of measures adopted since 1992 to deal with falling agricultural production. Overall, results

TABLE 6.11 Determinants of Changes in Returns, 1994-1997 vs 1986-1990 (percent)

Commodity	Return	World CIF Price	Real Exch. Rate	Policies and others	Input CIF Prices	Wages
Cotton	0	-8	-9	7	6	1
Bananas	-35	-16	-13	-11	3	1
Coffee	-15	-12	-15	6	4	0
Sugar	29	-5	-5	21	9	2
Cocoa	-46	-42	-14	6	3	1
Rice	1	-34	-5	29	8	1
Maize	-49	-37	-19	9	0	-1
Oil Palm	-72	-6	-10	-64	5	1
Sorghum	-23	-41	-6	14	7	1
Soybeans	-32	-40	-4	-1	9	1
Wheat	-38	-34	-5	-8	7	0

Source: Author's own calculations.

conform to the political economy reasons underlying differential protection results described in Chapter 5.

The Colombian Bout of Dutch Disease

Falling returns for tradable crops after 1990 were mostly a result of declining world prices and real exchange rate appreciation. Rural wages, the most important cost item for many crops, did not fall to compensate the effects of these depressing forces. The decline in world prices simply reflected a well-known long-term trend, related to rapid growth in global agricultural productivity. However, the causes underlying the behavior of exchange rates and wages in the 1990s are less obvious. In this section, the reasons behind the appreciation of the Colombian peso of the 1990s are presented. In the following section, some light is shed on the determinants of rural wage trends.

The literature on the determinants of real exchange rates is extensive. On the whole, the consensus view is that there are certain key fundamental factors that determine the medium and long-run levels of the exchange rate.[7] (There is more disagreement about why it can vary from its long-run value in the short run). Some factors are not easily controllable by policy-makers, such as productivity growth and the terms of trade. Others fall under state purview, such as the size of government expenditures and trade policies.

Productivity growth in tradable sectors usually leads to an appreciation of the exchange rate. The idea is that it leads to increasing real wages in the tradable sector; non-tradable producers must increase their relative prices (i.e., an alternative definition of the real exchange rate) if they are to remain competitive in the labor market. In a similar fashion, positive terms of trade shocks (such as a surge in coffee prices) lead to higher wages in the booming tradable sector. Furthermore, increased incomes in the booming sector generate a domestic spending effect, which puts further upward pressure on prices of non-tradable sectors. This relative prosperity of non-tradable sectors of the economy, at the expense of tradable activities (excluding the booming sector) is what has been known in the literature as the Dutch disease effect.[8]

Governments usually spend more on non-tradable sectors (including wages) than private agents. This explains why greater government expenditures are associated with increasing relative prices of non-tradable goods. On the other hand, trade policy has a well-known effect on exchange rates. Higher tariff levels discourage imports and tend to appreciate the value of the currency. This was precisely the effect of import substitution industrialization policies across much of Latin America since the 1950s, as explained in Chapter 1.

If other things would have remained constant, the tariff reduction associated with *Apertura* should have acted in favor of the depreciation of the exchange rate. Why then did the Colombian peso appreciate after 1990? Studies have advanced essentially four arguments to explain the appreciation: the excessive devaluation of the 1989-90, the discovery of large oil deposits in 1991 (a type of terms of trade effect), the exogenous increase of capital inflows (for loans and direct investment), and, the massive increase in government spending after 1990.

As explained in Chapter 1, macroenomic policy-makers devalued the peso pre-emptively in 1989 and early 1990, expecting a large shortfall of foreign exchange due to falling coffee prices and greater demand for imports after *Apertura*. This devaluation turned out to be unnecessary and was quickly corrected by increasing inflation. Hence, the excessive devaluation of 1989-90 explains the appreciation of 1991 but not the longer-term appreciation observed until mid-1997.

Chapter 1 also illustrated how the increase in capital inflows affected most of the major economies of Latin America. This was a result of changing attitudes of international banks and foreign investors about the risks inherent in the region after the debt crisis of the 1980s. In Colombia, foreign perceptions were colored by news of liberal economic reforms as well as oil findings, which boosted economic prospects and diminished balance of payments risks. Capital inflows were facilitated by reforms that removed obstacles to capital markets. It has been argued that this also facilitated the repatriation of drug-trafficking profits, a factor that may have contributed to appreciation pressures.

Increasing capital inflows in the early 1990s have been associated with a consumption boom which took place between 1992 and 1995. Much of this boom reflected a sudden change in the behavior of private agents, who were eager to consume and invest in consumer durables. This spending boom was accentuated by lax monetary policies and by a surge in local credit flows for consumption.

Contrary to developments in other Latin American countries at the time, *Apertura* in Colombia was accompanied by a rapid increase of government expenditures. Growing fiscal outlays were largely a result of three factors. First, higher investment in social programs by local governments. Second, enlarged expenditures by the social security system. And third, greater judicial and defense expenditures. The enlargement of expenditures in all three fronts responded to enlarged government responsibilities, emanating from the 1991 Constitution. Most significantly, new constitutional provisions mandated a gradual increase in the share of tax revenues to be transferred to local governments for investments in education and health.

The mix of growing government expenditures with lax monetary policy and the spending mood of consumers led to a massive domestic demand boom. As a consequence, demand grew at an average annual rate of 11 percent between 1992 and 1994. Furthermore, a rapid appreciation of the Colombian peso ensued. Between 1991 and 1997, it appreciated at an annual rate of 6.7 percent.[9] By contrast, the exchange rate had depreciated at a rate of 7.1 percent annually in the 1980s. The appreciation of the 1990s may have gone beyond what may have been justified by medium run fundamental forces. According to Quiroz

(1997), sustainable capital inflows would have justified an appreciation of 3 percent between 1990 and 1996; instead, the peso strengthened by 25 percent in that period. Cárdenas (1995) argues that the CPI-based real exchange rate by the end of 1996 was overvalued by 18.7 to 24.9 percent with respect to a level consistent with medium-run sustainable public expenditures.

As in textbook analyses of Dutch disease, the rapid appreciation of the Colombian peso between 1990 and mid-1997 was associated with a rapidly expanding service sector (e.g., construction, financial, commerce) and a recession in industrial and tradable agricultural markets. Returns to export activities fell, as evidenced by a slowing rate of growth. The high labor content of the booming service sector exerted upward pressure on urban (and later, rural) wages. Remuneration for highly qualified individuals in urban areas grew significantly faster than for unqualified segments of the labor force.[10] Upward pressure on both rural and urban wages may have been intensified by the growth of illicit crop activities during the 1990s (see "Illicit Drugs and Agriculture in the 1990s" below).

Colombian authorities adopted some of the policies usually recommended to avoid excessive costs from appreciation. Capital inflows were limited by a series of Central Bank regulations, aimed at slowing down the rapid influx of loans from abroad. In particular, short-term loans were penalized with taxes intended to make them unattractive. The value added tax was increased, partly with the intent of penalizing consumption and stimulating savings. An oil stabilization fund was established in 1995 to prevent the rapid monetization of annual export revenue. However, in the final analysis, most observers agree that these measures were nullified by the overwhelming effect of greater government expenditures. Not surprisingly, the prominent issue of debate among Colombian economists since 1996 has been how to reduce fiscal expenditure.

Social Conditions in the Countryside and *Apertura*

Widespread opposition to *Apertura* measures during the 1992 crisis and its aftermath was in part justified by beliefs that declining annual crop output affected directly the living conditions of the rural population. Despite output gains in permanent crops and livestock activities, critics of liberalization charged that the overall effect of *Apertura* had been a large loss in rural jobs, increasing unemployment and poverty levels in the countryside. Deteriorating incomes were, in turn, blamed for increasing migration to cities and to frontier areas, where it was linked to deforestation of valuable rainforests and fragile ecosystems. It was also claimed that the crisis had fueled rural violence, by increasing the pool of impoverished rural inhabitants.

Despite popular beliefs, the net effect of structural changes in agriculture of the 1990s seems more favorable for rural inhabitants than anticipated. Falling employment in annual crop cultivation was greatly compensated by increasing employment in permanent crops, rural non-agricultural activities and urban opportunities. An intense urban construction boom between 1992 and 1995 pushed urban wages sharply up, attracting many rural inhabitants to the cities. Furthermore, some rural and urban labor markets may have been affected by growing employment opportunities in illicit crop cultivation since 1991.

The dearth of statistics make it difficult to give a complete picture of the evolution of living standards in the Colombian countryside during the 1990s. This section attempts to analyze the available evidence, and to speculate about the possible causes of rural welfare trends after 1990. The striking conclusion is that despite widespread beliefs to the contrary, most of the data indicates that by the mid-1990s, the bulk of the rural population was enjoying substantially higher incomes than at the beginning of the decade. This seems largely a result of the boom in rural and urban non-tradable activities (i.e., services and some agricultural activities) that has been observed in Colombia since 1990.

Demographic Trends

According to census data, the population of Colombia grew at an annual average rate of 2.4 percent between 1985 and 1993. Urban areas grew faster (2.9 percent per year) than rural settings (1.2 percent). Hence, the rural population increased from 10.7 to 11.8 million between the two census years. Despite slower growth in rural areas, by 1993 a relatively high proportion of Colombians continued to inhabit the countryside: 31.3 percent of the population lived outside urban concentrations, down from 34.4 percent in 1985. If the inhabitants of towns of 10,000 or less are also counted as rural residents, the rural share of the population increases to 42.0 percent in 1993.

Migration flows from rural settings to urban areas have continued in the 1990s. However, information about the dynamics of these flows is poor. Census data indicate a slowdown in migratory flows between 1985 and 1993, although methodological differences between censuses prevent firm conclusions. Some analysts have pointed to indirect signs of increased migratory flows in the first half of the 1990s,[11] a trend that may be consistent with booming urban labor markets and growing wages (see "Wages" below).

In 1993, 51 percent of the rural population was accounted for by men, reflecting greater rural-urban migration of women. Female workers enjoy proportionally greater employment opportunities in urban areas. For instance, In 1995, women made up 48 percent of the economically active population in cities, while in rural areas the corresponding figure was 29.2 percent. Despite fewer opportunities, women have gradually augmented their participation in the rural labor force, increasing their share from 29 to 32 percent between 1988 and 1995.[12]

Employment

Despite the crisis in annual crop production, total employment in the country-side diminished only slightly between 1991 and 1997 (see Figure 6.1). In this period, rural household survey data indicate that nearly 80,000 jobs were lost, implying a decline of 1.3 percent with respect to 1991. In 1997, rural employment still contributed 38.1 percent of economywide employment, down only slightly from 40.2 percent in 1988.[13]

These changes seem consistent with structural changes in agricultural production. Using fixed employment coefficients, it has been estimated that the reduction in areas dedicated to annual crops between 1991 and 1996 should have resulted in a loss of 119,600 jobs.[14] On the other hand, increased areas for permanent crops (excluding coffee) should have led to the generation of some 131,000 new jobs. These two trends alone should have resulted in the creation of 11,000 net new jobs. However, in the same period, the substantial decline in coffee production reduced rural employment by about 108,000 jobs. Hence, total agricultural employment should have declined by about 98,000 net jobs, between 1991 and 1997, minus a small fraction that may have been generated by the expansion of poultry and cattle raising activities, for which no official figures are known.

Another important trend was the rapid rate of job creation displayed by rural non-agricultural activities (see "Income Diversification" below). Rural house-

FIGURE 6.1 Employment in Rural Areas, 1991-1997 (Million Jobs)

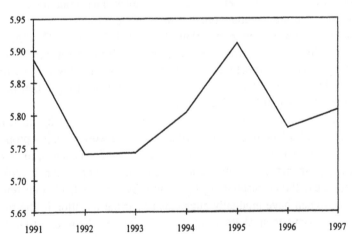

Source: Data from Departamento Administrativo Nacional de Estadística.

hold data suggest that between 1991 and 1995 some 257,000 jobs were created in non-agricultural activities. Most of these have been concentrated in service sectors, including commercial, financial, construction and transportation activities. The reasons for and consequences of the surge in service sector activities in the countryside will be discussed below.

Unemployment

Information about rural unemployment rates is notoriously defective. Such rates are often disproportionately low, because surveys deem a person unemployed only if she has not performed any work in the week before the survey. In rural areas, where jobs tend to be informal and farming families increase attention to fields when not otherwise employed, this exerts a downward bias in the figures. Survey methodologies also produce higher rates of unemployment for women, who tend to spend more time in domestic activities, which are not classified as "productive." For instance, in 1993, the average rate of unemployment of 4.7 percent was the result of a high proportion of unemployed women (12.0 percent) and a low share of men (2.2 percent).

Despite the above caveats, official figures reveal that unemployment rates in rural areas increased from 4.2 percent in 1991 to 5.4 in 1995 and to 6.5 in 1997. Growing unemployment between 1991 and 1997 reflects 140,000 newly unemployed, a consequence of the loss of 80,000 jobs and the appearance of 60,000 more jobs seekers.

Unemployment changes in the 1991-95 period exerted a differential effect by income class. Data from household surveys indicates that unemployment increased for the first eight deciles of the rural population, with only minimal changes for the wealthiest 20 percent (see Table 6.12). Women have also suffered disproportionately from the increase in unemployment: overall rates of unemployment for this gender increased from 8.5 to 10.6 percent in the 1991 to 1995 period. However, as will be discussed below, higher unemployment rates have been more than compensated by higher incomes among disadvantaged rural inhabitants.

Wages

Rural wage data show that, after exhibiting little growth during the latter half of the 1980s, wages dropped precipitously during the 1992 crisis. Real wages fell by 14 percent between the first quarter of 1990 and the third quarter of 1992. However, since early in 1993, remuneration for rural workers began a rapid recovery, growing at an annual rate of 4 percent between 1993 and 1997, and reaching record levels towards the end of the period (see Figure 6.2).

Rural wage information reveals important differences by region (see Table 6.13). For example, during the 1992 crisis, wages fell more sharply in the Coffee region, the Atlantic Coast and the Eastern Plains. In contrast, wages rose

TABLE 6.12 Unemployment Rates by Decile, 1991 and 1995 (percent)

Deciles	1991	1995
1-2	5.8	7.5
3-5	4.9	6.1
6-8	4.0	5.1
9	2.6	2.4
10	3.1	3.2

Source: Ocampo et al. (1998).

in the Central region, possibly reflecting the effect of a booming construction cycle in urban centers. In the 1993-96 period, wages have grown rapidly in the Eastern Plains, Amazon, Western, Southern and Central regions, with the lowest rates of increase in the Atlantic and Coffee regions.

Differential patterns of wage growth suggest that rural labor markets are still deeply segmented in Colombia. A recent detailed analysis of this issue concludes that there is very little correlation between rural wages across regions and between rural and urban wages.[15] Wages in the Atlantic coast region exhibit the

FIGURE 6.2 Rural Daily Wages, 1976-1996 (1988 Col pesos)

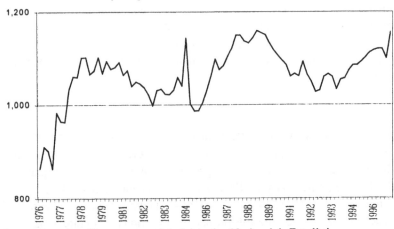

Source: Data from Departamento Administrativo Nacional de Estadística.

TABLE 6.13 Rural and Urban Wages, 1986-1996 (annual rates of growth, percent)

Zone	86-90	91-93	93-96
Rural	0.52	-3.51	4.06
Central	0.26	1.23	3.54
Atlantic	0.55	-6.70	1.12
Coffee	2.63	-6.90	2.09
Western	0.50	-2.36	4.98
Sothern	-0.22	-2.29	4.49
East. Plains	-4.59	-3.23	6.00
Other	-13.87	1.29	7.34
Urban	-2.77	-2.69	0.80

Source: Author's own calculations with data from Departamento Administrativo Nacional de Estadística.

least amount of correlation with other areas of the country. Rural market segmentation is consistent with independent findings of pervasive regional differences in poverty levels in the mid-1990s.[16] Such differences do not seem to be explained by household characteristics, suggesting that there are barriers to mobility across rural areas in Colombia. In many cases, this is probably because low income farmers and agricultural workers are too poor to muster the necessary investments to migrate. In other cases, it reflects strong cultural differences that limit migratory flows, in particular, between the Atlantic coast region and the rest of the country.

Income

Evidence from household surveys indicates that income per capita in rural areas fell at a rapid 5.7 percent annual rate between 1991 and 1995.[17] This negative performance contrasts with the increase of 1.2 percent per year observed in the 1978-91 period.

Given the skewed distribution of income exhibited in the Colombian countryside, overall income trends may hide important differences within the rural population. Disaggregating by income categories indicates that trends are reversed if the upper decile of the rural population is excluded from the calculation. In this case, rural income increases at an average rate of 1.4 percent between 1991 and 1995—2.5 percent annually for the first five deciles. By contrast, the apparently prosperous 1978-91 period turns out to be only favorable for the upper decile (see Table 6.14). All other deciles exhibit falling incomes in the same period. Excluding the highest decile, aggregate rural

TABLE 6.14 Growth in Rural per Capita Income (average annual growth rate, percent)

Deciles	78-91	91-95	91-95[a]
1-2	-0.1	4.1	5.7
3-5	-0.4	2.1	3.9
6-8	-0.7	1.1	2.8
9	-0.7	0.4	2.1
10	3.3	-14.3	-12.7
TOTAL	1.1	-5.7	-4.0
TOTAL[b]	-0.6	1.4	3.1

[a]Growth rates using food CPI as deflator.

[b]Excludes the uppermost decile.

Source: Ocampo et al. (1998) and Author's own estimates.

income fell at an annual average rate of 0.6 percent between 1978 and 1991.

The sharp differences between income growth of the wealthiest stratum and the remainder of the rural population has not yet been fully explained. There is consensus that falling incomes of the top decile are mainly a reflection of falling agricultural incomes due to the effect of *Apertura* on agricultural rents.[18] These include the remuneration to land and to the family labor of agricultural entrepreneurs. What is more difficult to explain is why per capita incomes of poorer groups increased rapidly. This is likely to respond to a combination of four important factors.

First, tight rural labor markets after 1992 may have been the consequence of fast-growing employment opportunities in urban areas and increased rural urban migration. A protracted urban building boom ensued during the ascending phase of the construction cycle, intensified by the effects of surging capital inflows and lax monetary policy between 1992 and 1995. It is also possible that wages in some areas increased in response to growing employment opportunities in illicit crop cultivation. This may have affected farmers in the South and Eastern Plains regions, due to the proximity of the coca growing frontier; farmers in some coffee growing areas may have been affected by the growth of poppy cultivation for heroin production in the Andean highlands.

Second, poorer rural groups include *campesino* producers of non-tradable crops and landless workers employed in the production of *campesino* crops, as well as in other agricultural activities which fared well after 1990 (e.g., oil palm, sugar, cattle). As shown earlier in this chapter, both production and returns increased for many of these crops after 1990.

Third, poorer rural families seem to have enjoyed greater income diversification opportunities in the post-*Apertura* period. In fact, rural household data suggest that lower income groups benefited most from the expansion of employment in non-agricultural sectors, concentrated in service sectors (see Table 6.15). The poorest 20 percent of the rural population increased their share in service jobs from 22 to 35 percent between 1991 and 1995. In addition, wages in rural service sectors earn substantially higher average incomes than both farmers and agricultural workers. For example, workers in rural construction activities earned 43.4 percent greater incomes than their counterparts in agriculture. A 1993 survey found that the per capita income for rural non-farm workers was US$740, while those for small farmers and landless workers were only US$413 and US$416.[19] The evidence also points to a widening of the service-agriculture earnings gap in rural areas. For instance, the premium of construction over agricultural incomes increased from 34.7 to 43.4 percent between 1988 and 1995.[20]

Fourth, the rural economy may have also been influenced by the large increase in local government expenditures since 1990. This surge in public expenditures was the result of increasing transfers from the central government for social investments, as dictated by the 1991 Constitution. Transfers to municipal and provincial governments increased fourfold in real terms, increasing from US$1.1 billion to US$4.6 billion between 1990 and 1997. Although this issue has not been thoroughly investigated in Colombia, increased expenditures at the local level are likely to have created rural jobs in non-agricultural activities which may have compensated for falling employment in agriculture.

Recent analyses of the microeconomic determinants of rural welfare in the 1990s indicate that experience, education and sex are the key factors that influence per capita incomes.[21] Males earn more for similar work, probably a result of traditional cultural norms, although the gap has been falling in the 1990s. A surprising finding is that education is not a high productivity investment for

TABLE 6.15 Share of Population Employed in Tertiary Sector (percent)

Decile	1991	1995
1-2	22.0	34.7
3-5	26.0	29.4
6-8	29.5	31.3
9	32.0	33.0
10	34.1	37.6
Total	28.2	32.5

Source: Ocampo et al. (1998).

those involved in agricultural activities. On the other hand, schooling yields much higher returns in non-agricultural employment.[22]

Poverty and Living Conditions

In Colombia, poverty is measured with two competing methodologies. The first measures the proportion of population under an appropriately defined income level, known as the poverty line—complemented some times with a lower "misery" line. According to this definition, rural poverty levels decreased steadily from 36.0 percent in 1988 to 26.2 percent in 1995[23] (see Table 6.16). These results seem consistent with findings of increasing per capita income for lower income groups after 1991. Indicators of indigence also reveal continuous improvement, from 14.6 percent in 1988 to 8.4 percent in 1995.

The continuous decline in poverty levels in the 1990s contrasts with deteriorating conditions between 1978 and 1988. In the latter period, poverty levels increased as a result of falling incomes for the poorest segments of the rural population, according to rural household survey data.[24]

The second measure of poverty often used in Colombia is an indicator built upon "unsatisfied basic needs" (UBN). According to this criterion, a rural inhabitant is classified as poor if she fails to meet any one of five essential needs: the quality of housing, the amount of living space per family member, access to basic sanitation services, schooling of children and economic dependence.[25] The needs-based indicator also reveals a substantive and continued improvement in the welfare of the poorer segments of the population in the 1990s (see Table 6.16). The proportion of the rural population not meeting any of the needs criteria fell from 37.4 to 31.5 percent between 1991 and 1995.

TABLE 6.16 Rural and Urban Poverty Indexes, 1988-1995 (percent)

Year	Rural			Urban		
	Poverty	Misery	UBN[a]	Poverty	Misery	UBN[a]
1988	36.0	14.6				
1991	31.4	11.5	37.4	11.0	2.2	15.0
1992	30.8	12.3	33.8	10.7	2.4	12.6
1993	30.0	10.2	32.3	8.4	1.8	10.7
1994	28.5	9.1	31.5	8.0	1.7	11.3
1995	26.2	8.4		7.5	1.7	

[a]UBN: Unsatisfied basic needs indicator.
Source: Poverty and misery indexes from Ocampo et al. (1998). UBN indexes from Leibovich et al. (1997).

Improvements have been mainly associated with widening access to sanitation and electrification services in rural areas.

Clearly, the evolution of poverty indicators is consistent with income trends showing greater gains for poorer segments of the rural population. Hence, the reduction of poverty is tightly linked to the same forces that have contributed to income growth. However, the reduction of extreme rural poverty is also a result of the increasing success of government programs in reaching the truly needy. Several studies have shown that government expenditures in social programs have increased their effectiveness in the 1980s and 1990s, thanks to improved targeting, which have made these expenditures more progressive than in the past.[26]

Distribution

A lot of controversy has surrounded the distributional effects of structural reforms and trade liberalization in Latin America. For some observers, reforms have opened proportionally greater opportunities for lower income groups, leading to improving distribution. For others, new opportunities stemming from liberalization have concentrated benefits among highly qualified workers while cutbacks in agricultural expenditures disproportionately affected the welfare of poorer groups.[27]

Despite controversies about the overall effect of liberalization reforms, the empirical evidence in Colombia unambiguously points to steady gains in equality in the countryside between 1991 and 1995 (the last year for which data is available). This is a direct result of the drop in per capita income of the upper decile and income gains in all other income groups. The drastic fall in the Gini coefficient—an index of inequality[28]—from 0.565 in 1988 to 0.441 in 1995 reflects greater income gains of the lowest deciles (see Table 6.17).

Increasing equality in the 1990s contrasts sharply with the deterioration of income distribution indicators recorded between 1978 and 1991, which has been attributed to protection policies for annual crops. As a result, the ratio of income

TABLE 6.17 Income Distribution, 1988-1995 (Gini coefficient)

	1978	1988	1991	1992	1993	1994	1995
Total	0.516	n.a.	0.532	0.532	0.523	0.529	0.534
Urban	0.515	0.492[a]	0.487	0.505	0.500	0.515	0.528
Rural	0.491	0.566	0.569	0.530	0.505	0.479	0.441

[a]Only includes seven major urban centers.

Source: Data from Ocampo et al. (1998).

of the top decile relative to the bottom two deciles increased from 22 to 33 between 1978 and 1988. In 1995, this ratio fell to 15, due to the effect of falling incomes for the upper decile and improving living standards of the poor.

In 1988, the Gini coefficient reflected greater inequality in rural areas compared to urban areas. By 1995, this result had been reversed. This shift was aided by the deterioration of the urban Gini in the 1990s. The evidence indicates that distributive shocks seem to affect rural and urban incomes in opposite directions. While structural changes in the 1990s improved incomes of all but the highest income groups in rural sectors, urban areas witnessed greater income gains for wealthier segments. This has been explained by the increasing premium for qualified labor that has been associated with structural reforms in many Latin American countries.[29]

Income Diversification

One of the most important trends revealed by rural household surveys during the 1990s was the rapid growth in non-agricultural sources of income. The diversification of economic activity in rural areas has been identified as a long-term trend across Latin American economies, usually associated with investments in rural infrastructure.[30] For the case of Colombia, however, forces associated with exchange rate appreciation as well as the substantial growth of local government expenditures accelerated this trend. As a result, the share of aggregate rural income derived from service sector jobs grew from 30 to 38 percent between 1991 and 1995. In the same period, the share of the rural population deriving its primary income from service sector jobs increased from 28.2 to 32.5 percent. By contrast, incomes derived from agricultural activities fell from 66 to 55 percent in the same period.

The dynamism of non-agricultural activities has offered diversification opportunities to low income rural families who had been overwhelmingly dependent in the past on farm incomes, which tend to be highly seasonal and unstable. As shown above, poorer segments of the population benefited disproportionately from the boom in service activities, explaining a great share of the income gains recorded.[31] The evidence also suggests that women have taken greater advantage of service sector opportunities. The proportion of women deriving their income from such jobs increased from 26 percent in 1988 to 34 percent in 1995.[32] This reflects greater participation by females in work activities areas in which they have traditionally exhibited advantages over men, including commercial activities, restaurants, hotel and domestic services.[33]

Illicit Drugs and Agriculture in the 1990s

As explained in Chapter 2, Colombia has been the host of a thriving illicit drug business, initiated with shipments of marihuana in the 1970s. By the late

1980s, it was estimated that between 70 and 80 percent of international supplies of cocaine originated in Colombia. In the 1990s, growing poppy cultivation has been associated with increasing shipments of heroin.

Official figures reveal that important changes have occurred in the structure of the Colombian cocaine industry during the 1990s.[34] In the 1980s, the development of this activity relied on shipments of coca paste from Bolivia and Peru. The processing was performed in Colombian laboratories, many of them located in remote areas of the Amazon rainforest in the Southeastern section of the country. However, since the second half of the 1980s, the areas planted in coca within Colombia have grown substantially. Estimations for 1994 suggest that Colombia had overtaken Bolivia as the second largest grower of coca leaf. This has been attributed to the increasing effectiveness of interdiction efforts in the border between Colombia and Peru and to increasing competition for supplies of coca paste in neighboring countries. As a result, official figures from the US government indicate that the areas planted in coca within Colombia increased from 14,000 to 50,000 hectares between 1985 and 1995.[35] Recent studies financed by the United Nations suggest that these figures are seriously underestimated and that coca plantations covered between 70,000 and 84,000 hectares in 1994-95.[36]

The growing cultivation of coca in Colombia has also given rise to a dichotomy of farmers, similar to that present in the rest of Colombian agriculture.[37] Small *campesino* farmers are estimated to account for nearly 50 percent of the areas dedicated to coca but only 35 percent of production. Commercial farmers, who plant larger areas and hire a large migrant labor force during the harvest, account for the remaining half of the area and 64 percent of production.

There is considerable controversy about the value of illicit crops in Colombia. The figures that appear in the mass media are usually widely exaggerated, including reports that average annual earnings have been in excess of US$7.0 billion. Recent studies estimate annual drug revenues at US$2.0 to US$2.5 billion a year, of which two-thirds originates in cocaine shipments.[38] This means that revenues from drug sales abroad have amounted only to about 3 percent of gross domestic product and between 23 and 34 percent of legal exports. There is greater controversy about how much of this figure actually makes its way back into the local economy.

United Nation's studies reveal that the value of the coca harvest in 1994 may have reached between US$700 and US$850 million, while that for poppy ranged from US$160 to US$330 million.[39] The marihuana crop is estimated to be worth about US$90 million per year. These figures place coca as the fifth most valuable agricultural activity, behind cattle, poultry, coffee, and sugar. The value of the poppy harvest is comparable to that of beans, cassava and sorghum.

The impact of illegal drugs on the Colombian economy has been subject to considerable controversy. For some analysts, the costs generated by the trade—violence, corruption and distortions associated with large inflows of drug revenues—have inflicted considerable damage to the economy.[40] For others, it may have prevented serious balance of payments imbalances throughout the 1980s.[41] The effects of illicit drugs on Colombian agriculture have been less explored. In theory, farming activities could be potentially affected by several direct and indirect effects of the drug trade, including competition for inputs (labor and land), macroeconomic distortions, violence, diversion of government resources and destruction of natural resources.

Illicit drugs use labor and land that could otherwise be used for legal agricultural activities. How important is this competition for Colombian farmers? With respect to land, the latest estimates indicate that about 100,000 hectares were planted in illicit drugs in the mid-1990s—80 percent in coca, 16 percent in poppy and the rest in marihuana.[42] This represents about 1.4 percent of the country's arable land. Moreover, much of the land used in illicit crops is located in frontier areas, with poor communications infrastructure and low population density. It is in these areas, far from government control, that illegal activities thrive. Most of the coca fields are located in remote areas of some of the least populated provinces (i.e., Caquetá, Guaviare, Putumayo, Meta, and Cauca). On the other hand, poppy is grown in the higher elevations of the Central Andean ranges, at altitudes of between 1,800 and 3,000 meters, and in very sparsely populated zones. Little agriculture has traditionally taken place at these altitudes. Hence, formal agriculture is probably little affected by direct competition for land with illegal crops.

Indirectly, illicit drug activities have exerted a stronger effect on rural land markets through money laundering activities. Purchases of farmland have been a favorite method of investing illegal funds by wealthy drug barons. Land transactions are not closely supervised by authorities, and real estate has been traditionally considered a safe asset for Colombian investors. Moreover, land taxes are low and transactions values are largely underestimated, to avoid taxes. Some studies suggest that purchases by drug barons since the mid-1980s may have helped inflate rural land prices in some agricultural areas.[43] Rising land prices stimulate investment in real estate for speculative purposes and reduces incentives for agricultural activities. Studies of these processes have shown, however, that much of the land acquisitions by drug barons have been concentrated in lands with an aptitude for extensive cattle grazing as well as in areas with strong potential for appreciation, such as those near urban perimeters.[44] Few purchases of prime arable land with drug money have been documented. Thus, it is likely that the effect of land acquisition practices with illicit funds may have led to the replacement of traditional landowners by drug barons, most of whom have continued with extensive cattle operations.

There is substantially less evidence about the potential effect of illicit drugs on rural labor markets. United Nations studies indicate that illegal crops may have generated up to 40,000 permanent jobs annually in the mid-1990s, a small amount relative to the 5.8 million jobs generated by legal agricultural activities.

A large share of these jobs are seasonal, mostly in remote coca growing areas, attracting young unemployed men and women from urban centers. If this is the case, the impact on rural labor markets may be very indirect and largely limited to provinces adjacent to coca growing regions.

Although exact figures are unavailable, it is estimated that between US$2.0 and US$2.7 billion enter Colombia annually from illicit drug revenues—while legal agricultural exports amount to about US$2.5 billion and total exports to US$10.5 billion.[45] About 65 percent of revenues originates in cocaine sales, 30 percent from heroin and the remainder from marihuana. Substantial year-to-year variations in revenues have been detected due to price fluctuations, often related to the intensity of anti-drug efforts. Macroeconomists agree that illicit dollar flows have helped maintain a more appreciated peso than would have been the case otherwise. Thus, drug trafficking has probably increased the prices of non-tradables with respect to tradables, including those within agriculture.

Are drug revenues responsible for exchange rate appreciation in the 1990s? The uncertain nature of the amount of revenues that are actually brought back into the economy does not allow firm answers to this question. However, studies on the recent appreciation of the exchange rate observed in Colombia point to strong similarities with other Latin American countries (see Chapter 1), including many where drug money has had a negligible impact.[46] On the other hand, drug activities can be blamed for the rapid growth of the service sector relative to agriculture and industry in some producing provinces.[47]

It is an established fact that the growth of the drug trafficking business has been associated with increasing violence in Colombia. In the years when Pablo Escobar and the Medellín Cartel dominated the industry, murders, kidnappings and terrorist acts were commonplace. In the 1980s, drug lords developed the practice of hiring private armies to eradicate guerrillas from rural areas where they possessed extensive land holdings, such as the Central Magdalena River Valley and the Northwestern area adjacent to the Gulf of Urabá. In the 1990s, this practice was extended to many areas affected by guerrilla presence, with the support of private landowners and businessmen. The unfortunate result has been small-scale civil wars, which are responsible for the growing rural death toll in recent years.

In other areas of the country, a more permanent alliance has been forged between some guerrilla groups and drug traffickers. This is particularly the case in the Southeastern provinces of Meta, Guaviare, Putumayo and Caquetá, where most coca production is concentrated. In these sparsely populated regions, guerrillas have found a new source of revenue in the drug trade, especially important at a time when ideological support dwindled due to the collapse of the Communist Block. Traffickers have been willing to pay large sums to armed groups in exchange for protection of drug plantations and laboratories. For example, in Miraflores, a key coca growing area of the Guaviare province, it was estimated that the drug tax in 1995 amounted to some US$27,000 to

US$36,000 per guerilla soldier.[48] In these areas, guerrillas have forged a close alliance with the coca growing population, fighting government efforts to eradicate illicit crops. Helicopters in charge of fumigation of coca plantations are a favorite target of guerrilla attacks.

Drug money has strengthened the military capacity of guerrilla groups in Colombia during the 1990s. Renewed vigor has allowed them to expand their presence in many rural areas of the country, attempting daring attacks on military targets. Farmers living in areas where guerrillas are present are usually forced to pay contributions in cash or in kind. Moreover, guerrillas operate a thriving kidnapping industry, which affects disproportionately farming families. The intensification of rural violence in this period, although unquantifiable, has represented a substantial cost to farmers in recent years.

Pressures stemming from drug-trafficking have distracted government attention and resources from agricultural problems. Public funds used directly in anti-drug campaigns have been increasing as a share of the national budget, although they still only amount to 1.5 to 2.0 percent of total expenditures. However, the cost of fighting drugs does not include the substantial increases in defense spending that have been necessary to counteract growing guerrilla activities in the 1990s. Additionally, scarce government resources have been increasingly used to implement programs to provide alternative income-earning opportunities to growers of illicit crops, most of which have failed due to the lack of profitable productive alternatives in the remote areas where they are grown. During the Samper administration nearly US$100 million were spent on investments in infrastructure (e..g., roads, rural electrification), crop purchases and credit. By mid-1998, no noticeable decline in the areas dedicated to illicit crops had been detected.

Illicit crops have also exerted a heavy toll on natural resources. The cultivation of the 16,000 hectares of poppy in the mid-1990s has been associated with the destruction of large preserves of Andean highland forests. Apart from the loss of the intrinsic value of these unique forests, the destruction has created water shortages downstream, with still unquantified effects on traditional farms. In addition, the spread of coca plantations has been associated with the deforestation of huge areas of valuable tropical rainforests. For every hectare of coca planted, it has been estimated that four hectares of rainforest are burned, indicating that coca may be responsible for the loss of over 300,000 hectares of virgin rainforests in the Colombian Amazon region. While this is not a direct cost on Colombian farmers, it is a large loss for the society as a whole.

In sum, illicit drug cultivation has likely exerted significant negative impacts on Colombian agriculture. The sustained flow of foreign exchange has supported a more appreciated exchange rate, favoring prices of non-tradable sectors. It is also probable that the growth in coca areas observed in the 1990s raised rural wages in agricultural zones located near growing regions, as well as land prices in some cattle-growing areas. Most significantly, it is likely that this growth is responsible for the military strengthening of guerrilla groups and the intensification of rural violence, which imposed substantial costs to Colombian farmers during the 1990s.

Conclusions

The 1990s have been a time of mediocre economic performance for Colombian agriculture. The production of annual crops fell almost uninterruptedly between 1990 and 1997. By contrast, most permanent crops displayed moderate growth while livestock activities displayed fast-growing production, led by a very dynamic poultry sector. In the aggregate, farm output grew substantially below historical averages.

In the same period, production of importable (mostly annual) crops declined while that of exportables (mostly permanent crops) remained stagnant. By contrast, non-tradable activities recorded significant growth. These trends produced important changes in the structure of Colombian agriculture. Non-tradable (and permanent) activities gained output share, mostly at the expense of importable (and annual) crops.

Trade figures broadly confirm production trends. Growth rates for agricultural exports were moderate and significantly lower than those observed in the second half of the 1980s. On the other hand, agricultural imports increased at historically unprecedented rates. This has been the result of booming domestic demand and diminished domestic availability. The poor performance of importables has been accentuated by lagging relative productivity, in part caused by institutional and funding problems in research institutions.

Diverging performance across agricultural subsectors has been largely a result of changing relative incentives. Returns for most tradable farming activities fell substantially, with greater intensity for importable crops. On the other hand, those for non-tradables increased. Two tradable crops (i.e., sugar and rice) also experienced increasing returns as a result of special support measures. Declining international prices and the real appreciation of the exchange rate explain weakening incentives for most tradable crops. Agricultural trade policies were not neutral across commodities. Government interventions supported commodities like rice, sugar, maize and barley, remained neutral for most exportable crops and reduced protection for crops like soybeans and wheat.

The appreciation of the exchange rate has been a critical factor in explaining decreasing returns for tradables and the structural transformation of Colombian agriculture of the 1990s. Appreciation of the currency has been the result of several factors, including surging capital inflows, oil findings and the massive increase in government expenditures after 1990.

Despite widespread beliefs to the contrary, the 1990s have been a time of continuously improving living standards for most rural inhabitants. Aggregate rural income fell, due to the sharp fall in the revenues of the wealthiest decile.

By contrast, the remaining 90 percent of the rural population enjoyed improving incomes, with greater gains for the poorest families. Income trends are consistent with rural wage data and poverty indicators. As a result, steady gains in equality in the countryside during the 1990s have been observed. Improving welfare levels for the majority of the rural population seems to be related to booming urban labor markets, growth in non-tradable *campesino* crops, expanding job opportunities in rural service sectors and the effects of rapidly-growing expenditures by local governments. Income reductions among high-income farmers are a result of falling rents, associated with the results of trade liberalization and the appreciation of the exchange rate.

The cultivation of illicit drugs has had negative repercussions on Colombian agriculture. The growth in coca areas observed in the 1990s is largely responsible for the military strengthening of guerrilla groups and the intensification of rural violence, which has imposed growing costs to Colombian farmers and to the national budget, diverting resources which otherwise could be used to support agricultural activities. It is also likely that this growth raised rural wages in areas adjacent to coca growing regions, as well as land prices in some cattle-growing zones.

Notes

1. A comparison of yields in Colombia and in other major competitors appears in Balcázar (1998).

2. The comparison is drawn from Balcázar (1998).

3. This argument is developed in Urrutia (1997).

4. Estimates of supply response elasticities for Colombian crops appear in García and Montes (1988) and in Departamento Nacional de Planeación (1990).

5. The elasticities reported were calculated using Nerlove's classic method, as described in García and Montes (1988).

6. The algebraic derivation yields:

$$I\hat{R} = \hat{P}^b + (1-\lambda)R\hat{E}R - \alpha\hat{P}_f^{cif} - \beta\hat{P}_i^{cif} - \delta\,\hat{P}_p^{cif} - \gamma\hat{P}_m^{cif} - \gamma\,\hat{I} - \lambda\hat{W}$$

$$-\alpha(1+\hat{\varepsilon}^f) - \beta(1+\hat{\varepsilon}^i) - \delta(1+\hat{\varepsilon}^p) - \gamma(1+\hat{\varepsilon}^m).$$

7. Some classic references are Balassa (1964) and Samuelson (1964). For the Colombian context, the discussion draws from Calderón (1995), Cárdenas (1997) and the collection of articles in Montenegro (1997).

8. The Dutch disease is explained in Corden and Neary (1982).

9. The appreciation rate refers to the definition of the exchange rate using Colombian and international consumer price indexes as deflators.

10. See Nuñez and Sánchez (1997) and Robbins (1996).

11. See for example Londoño (1997).

12. Figures taken from Leibovich et al. (1997).

13. Data from Gómez (1998).

14. Employment data reported in Balcázar (1998).

15. The study is by Nupia (1997).

16. López and Valdés (1998) reach this conclusion in their study of the micro determinants of rural poverty levels across regions in Colombia, with 1993 data.

17. Figures derived from Ocampo et al. (1998).

18. This explanation is given by Lora and Herrera (1994) and Ocampo et al. (1998).

19. Data taken from López and Valdés (1998).

20. Primary information drawn from Leibovich et al. (1997).

21. Recent studies on the microeconomic determinants of rural per capita incomes in Colombia include Leibovich et al. (1997) and López and Valdés (1998).

22. This result is highlighted by López and Valdés (1998).

23. The indexes displayed use a poverty line level compatible with international standards. The Colombian government uses a domestic poverty line which yields higher poverty levels. However, with the Colombian line, the declining poverty trend after 1991 is also detected (Ocampo et al., 1998).

24. See Ocampo et al. (1998).

25. An economic dependence ratio is constructed by dividing the number of family members by the number of working adults. A high ratio of dependence is interpreted as an indicator of poverty.

26. On the increased progressivity of social expenditures in the countryside see World Bank (1994a) and May (1996).

27. Among those proclaiming that reforms have improved income distribution are Londoño and Székely (1997). Reforms are seen as inducing greater income inequality in Comisión Económica para América Latina (1997).

28. The Gini coefficient is a commonly used index of income inequality. Its value ranges from zero to one, with lesser values signaling greater equality.

29. See Nuñez and Sánchez (1997).

30. Recent growth in non-agricultural rural activities is noted in several countries of Latin American by López and Valdés (1998).

31. Despite gains by poor segments, by 1995, the wealthiest 10 percent of the rural population maintained the highest rate of participation in the service sector (38 percent).

32. Data from Gómez (1998).

33. Men have usually benefited most from expansion of manufacturing jobs in rural areas.

34. Much of the material for this section come from the studies financed by the United Nation's Development Program edited by Thoumi (1997).

35. Data appears in Uribe (1997).

36. See Uribe (1997).

37. The dichotomy is explained in Uribe (1997).

38. See Steiner (1996).

39. See Uribe (1997).

40. See for example Urrutia (1990).

41. See for example Kalmanovitz (1992).

42. Figures from Uribe (1997).

43. Reyes (1997).

44. See Reyes (1997)

45. Estimates taken from Steiner (1996).

46. See Calvo et al (1992).
47. See Rocha (1997).
48. See Uribe (1997).

7

Conclusions and Lessons

This study has presented a detailed account of the Colombian experience with the adoption of a market-oriented regime in agriculture and the removal of import substitution policies since 1990. Similar reforms have been implemented in recent years across Latin America. The Colombian experience is particularly valuable due to the continuing importance of agriculture in the overall economy and the complex nature of its farming sector.

The account has shown that the timing of Colombian trade liberalization reforms was not ideal. Shortly after liberalization measures were adopted, world prices dropped precipitously and capital inflows surged. These factors exerted a negative influence on tradable sectors in agriculture, compounded in 1992 by the effects of an intense drought. The 1992 crisis generated an adverse reaction against the reforms among farmers who were convinced that liberalization measures were responsible for falling farm incomes. Strong political pressures were followed by a wide array of government measures designed to cushion farm incomes. In the end, decision-makers resorted to selective policies, favoring some agricultural activities over others.

This chapter summarizes the most important conclusions of preceding chapters and draws some overall lessons from the Colombian experience. First, a brief review of the context and breadth of the policy changes of 1990-91 is presented. Second, the most important factors underlying the 1992 crisis are reviewed. Third, the impact of post-crisis government measures on liberalization efforts is assessed. Fourth, a description of structural changes in Colombian agriculture between 1990 and 1997 and their impact on the welfare of rural inhabitants is presented. The final section highlights some important lessons from the experience of Colombian agriculture in the 1990s.

Colombian Agriculture and *Apertura* Reforms

Agriculture has traditionally been the most important sector within the Colombian economy. In the mid-1990s, it contributed nearly a fifth of value added, over a third of foreign exchange earnings and over 30 percent of overall employment in the economy.

Prior to 1990, import substitution policies had discriminated against agriculture. Nonetheless, a number of importable (most of them annual) crops were protected and enjoyed the bulk of benefits from government action, including subsidized credit and technical assistance. Exportable crops benefited from export subsidies as well as credit programs. By contrast, non-tradable (mainly *campesino*) crops were mostly ignored, until the mid-1970s, when integrated rural development efforts were launched. Under the import substitution regime (1950-1990), Colombian agriculture displayed a positive growth record. However, unequal land distribution and promotion of mechanical innovations resulted in slow employment generation and few benefits for the poorer segments of the rural population.

Starting in August of 1990, a reformist administration replaced import substitution policies with a new market-oriented strategy, featuring trade liberalization for all sectors, including agriculture. *Apertura* reforms were introduced to combat slow overall growth and declining productivity in the 1980s. The new framework was expected to expand markets for Colombian products, reinvigorate capital accumulation and foster technological improvements.

Reforms were designed to be applied neutrally to all sectors of the economy. However, political and economic considerations led to special treatment for agriculture. In particular, farmers of sensitive importable crops benefited from the operation of stabilizing price bands.

As in other areas of the economy, *Apertura* implied ambitious changes in agriculture. These were reflected in new policies, new legal provisions and momentous institutional changes. Overall, they constituted the most ambitious agenda for change that had been presented to Colombian farmers in several decades. Critical changes included measures to liberalize trade, boost public investment in irrigation and drainage, negotiate trade agreements, increase credit flows to farmers and overhaul agricultural agencies. Furthermore, *Apertura* included policies to aid disadvantaged *campesinos*, including special subsidies for irrigation and infrastructure, technical assistance and a new approach to land reform. The strategy for rural development was reformed, with an emphasis on decentralization of decision-making and project implementation, as instructed by the 1991 Constitution. The effectiveness of expenditures aimed at reducing rural poverty were enhanced through improved targeting methods.

Most of the efforts of the Gaviria administration in the agricultural sphere were spent in formulating and designing reforms in policies, institutions and regulations. Little time was left to implement investment plans and new policies in areas such as irrigation, research and land reform. The responsibility to carry out investment under new policy priorities was left to future administrations. With the benefit of hindsight, it seems that reformist policy-makers underestimated the amount of time and political capital required to obtain desired institutional changes. This was the case of the new strategies for investment in irrigation projects, agricultural research, modernization and diversification, rural infrastructure, agricultural credit and land reform. Most of the agencies in charge of these areas had become a refuge to entrenched political interests that opposed reforms because they threatened traditional patron-client relationships.

The market-oriented reforms put in place in 1990 and 1991 were expected to favor agriculture, a sector that had been discriminated by the import substitution regime. However, policy-makers underestimated the severe lack of competitiveness of many producers of importable crops. Also, few predicted the severity with which macroeconomic forces and world markets were to depress economic incentives for tradable crops after 1991.

Interpreting the 1992 Crisis

A few months after *Apertura* reforms were implemented, many farmers were affected by what was later known as the agricultural crisis of 1992. This crisis was the result of a coming together of factors that depressed agricultural incentives and production levels. One of the worst droughts on record affected much of the country in that year, as a result of the weather phenomenon, *El Niño*. International prices of most commodities of importance to the Colombian economy collapsed since 1991. Moreover, the exchange rate appreciated, rebounding from the levels attained at the end of 1990. In addition, many importable crops faced diminished protection as a result of *Apertura* reforms. The situation was also aggravated by the interruption in the flow of farming credit due to financial difficulties at Caja Agraria, the growing gap between domestic and international interest rates (and its effect on domestic storage and harvest prices) and increasing rural violence. These factors affected many regions and agricultural activities, creating a sense of generalized crisis among farmers.

However, the crisis was in fact concentrated in a number of annual, importable crops, representing about a fifth of agricultural gross domestic product. For this sector of Colombian agriculture, production and prices fell as a result of several mutually reinforcing factors, including declining world prices, exchange rate appreciation and tariff reductions. Harvest levels contracted sharply, as a result of poor weather conditions and declining returns for marginal farmers. The latter had been lured into producing importable crops during the boom of 1985-90, when high international prices, a devalued exchange rate and a government-sponsored Selective Supply Plan boosted incentives for farmers.

The 1992 crisis provided a glimpse of things to come later in the decade. Some of its causes reflected factors that would continue to influence economic incentives for several years. These included the appreciation of the exchange rate and the removal of trade barriers in agriculture. The persistence of these factors explains why some of the changes in production trends that were evident in 1992—the relative success of permanent and non-tradable crops over annuals and tradable commodities—would continue in later years. Also among the winners were those that managed to obtain disproportionately high protection levels, such as producers of rice and sugar.

The 1992 crisis created a hostile atmosphere for *Apertura* policies among most farming groups. This embittered the relationship between the private sector and the government and slowed down advances in some of the joint efforts necessary to deepen the long-term competitiveness of Colombian agriculture. Weak public-private collaboration was at the root of the poor results of investment in fields like irrigation and agricultural research.

Reforming *Apertura*

In the aftermath of the 1992 agricultural crisis, political pressures to undo *Apertura* policies in agriculture and rescue affected farmers were intense. As a result, massive government efforts were undertaken to facilitate recovery, as reflected in the ad hoc measures of 1992, the Recovery Plan of 1993, the implementation of *Ley Agraria* in 1994 and the revamped efforts to reactivate agriculture during the Samper administration. Some government actions reversed initial *Apertura* announcements, including those related to the reduction of government involvement in agricultural markets and the phasing out of interest rate limits. Nonetheless, despite intense public efforts, at the time of this writing (June of 1998), production of annual crops still showed no signs of recovery. On the contrary, for most of the crops affected by the 1992 crisis, output continued to drop after 1993 period, a result of deeper economic forces that are identified below.

The ineffectiveness of government efforts is also partially attributable to the deep-seated flaws in the institutional setup of government action in Colombian agriculture. Most agencies resisted *Apertura*-related changes and only adopted new policies in a half-hearted manner. Private farming groups often supported resistance efforts, particularly since they derived significant benefits from traditional arrangements. During much of the Samper administration, the situation was aggravated by the weakness of the executive branch of government. By 1996, the government acknowledged a massive institutional collapse, which affected the agencies in charge of land reform (INCORA), rural development (DRI), irrigation (INAT), agricultural credit (Caja Agraria) and marketing (IDEMA). As of this writing, serious measures to deal with this situation had not been taken.

Despite the long list of government policies announced in the aftermath of the 1992 crisis, protection levels in the 1994-97 period were only increased significantly for three crops: rice, maize and sorghum. These crops, jointly with sugar, obtained greater support levels after *Apertura* reforms. Political economy arguments suggest that these crops were favored because they are mostly import-competing, they face distorted markets and processors and producers are strongly allied. In addition, there may be some policy inertia, in that these crops have been traditionally supported in the past. For the case of maize, policy-makers may have taken into account the low average income of producers in decisions to extend generous protection measures.

Agricultural trade liberalization in Colombia was partial and incomplete. Econometric tests demonstrate that traditionally low integration levels between domestic and foreign markets did not change substantially after *Apertura*—largely a result of price bands, import restrictions, absorption agreements and other market imperfections. Price stabilization and protection (or taxation, for the case of coffee) for agricultural products have remained as important policy priorities, despite *Apertura* reforms and the apparent removal of import substitution policies. Moreover, the comparison of pre-*Apertura* and post-crisis protection levels reveals that, on aggregate, liberalization measures resulted only in a slight decline in support levels for importable crops (including sugar). Protection levels after *Apertura* exhibit wide dispersion across commodities, indicating that policies have continued to be far from neutral, as was the case before 1990. Crops like rice, maize, sorghum and sugar enjoyed higher protection levels after 1990. In the same period, milk, oil palm, wheat, and bananas saw their protection levels decline. Others like cocoa, cotton, soybeans and barley did not experience significant changes in support levels. Coffee farmers have continued to be subject to taxation of about 20 percent of export revenues.

Structural Changes and Rural Welfare

The 1990s have been a time of mediocre economic performance for Colombian agriculture. The production of annual crops fell almost uninterruptedly between 1990 and 1997. By contrast, most permanent crops displayed moderate growth output gains, while livestock activities grew rapidly. In the aggregate, farm output preformed substantially below historical averages.

Up until 1990, long-term production trends displayed higher rates for tradable (and annual) commodities. This was the expected result of decades of government attention, including protection and stabilization schemes. After 1990, economic incentives have favored permanent crops and livestock activities. Also, non-tradable crops, including those produced overwhelmingly by *campesino* producers, have benefited from favorable relative price trends. Output of importable crops (mostly annual) contracted while that of exportable activities (mostly permanent) stagnated. Among the latter, two important exceptions should be noted: sugar, which received substantial protection, and oil palm, in which farmers were able to maintain competitiveness with important technological advances. These trends generated important changes in the structure of Colombian agriculture in the 1990s. Non-tradable (and permanent) activities gained output share, mostly at the expense of importable (and annual) crops.

Changing relative incentives explain the widely disparate performance across groups of agricultural activities observed since 1990. Returns for most tradable farming activities and, in particular, importable crops, fell substantially between 1990 and 1997. On the other hand, profit indexes for non-tradables increased. Sugar and rice, also experienced rising incentives, the result of special support measures. Declining international prices and the real appreciation of the exchange rate were the key factors depressing returns for tradable crops. Most significantly, trade policy was not neutral across commodities. Government actions supported commodities like rice, sugar, maize and barley, remained neutral for most exportable crops and reduced protection for crops like soybeans and wheat.

A great deal of the structural changes observed after 1990 in Colombian agriculture can be associated with the appreciation of the exchange rate. In particular, this phenomenon is responsible for decreasing relative returns for tradable crops. The rising value of the peso has been the result of several factors, including surging capital inflows, oil findings and the massive increase in government expenditures after 1990. Other things equal, some depreciation is expected in coming years due to the unsustainable nature of government spending levels

Despite poor overall agricultural performance, living standards improved significantly for most rural inhabitants between 1990 and 1997. The bulk of the rural population enjoyed growing incomes, with the greatest gains going to the poorest families. Improving welfare levels seem to be related to booming urban labor markets, growth in non-tradable *campesino* crops, expanding job opportunities in rural service sectors and rapidly-growing expenditures by local governments. Other evidence indicates that poverty levels have been declining steadily since 1991 and that rural wages have been increasing since mid-1992. Ironically, the 1990s have been a time of steady improvement in equality in the Colombian countryside, despite the mediocre performance of the agricultural sector.

Learning from the Colombian Experience

Two important lessons stand out from the Colombian experience with agricultural policy reform in the 1990s. The first is that macroeconomic factors are a critical determinant of developments in agriculture. The Colombian experience demonstrates that even after removal of trade barriers (which had favored manufacturing) and the adoption of a more neutral trading regime, economic incentives for tradable crops declined. Evidently, the persistent appreciation of the real exchange rate from late 1990 until mid-1997 exerted a strong negative effect on incentives for these activities. The effect was strongest for importable crops, some of which saw their protection levels diminished after 1990. Moreover, farming policies, regardless of how supportive, are not enough to fully determine relative prices between different crops or those between agricultural and non-agricultural sectors. The wide array of measures adopted after 1992 to assist farmers of depressed importable crops were for the most part over-whelmed by the intense effects of exchange rate appreciation, including in-creasing rural and urban wages and falling prices of domestic crops relative to imported ones.

What can farmers do on the face of declining incentives due to real exchange rate appreciation? Colombian farmers followed tradition by pressing for policy concessions and compensatory measures. In some cases, protection levels were increased, in others, farmers obtained refinancing facilities, and for some, the pressures went unanswered. Undoubtedly, many suffered significant financial losses and curbed their farming activities. For those who survived, coping with falling relative prices meant cutting production costs, increasing productivity and adopting new technologies. This, of course, is the ideal method to regain lost competitiveness in an appreciation scenario. However, Colombian farmers did not have access to many new agricultural technologies in the 1990s, largely as a consequence of the traumas caused to research and development institu-tions. Preoccupied with short-term profitability problems, farming groups did little to promote the resolution of the problems facing agricultural research institutions. However, the future of important segments of Colombian agricul-ture depends on a successful resolution of these problems, which will likely entail greater public and private funding and stronger collaboration between government and farming groups in these areas.

Macroeconomic forces associated with exchange rate appreciation greatly determined outcomes in Colombian agriculture after 1990. Much of the appre-ciation responded to fundamental factors outside the control of the government. However, growing government expenditures after 1991 have been identified as a key source of appreciation. Moreover, there is increasing evidence that expen-ditures have grown beyond sustainable levels, indicating that part of the appre-ciation may be reversed in the not-too-distant future.

Under this scenario, Colombian farming groups representing tradable crops should have pressed for policies to ameliorate exchange rate appreciation, including a slower rate of increase of government expenditures. However, in the early 1990s, few farming groups understood the strong link between macroeco-nomic developments and agricultural incentives. Fewer still understood the link between the appreciation of the peso and public expenditure levels. In the future, a better understanding of the macroeconomic workings of a small, open economy may improve greatly the effectiveness of lobbying efforts of Colom-bian farming groups.

A second lesson from the Colombian experience of the 1990s is that the fate of agriculture (especially, tradable crops) does not necessarily determine the welfare of most rural inhabitants. This is particularly true of rural economies like Colombia's, in which inequality levels are high. In such an environment, protection of tradable crops prior to 1990 meant increasing rents for the elite, sluggish growth in agricultural employment and stagnant living standards for the bulk of the rural population. Clearly, agricultural progress in Colombia has not promoted an egalitarian pattern of growth. This stands in sharp contrast with the historical experiences of those countries where land ownership was widely distributed (e.g., Japan, Korea, Taiwan and the US).

The experience of the last decades in Colombia suggests a classic dichotomy of interests. The favorable effects of policies that protect agricultural incomes are disproportionately captured by landowners. This is stronger when protected crops tend to be grains or oilseeds, produced in large-scale, mechanized operations. By contrast, policies that boost employment opportunities for the rural poor, such as rapidly growing urban or service sectors, are not favorable for landowners, who have to compete for scarce labor at higher costs.

Further studies will need to be performed to gain a better understanding of the causes behind the dramatic increase of incomes of the rural poor in the 1990s in Colombia. Research will have to assess the extent of rural-urban migration and the impact of booming construction activities in cities on rural wages. The impact of illicit crop cultivation needs to be better understood. Moreover, additional research should address the causes and manifestations of the recent growth of service sector jobs (and incomes) in rural areas, as well as the effect of growing expenditures by local governments on the rural economy.

The Future of Colombian Agriculture

Colombian agriculture will face difficult challenges in the next decade. First, the forces behind increasing trade globalization will require a significant boost in the competitiveness level of most tradable crops. Greater investments will need to be made in research efforts and stronger ties will need to be developed between producers, processors and government agencies in order to increase the effectiveness of these activities. Farmers and policy-makers will probably need to rethink the strategy of extending high levels of protection to some crops at the expense of others. Such policies will likely entail increasing social and financial costs and will come under attack in international trade negotiations. Efforts can be more usefully directed to providing farmers with more stable sources of long-term competitiveness.

Second, farmers will need to lobby policy-makers for more stable and neutral macroeconomic policies. Improved productivity gains in tradable crops can be quickly wiped out by negative macro trends. Authorities should strive to regulate macroeconomic conditions to accommodate gradual structural changes. However, Colombian farmers need to learn to cope with reasonable levels of instability, stemming from macroeconomic variables and international commodity prices. Markets for risk-management instruments need to be developed and institutions should be designed to reduce uncertainty without distorting economic signals. Advantage should be taken of the experience associated with the relative success of coffee stabilization efforts prior to 1990.

Third, market-oriented policies are unlikely to solve the pressing problems associated with inequality and poverty in rural areas. New creative solutions are needed to attack the vicious circles that tend to perpetuate low-income levels for over a quarter of the rural population. Recent approaches to redistribute assets efficiently to the rural poor (such as market-assisted land reform) need to be tested. A greater understanding is also required of the potential of non-tradable crops and service activities in providing jobs for the rural poor.

Finally, it is unlikely that Colombian agriculture can regain its growth path without a drastic reduction in rural violence levels. Instability stemming from constant violent threats has prevented many farmers from undertaking many of the required investments to survive in an era of increased competition. Violence has been fueled in the 1990s by the boom in illicit crop cultivation, which has also generated problematic distortions in rural labor and land markets. Part of the solution is likely to involve the generation of greater employment opportunities in rural sectors and the reduction of gross inequalities in land ownership.

Bibliography

Baffes, John. 1997. "World Price Signals, Policy Reforms, and Domestic Commodity Price Behavior." Occasional Paper, International Economics Department. Washington: The World Bank.

Bairoch, Paul. 1975. *The Economic Development of the Third World Since 1990.* Berkeley: University of California Press.

Balassa, Bela. 1964. "The Purchasing Power Parity Doctrine: A Reappraisal." *Journal of Political Economy* 72 (December): 584-596.

Balcázar, Alvaro. 1998. "Agenda de Modernización Productiva." Occasional Paper. Bogotá: Misión Rural and Instituto Interamericano de Cooperación Agrícola.

Barbosa, Judith Helena and Carlos Felipe Jaramillo. 1995. "La Evolución de la Política Agrícola Colombiana y el Equivalente del Subsidio al Productor (ESP)." *Planeación y Desarrollo* 25 (January-April): 115-164.

Bejarano, Jesús Antonio. 1988. "Efectos de la Violencia en la Producción Agropecuaria." *Coyuntura Económica* 18 (September): 185-185.

Berry, Albert. 1973. "Land Distribution, Income Distribution, and the Productive Efficiency of Colombian Agriculture." *Food Research Institute Studies* 12 (September): 199-232.

_____. 1991. "Colombian Agriculture in the 1980s," in Michael J. Twomey and Ann Helwege, eds., *Modernization and Stagnation: Latin American Agriculture into the 1990s.* New York: Greenwood Press.

_____. 1992. "Agriculture During the Eighties' Recession in Colombia: Potential Versus Achievement," in A. Cohen and F.R. Gunter, eds., *The Colombian Economy: Issues of Trade and Development.* Boulder, Colorado: Westview Press.

Bivings, Elizabeth. 1992. "Price Seasonality and Trade Liberalization: A Dynamic Spatial Model of the Mexican Foodgrains Sector." Ph.D. Thesis, Stanford University, Stanford.

Bulmer-Thomas, Victor. 1994. *The Economic History of Latin America Since Independence.* Cambridge: Cambridge University Press.

Calderón, Alberto. 1995. "La Tasa de Cambio Real en Colombia: Mitos y Realidades." *Coyuntura Económica* 25 (June): 101-118.

Calvo, Guillermo A., Leonardo Leiderman and Carmen Reinhardt. 1992. "Capital Inflows and Real Exchange Rate Appreciation in Latin America: The Role of External Factors." Occasional Paper. Washington: International Monetary Fund.

Cárdenas, Mauricio. 1995. "On the Effectiveness of Capital Controls in Colombia." Paper presented at the 8th Annual Inter-American Seminar on Economics of the National Bureau of Economic Research. Bogotá.

_____. 1997. *La Tasa de Cambio en Colombia*. Bogotá: Tercer Mundo.

Cepeda, Fernando. 1994. *Dirección Política de la Reforma Económica*. Bogotá: FONADE.

Comisión Económica para América Latina (CEPAL). 1992. *Economic Survey of Latin America*. Santiago: CEPAL.

_____. 1997. *La Brecha de la Equidad*. Santiago: CEPAL.

Consejería para la Paz. 1994. "Dimensión Económica de la Violencia y la Criminalidad en Colombia." Presidencia de la República, Bogotá.

Consejo Nacional de Política Económica y Social (CONPES). 1991a. "Programa de Modernización y Diversificación del Sector Agropecuario," Documento DNP-2558-UDA-MINAGRICULTURA. Bogotá: Departamento Nacional de Planeación.

_____. 1991b. "Programa de Adecuación de Tierras, 1991-2000," Documento DNP-2538-UDA-MINAGRICULTURA. Bogotá: Departamento Nacional de Planeación.

_____. 1992a. "Nuevo Impulso a la Reforma Agraria," Documento DNP-2590-UDA-MINAGRICULTURA. Bogotá: Departamento Nacional de Planeación.

_____. 1992b. "Medidas de Emergencia para Créditos a la Industria Bananera," Documento DNP-2629-UDA. Bogotá: Departamento Nacional de Planeación.

_____. 1993a. "Política para el Desarrollo Rural Campesino," Documento CONPES SOCIAL-008-DNP-UDA-MINAGRICULTURA. Bogotá: Departamento Nacional de Planeación.

_____. 1993b. "Nuevas Medidas para Créditos de Emergencia a la Industria Bananera," Documento DNP-IFI-2653-UDA. Bogotá: Departamento Nacional de Planeación.

_____. 1994. "Política para el Desarrollo de la Mujer Rural," Documento CONPES SOCIAL-23-DNP-UDA-MINAGRICULTURA. Bogotá: Departamento Nacional de Planeación.

Consejo Superior de Comercio Exterior. 1992. "Coyuntura Agropecuaria y Medidas de Comercio Exterior," Documento de Asesores. Bogotá: Ministerio de Comercio Exterior.

Corden, W. Max and Peter Neary. 1982. "Booming Sector and Deindustrialization in a Small Open Economy." *Economic Journal 92* (December): 825-848.

de Janvry, Alain and Elisabeth Sadoulet. 1993. "Path-Dependent Policy Reforms: From

Land Reform to Rural Development in Colombia," in Karla Hoff, Avishay Braverman and Joseph E. Stiglitz, *The Economics of Rural Organization: Theory, Practice and Policy*. New York: Oxford University Press.

de Janvry, Alain, Nigel Key and Elisabeth Sadoulet. 1997. "Agricultural and Rural Development Policy in Latin America: New Directions and New Challenges." Working Paper No. 815, Department of Agriculture and Resource Economics, University of California. Berkeley: University of California.

Deininger, Klaus. (1997). "Making Market-Assisted Land Reform Work: The Case of Colombia." Occasional Paper. Washington: The World Bank.

Departamento Administrativo Nacional de Estadística. 1997. "Cuentas Nacionales 1990-96." *Boletín de Estadística* No. 5341. Bogotá: DANE.

Departamento Nacional de Planeación. 1990. *El Desarrollo Agropecuario en Colombia*. Bogotá: Editorial Presencia.

Dinar, Ariel and Andrew Keck. 1995. "Inversión Privada en Riego en Colombia: Efectos de la Violencia, la Política Macroeconómica y las Variables Ambientales." *Planeación y Desarrollo* 25 (January-April): 203-224.

Edwards, Sebastián. 1984. "Coffee, Money and Inflation in Colombia." *World Development* 12 (November/December): 1107-1117.

_____. 1994. "Trade Liberalization Reforms in Latin America: Recent Experiences, Policy Issues and Future Prospects," in Graham Bird and Ann Helwege, eds., *Latin America's Economic Future*. London: Academic Press.

_____. 1995. *Crisis and Reform in Latin America: From Despair to Hope*. New York: Oxford University Press.

Errázuriz, María. 1987. "Evolución del Empleo Cafetero en Colombia," in José Antonio Ocampo, ed., *Lecturas de Economía Cafetera: 1970-1985*. Bogotá: Tercer Mundo.

Furtado, Celso. 1976. *Economic Development of Latin America*. New York: Cambridge University Press.

Gaitán, Fernando. 1994. "Cifras de Homicidios por cada 100,000 Habitantes." Personal comunication. Bogotá.

García, Jorge. 1991. "Colombia," in Anne O. Krueger, Maurice Schiff and Alberto Valdés, eds., *The Political Economy of Agricultural Pricing Policy*. Vol. 1. Baltimore: The Johns Hopkins University Press.

García, Jorge and Gabriel Montes. 1988. *Coffee Boom, Government Expenditure and Agricultural Prices: The Colombian Experience*. Research Report 68. Washington: International Food Policy Research Institute.

_____ and _____. 1989. *Trade, Exchange Rate and Agricultural Pricing Policies in Colombia*. World Bank Comparative Studies. Washington: The World Bank.

Gardner, Bruce L.. 1987. "Causes of U.S. Farm Commodity Programs." *Journal of Political Economy* 95 (April): 290-310.

Gómez, Alcides. 1998. "Agenda de Pobreza Rural." Occasional Paper. Bogotá: Misión Rural y Instituto Interamericano de Cooperación Agrícola.

Gómez-Oliver, Luis. 1994. *La Política Agrícola en el Nuevo Estilo de Desarrollo Latinoamericano*. Santiago: Food and Agriculture Organization.

Grindle, Merilee S. 1986. *State and Countryside: Development Policy and Agrarian Politics in Latin America*. Baltimore: The Johns Hopkins University Press.

Hazell, Peter, Mauricio Jaramillo and Amy Williamson. 1990. "The Relationship Between World Price Instability and the Prices Farmers Receive in Developing Countries." *Journal of Agricultural Economics* 41 (May): 227-241.

Heath, John and Hans Binswanger. 1996. "Natural Resource Degradation Effects of Poverty and Population Growth are Largely Policy-Induced: The Case of Colombia," *Environment and Development Economics* 1 (February): 65-84.

Hendry, D.F., A.R. Pagan and J. Sargan. 1984. "Dynamic Specification," in Zvi Griliches and Michael D. Intriligator, eds., *Handbook of Econometrics*, Vol. 2. Amsterdam: North-Holland.

Hernández, Antonio. 1991. "La Política de Crédito y la Comercialización de Productos Agrícolas." Economistas Consultores Asociados. Bogotá.

_____. 1992. "Caja Agraria: Racionalización de la Red de Oficinas." Economistas Consultores Asociados, Bogotá.

_____. 1995. "Memorias 1994-1995 del Ministerio de Agricultura." Bogotá: Ministerio de Agricultura y Desarrollo Rural.

HIMAT. 1993. "Características Climáticas Observadas en el Territorio Nacional Durante el Año de 1992." Occasional Paper, HIMAT, Ministerio de Agricultura. Bogotá: HIMAT.

Hirschman, Albert O. 1958. *The Strategy of Economic Development*. New Haven: Yale University Press.

_____. 1968. "The Political Economy of Import-Substituting Industrialization in Latin America." *Quarterly Journal of Economics* 82 (February): 1-32.

_____. 1987. "La Economía Política del Desarrollo en América Latina: Siete Ejericios en Retrospectiva," *El Trimestre Económico* 54 (October/December): 769-804.

Hollinger, Frank. 1998. "Reforma Agraria a través del Mercado: Lecciones de Colombia."

Occasional Paper. Bogotá: Centro de Estudios Ganaderos y Agrícolas, CEGA.

Hommes, Rudolf, Armando Montenegro and Pablo Roda. 1994. *Una Apertura Hacia el Futuro*. Bogotá: Ministerio de Hacienda y Crédito Público and Departamento Nacional de Planeación.

Ingco, Merlinda D. 1995. "Agricultural Trade Liberalization in the Uruguay Round." Policy Research Working Paper No. 1500, International Economics Department. Washington: The World Bank.

Inter-American Development Bank. 1996. *Economic and Social Progress*. Baltimore: The Johns Hopkins University Press.

_____. 1997. *Economic and Social Progress*. Baltimore: The Johns Hopkins University Press.

International Monetary Fund. 1998. *International Financial Statistics*. Washington: International Monetary Fund.

Jaramillo, Carlos Felipe. 1994. *Apertura, Crisis y Recuperación: La Agricultura Colombiana entre 1990 y 1994*. Bogotá: Tercer Mundo.

Jaramillo, Carlos Felipe and Roberto Junguito. 1993. "Crisis Agropecuaria y Política Macroeconómica", *Debates de Coyuntura Económica* 29 (October): 47-66.

Johnston, Bruce F. and Peter Kilby. 1980. *Agriculture and Structural Transformation*. New York: Oxford University Press.

Kalmanovitz, Salomón. 1978. *Desarrollo de la Agricultura en Colombia*. Bogotá: Editorial La Carreta.

_____. 1992. "Análisis Macroeconómico del Narcotráfico en la Economía Colombiana." Occasional Paper, Centro de Investigaciones para el Desarrollo (CID). Bogotá: Universidad Nacional.

Kamas, Linda. 1986. "Dutch Disease Economics and the Colombian Export Boom," *World Development* 9 (September): 1177-1198.

Krueger, Anne O., Alberto Valdés and Maurice Schiff. 1992. *The Political Economy of Agricultural Price Intervention in Latin America*. San Francisco: International Center for Economic Growth.

Lavergne, R. 1983. *The Political Economy of U.S. Tariffs: An Empirical Analysis*. New York: Academic Press.

Legrand, Catherine. 1986. *Frontier Expansion and Peasant Protest in Colombia: 1850-1936*. Albuquerque: University of New Mexico Press.

Leibovich, José, Luis Angel Rodríguez and Oskar Andrés Nupia. 1997. "El Empleo en el Sector Rural Colombiano: Qué ha Pasado en los Últimos Años? Qué se Puede Prever?" Occasional Paper, Centro de Estudios para el Desarrollo Económico. Bogotá: Universidad de Los Andes.

Londoño, Juan Luis. 1997. "Social Rifts in Colombia." *CEPAL Review* 61 (April): 19-40.

Londoño, Juan Luis and Miguel Székely. 1997. "Sorpresas Distributivas Tras de una Década de Reformas: América Latina en la Década de 1990, " in *Tras una Década de Reformas en América Latina. Cuáles son los Próximos Pasos?* Washington: Inter-American Development Bank.

López, Cecilia and Antonio Gómez. 1997. *Memorias 1996-1997 del Ministerio de Agricultura.* Bogotá: Ministerio de Agricultura y Desarrollo Rural.

López, Ramón and Alberto Valdés. 1998. "Determinants of Rural Poverty in Colombia," in Ramón López and Alberto Valdés, eds., *Rural Poverty in Latin America.* Baltimore: The Johns Hopkins University Press.

Lora, Eduardo and Ana María Herrera. 1994. "Ingresos Rurales y Evolución Macroeconómica," in Clara González and Carlos Felipe Jaramillo, eds., *Competitividad sin Pobreza: Estudios para el Desarrollo del Campo en Colombia.* Bogotá: Tercer Mundo.

May, Ernesto, ed. 1996. *La Pobreza en Colombia: Un Estudio del Banco Mundial.* Bogotá: Tercer Mundo.

Ministerio de Agricultura. 1992. "Medidas para el Sector Agropecuario." Bogotá: Ministerio de Agricultura.

_____. 1993. "El Balance del Sector en 1993: La Política de Reactivación y sus Frutos." *Boletín de Coyuntura*, No. 1. Bogotá: Ministerio de Agricultura.

_____. 1998. "Producción, Areas y Rendimientos de la Agricultura Colombiana, 1950-1998." Bogotá: Ministerio de Agricultura.

Ministerio de Comercio Exterior. 1998. "Cifras de Comercio Externo." Bogotá: Ministerio de Comercio Exterior.

Montenegro, Santiago, ed. 1997. *Los Determinantes de la Tasa de Cambio Real en Colombia.* Bogotá: Universidad de Los Andes.

Mora, Humberto and Jairo Cortés. 1993. "Efectos de la Apertura Comercial y del Crédito sobre el Sector Agropecuario." Working Paper DIE-0493-067-5, Banco de la República. Bogotá: Banco de la República.

Mundlak, Yair and Donald Larson. 1992. "On the Transmission of World Agricultural Price." *The World Bank Economic Review* 6 (September): 399-422.

Nuñez, Jairo and Fabio Sánchez. 1997. "Educación y Salarios Relativos en Colombia: Determinantes y Evolución: 1976-1995." Occasional Paper, Unidad de Análisis Macroeconómico. Bogotá: Departamento Nacional de Planeación.

Nupia, Oskar Andrés. 1997. "Integración Espacial en los Mercados Laborales: Evidencia para las Regiones Colombianas." Working Paper CEDE 97-09. Bogotá: Universidad de Los Andes.

Nurkse, Ragnar. 1953. *Problems of Capital Formation in Underdeveloped Countries.* Oxford: Blackwell.

Ocampo, José Antonio. 1993. "La Crisis y la Política de Reactivación del Sector Agropecuario." *Debates de Coyuntura Económica* 29 (December): 7-45.

_____. 1994a. *Memoria: 1992-1993.* Bogotá: Ministerio de Agricultura.

_____. 1994b. *Memorias del Señor Ministro de Agricultura y Desarrollo Rural.* Bogotá: Ministerio de Agricultura y Desarrollo Rural.

Ocampo, José Antonio and Leonardo Villar. 1992. "Trayectorias y Visicitudes de la Apertura Económica Colombiana." *Pensamiento Iberoamericano* 21 (January/June): 165-186.

Ocampo, José Antonio, Maria José Perez, Camilo Tovar and Francisco Javier Lasso. 1998. "Macroeconomía, Ajuste Estructural y Equidad en Colombia: 1978-1996." Archivos de Macroeconomía, No. 79. Bogotá: Departamento Nacional de Planeación.

Olson, Mancur. 1985. "Space, Agriculture, and Organization." *American Journal of Agricultural Economics* 67 (December): 928-937.

Oquist, Paul. 1980. *Violence, Conflict, and Politics in Colombia.* New York: Academic Press.

Prebisch, Raúl. 1950. *The Economic Development of Latin America and Its Principal Problems.* New York: United Nations.

Presidencia de la República and Departamento Nacional de Planeación. 1991. *La Revolución Pacífica.* Bogotá: Departamento Nacional de Planeación.

Quiroz. Jorge A. 1997. "Reformas Económicas y Precios Agrícolas en Colombia: 1991-1996." Report to the Inter-American Development Bank. Washington: Inter-American Development Bank.

Quiroz, Jorge A. and Raimundo Soto. 1993. "International Price Signals in Agricultural Markets: Do Governments Care?" Occasional Paper. Washington: The World Bank.

Quiroz, Jorge A. and Alberto Valdés. 1994. "Price Bands for Agricultural Price Stabilization: The Chilean Experience." Working Paper I-64, Programa de Postgrado en Economía. Santiago: ILADES, Georgetown.

Ramirez, Alvaro. 1998. "Análisis de la Política de Adecuación de Tierras." Occasional Paper, Unidad de Desarrollo Agrario. Bogotá: Departamento Nacional de Planeación.

Reyes, Alejandro. 1997. "Compra de Tierras por Narcotraficantes," in Francisco Thoumi, ed., *Drogas Ilícitas en Colombia: Su Impacto Económico, Político y Social*. Bogotá: Editorial Ariel.

Reyes, Alvaro and Jaime Martínez. 1994. "Funcionamiento de los Mercados de Trabajo Rurales en Colombia," in Clara González and Carlos Felipe Jaramillo, eds., *Competitividad sin Pobreza: Estudios para el Desarrollo del Campo en Colombia*. Bogotá: Tercer Mundo.

Robbins, Donald. 1996. "Trade Liberalization and Wages in Colombia, 1976-1994." Occasional Paper, Harvard Institute for International Development. Cambridge: HIID.

Rocha, Ricardo. 1997. "Aspectos Económicos de las Drogas Ilegales," in Francisco Thoumi, ed., *Drogas Ilícitas en Colombia: Su Impacto Económico, Político y Social*. Bogotá: Editorial Ariel.

Rueda, Ximena. 1995. "La Transmisión de los Precios Externos a los Mercados Domésticos en la Agricultura Colombiana: 1970-1992." *Planeación y Desarrollo* 25 (January-April): 69-90.

Ruiz, Maria del Pilar. 1995. "El Diferencial de Tasas de Interés Interna y Externa y los Precios Domésticos al Productor Agrícola en Colombia." *Planeación y Desarrollo* 25 (January-April): 91-114.

Samuelson, Paul. 1964. "Theoretical Notes on Trade Problems." *Review of Economics and Statistics* 46 (May): 145-154.

Sanint, Luis Roberto. 1993. "Efecto de la Apertura Económica sobre la Rentabilidad de las Actividades Agropecuarias en Colombia, 1989-93: Estudio de Casos." Occasional Paper, Ministerio de Agricultura. Bogotá: Ministerio de Agricultura.

Schadler, Susan, Marla Carkovic, Adam Bennett and Kahn, Robert. 1993. "Recent Experiences with Surges in Capital Inflows", Occasional Paper No. 108. Washington: International Monetary Fund.

Sheahan, John. 1987. *Patterns of Development in Latin America: Poverty, Repression and Economic Strategy*. Princeton: Princeton University Press.

Shonkwiler, Larry. 1994. "Desarrollo de Mercados Agrícolas," in Clara González and Carlos Felipe Jaramillo, eds., *Competitividad sin Pobreza: Estudios para el Desarrollo del Campo en Colombia*. Bogotá: Tercer Mundo.

Silva, Alvaro. 1994. "El Desarrollo de la Comercialización de Cereales," in Clara González and Carlos Felipe Jaramillo, eds., *Competitividad sin Pobreza: Estudios para el Desarrollo del Campo en Colombia*. Bogotá: Tercer Mundo.

Steiner, Roberto. 1996. "Cuantificación de Flujos del Narcotráfico." *Coyuntura Económica*

26 (December): 73-108.

Thomas, Vinod. 1985. *Linking Macroeconomic and Agricultural Policies for Adjustment and Growth.* Baltimore: The Johns Hopkins University Press.

Thoumi, Francisco E., ed. 1997. *Drogas Ilícitas en Colombia: Su Impacto Económico, Político y Social.* Bogotá: Editorial Ariel.

Timmer, C. Peter. 1988. "The Agricultural Transformation," in Hollis B. Chenery and T.N. Srinivasan, eds., *Handbook of Development Economics*, Vol. I. Amsterdam: North-Holland.

Tobón, Santiago. 1994. "Informe de Gestión." Informe de Gerencia. Bogotá: Caja de Crédito Agrícola, Industrial y Minero.

Torres, Luis Alfonso. 1994. "La Reforma del Régimen de Comercio y la Apertura Económica," en Olga Lucia Acosta and Israel Fainboim Yaker, eds., *Las Reformas Económicas del Gobierno del Presidente Gaviria: Una Visión Desde Adentro.* Bogotá: Ministerio de Hacienda y Crédito Público.

Torres, Luis Alfonso and Horacio Osorio. 1998. "El Sistema Andino de Franjas de Precios: Evaluación de Resultados." Occasional Paper, Centro de Estudios para el Desarrollo Económico. Bogotá: Universidad de Los Andes.

Uribe, Claudia and Florencia Leal. 1994. "Antidumping, Salvaguardia, Derechos Compensatorios y Reforma Aduanera," in Clara González and Carlos Felipe Jaramillo, eds., *Competitividad sin Pobreza: Estudios para el Desarrollo del Campo en Colombia.* Bogotá: Tercer Mundo.

Uribe, Sergio. 1997. "Los Cultivos Ilícitos en Colombia," in Francisco Thoumi, ed., *Drogas Ilícitas en Colombia: Su Impacto Económico, Político y Social.* Bogotá: Editorial Ariel.

Urrutia, Miguel. 1990. "Análisis Costo-Beneficio del Tráfico de Drogas para la Economía Colombiana." Coyuntura Económica 20 (October): 115-126.

_____. 1991. "Twenty-Five Years of Economic Growth, 1960-1985," in Miguel Urrutia, ed., *Long-term Trends in Latin American Economic Development.* Washington: The Johns Hopkins University Press.

_____. 1997. "Nota Editorial: Importaciones Agropecuarias." *Revista del Banco de la República* 70 (November): 5-21.

Valdés, Alberto. 1996. Surveillance of Agricultural Price and Trade Policy in Latin America During Major Policy Reforms. World Bank Discussion Paper No. 349. Washington: The World Bank.

Valdés, Alberto and Barry Schaeffer. 1995. "Surveillance of Agricultural Price and Trade: A Handbook for Colombia." World Bank Technical Paper Number 268. Washington: The

World Bank.

Vargas, Ricardo. 1994. "El Desarrollo Rural en Colombia (1961-1993): Apuntes y Notas para una Historia del Fondo DRI," in Absalón Machado, ed., *El Agro y la Cuestión Social*. Bogotá: Tercer Mundo.

World Bank. 1986. *World Development Report*. Oxford: Oxford University Press.

_____. 1993. *The East Asian Miracle: Economic Growth and Public Policy*. New York: Oxford University Press.

_____. 1994a. *Colombia, Poverty Assessment Report*. Washington: The World Bank.

_____. 1994b. *Commodity Markets and the Developing Countries: A World Bank Quarterly*. Washington: The World Bank.

_____. 1996. *Review of Colombia's Agricultural and Rural Development Strategy*. Washington: The World Bank.

Index